IN THE BEGINNING

To Henriette

God's gift of a companion, a helper fit for me
(Gn. 2:18)

IN THE BEGINNING

The opening chapters of Genesis

Henri Blocher

Translated by
David G. Preston

INTER-VARSITY PRESS
LEICESTER, ENGLAND
DOWNERS GROVE, ILLINOIS, U.S.A.

Inter-Varsity Press
38 De Montfort Street, Leicester LE1 7GP, England
Box 1400, Downers Grove, Illinois 60515 U.S.A.

First published in French 1979 with the title *Révélation des origines*
by Presses Bibliques Universitaires, Lausanne
First published in English 1984

British Library Cataloguing in Publication Data
Blocher, Henri
In the beginning.
  1. Bible O.T. Genesis – Commentaries
  I. Title II. Révélation des origines. *English*
222'. 1106   BS1235.3

UK ISBN 0-85111-321-4

Library of Congress Cataloging in Publication Data

Blocher, Henri.
  In the beginning.
  Translation of: Révélation des origines.
  Bibliography: p.
  Includes index.
  1. Bible. O.T. Genesis I-III–Criticism, interpretation, etc. 2. Creation–Biblical teaching. 3. Human evolution–Biblical teaching. 4. Man (Christian theology)–Biblical teaching. I. Title.
BS651.B5713 1984   222'.1106   84-12800

USA ISBN 0-87784-325-2

Typeset in Great Britain by Nuprint Services Ltd, Harpenden, Herts.
Printed in Great Britain by Richard Clay (The Chaucer Press) Ltd, Suffolk.

Inter-Varsity Press, England, is the publishing division of the Universities and Colleges Christian Fellowship (formerly the Inter-Varsity Fellowship), a student movement linking Christian Unions in universities and colleges throughout the United Kingdom and the Republic of Ireland, and a member movement of the International Fellowship of Evangelical Students. For information about local and national activities write to UCCF, 38 De Montfort Street, Leicester LE1 7GP.

InterVarsity Press, U.S.A., is the book-publishing division of Inter-Varsity Christian Fellowship, a student movement active on campus at hundreds of universities, colleges and schools of nursing. For information about local and regional activities, write IVCF, 233 Langdon St., Madison, WI 53703.

17   16   15   14   13   12   11   10   9   8   7   6   5   4
99   98   97   96   95   94   93   92

Contents

Translator's preface 7

Abbreviations 10

Select bibliography 12

1. Approaching Genesis 15

2. The week of creation 39

3. Being, order and life 60

4. The image of God 79

5. Man and woman 95

6. The covenant in Eden 111

7. The breaking of the covenant 135

8. The wages of sin 171

9. The aftermath and the promise 196

Appendix: Scientific hypotheses and the beginning of Genesis 213

Index of biblical references 232

General index 237

Translator's preface

Luther described the opening of Genesis as 'certainly the foundation of the whole of Scripture'. More recently, Francis Schaeffer has written: 'In some ways these chapters are the most important ones in the Bible.' Nevertheless – or, perhaps, therefore – there is no section of Holy Scripture over which the storms of theological and philosophical controversy have raged more fiercely. Positions have changed with the exaggeration, if not the speed, of women's fashions. Any properly representative theological library will carry the full spectrum of views on these chapters, from extreme scepticism to dogged literalism, all presented by scholars of the first order. The last decade has witnessed a significant resurgence of the latter, though in some quarters it is expressed with an unbecoming (yet understandable) belligerence which threatens with the name of apostate those who step out of line.

To write with any understanding and authority requires mastery of a range of disciplines, caution and humility before such varied and sincere opinions, and also courage to face possible misunderstanding, even excoriation, from fellow Christians. The author, therefore, deserves our thanks as well as respect for venturing upon this veritable minefield.

It is necessary to underline what this publication does and does not seek to achieve. '*Etablir le sens*', wrote the author at the start of his own preface: '*to establish the original meaning*'. This book attempts to provide a self-consistent and biblically consistent interpretation of the opening chapters of Genesis, making

7

practical application whenever possible, and taking careful and critical account of the whole range of writing on them – no more than that. It is certainly not put forth as a definitive statement, let alone as the official stance of the Christian organization of which Inter-Varsity Press is the publishing division. Rather, it is offered to the public as a piece of biblical scholarship which should, like any other, be brought to the bar of Holy Scripture itself. Inevitably some will find here material with which they disagree; but we dare to hope that all who read it will find much of great interest and personal profit. Manifestly, an enormous amount of work remains to be undertaken on these chapters and we should be gratified if this volume were to encourage such endeavours.

Henri Blocher is at last becoming known in the English-speaking world. He has published a small study in Isaiah, *Songs of the Servant*, and has given lectures and biblical expositions at a number of international conferences. His scholarly and pastoral gifts will be plain enough to the reader. For those who like credentials, he is Lecturer in Systematic Theology and Philosophy at the Faculté Libre de Théologie Evangélique, Vaux-sur-Seine, and an elder at the Baptist Church, L'Eglise du Tabernacle (163 bis, rue Belliard) in the north of Paris.

Certain continental features of the original French work survive in the translation. There are frequent references to French scholars whose writings are little known in the English-speaking world; the vast majority of these I have retained. Two sizes of print are used, the smaller distinguishing more specialist material and detailed argument that some readers will wish to pass over. In a few rare cases I have been unable to trace an English work referred to and have been obliged to translate back into the original language.

One or two changes have been made. The French original contained a short appendix discussing source criticism, summarizing material that is readily available in English. A few adjustments have been made to the appendix on scientific hypotheses, though it has not been possible to bring this up to date. It should be evident that it is written by a non-scientist for other non-scientists in order to give them some appreciation not only of the recent state of play but also of the bewildering complexity of the multifarious issues.

The manuscript of this English translation has been read by Dr Gordon McConville and Dr Oliver Barclay. They have made a considerable number of invaluable suggestions and to them I owe a debt of great gratitude. Needless to say, they are not responsible for, nor do they completely identify with, Henri Blocher's work, though they hold it in high esteem; nor are they to blame for the infelicities of expression that have accompanied its choppy passage across the English Channel.

Abbreviations

AV	Authorized (King James) Version of the Bible (1611)
BETS	*Bulletin of the Evangelical Theological Society*
Bib.	*Biblica*
BJRL	*Bulletin of the John Rylands Library*
BT	*The Bible Translator*
CBQ	*Catholic Biblical Quarterly*
CD	*Church Dogmatics*
CTJ	*Calvin Theological Journal*
EQ	*Evangelical Quarterly*
FV	*Foi et Vie*
GNB	Good News Bible (1976)
IBD	*Illustrated Bible Dictionary* (IVP, 1980)
JB	Jerusalem Bible (1966)
JBL	*Journal of Biblical Literature*
NASB	New American Standard Bible (1971)
NEB	The New English Bible, 1970
NIV	New International Version of the Bible (1978)
PCSR	*Presbyterion, Covenant Seminary Review*
PRPC	Presbyterian and Reformed Publishing Co.
RB	*Revue Biblique*
RR	*Revue Réformée*
RSPT	*Revue des Sciences Philosophiques et Théologiques*
RSV	Revised Standard Version of the Bible (1952, 1971)
RTL	*Revue Théologique de Louvain*
RV	Revised Version of the Bible (1885)
SC	*Scientific Creationism* (see bibliography)

SSt	*Scientific Studies in Special Creation* (see bibliography)
TB	*Tyndale Bulletin*
VT	*Vetus Testamentum*
WTJ	*Westminster Theological Journal*

Select bibliography

The literature available on the opening chapters of Genesis is most extensive. The following selection covers the full spectrum of approaches, from Protestant, Catholic and Jewish writers. They are those most commonly discussed in this study, and are cited in footnotes simply by the author's surname, except for the four symposia grouped at the end of this list, which are denoted by the abbreviations indicated.

Barth, K., *CD* III.1, *The Doctrine of Creation,* Edinburgh: T. & T. Clark, 1958.

Beauchamp, P., *Création et séparation: étude exégétique du premier chapître de la Genèse,* Paris: Aubier-Montaigne, Cerf, Delachaux & Niestlé, Desclée de Brouwer, 1969.

Bonhoeffer, D., *Creation and Fall,* London: SCM, 1959.

Calvin, J., *Genesis* (1563), Edinburgh: Banner of Truth, 1965.

Cassuto, U., *A Commentary on the Book of Genesis, Part I: From Adam to Noah, Genesis I – VI 8,* Jerusalem: The Magnes Press, Hebrew University, 1961.

Chaine, J., *Le livre de la Genèse,* Paris: Cerf, 1949.

Dubarle, A. M., *Le péché originel dans l'Ecriture,* Paris: Cerf, ²1967.

Goldstain, J., *Création et péché (Genèse 1 – 11),* Paris: Desclée de Brouwer, 1968.

Heidel, A., *The Babylonian Genesis,* University of Chicago Press, ²1963.

Keil, C. F., *Commentary on the Old Testament* 1 (The Pentateuch), Edinburgh: T. & T. Clark, 1878. Reprinted Grand Rapids: Eerdmans, 1975.

Kidner, D., *Genesis: An Introduction and Commentary (Tyndale Old Testament Commentaries)*, London: Inter-Varsity Press, 1967.

Kierkegaard, S., *The Concept of Anxiety* (1844), Princeton University Press, 1980.

Kline, M. G., 'Because it had not rained', *WTJ* 20 (1957–58), pp.146-157.

Loretz, O., *Die Gottenbildlichkeit des Menschen*, Munich: Kösel Verlag, 1967.

Michaëli, F., *Le livre de la Genèse, chapitre 1 à 11*, Paris/Neuchâtel: Delachaux & Niestlé, 1957.

Payne, D. F., *Genesis One Reconsidered*, London: Tyndale Press, 1964.

Pearce, E. K. V., *Who Was Adam?*, Exeter: Paternoster Press, ²1976.

Ramm, B., *The Christian View of Science and Scripture*, Exeter: Paternoster Press, 1955.

Renckens, H., *Israel's Concept of the Beginning. The Theology of Genesis 1 – 3*, New York: Herder & Herder, 1964.

Ricoeur, P., *The Symbolism of Evil*, New York: Harper & Row, 1967.

Speiser, E. A., *Genesis (Anchor Bible)*, Garden City: Doubleday, 1964.

Thompson, J. A., 'Genesis 1: Science? History? Theology?', *TSF Bulletin* 50 (Spring, 1968), pp.12–23.

Von Rad, G., *Genesis*, London: SCM, ²1963.

Waltke, B. K., 'Genesis 1' in *Bibliotheca Sacra* 132 (1975), pp.25–36, 136–144, 216–228, 327–342, and *ibid.* 133 (1976), pp.28–41.

Weeks, N., 'The hermeneutical problem of Genesis 1 – 11', *Themelios* 4.1 (September, 1978), pp.12–19.

Westermann, C., *Creation*, London: SPCK, 1971 (below = Westermann *C*).

Westermann, C., *Genesis, Band I (Biblischer Kommentar)*, Neukirchen: Neukirchener Verlag des Erziehungsvereins, 1974 (below = Westermann *G*).

Young, E. J., *Studies in Genesis One*, Grand Rapids: Baker Book House, 1964 (below = Young I).

Young, E. J., *Genesis 3: A devotional and expository study*, London: Banner of Truth, 1966 (below = Young III).

In Principio = *In Principio: Interprétation des premiers versets de la Genèse,* Paris: Etudes Augustiennes, 1973.

Mélanges Robert = *Mélanges rédigés en l'honneur d'André Robert,* Paris: Bloud & Gay, 1956.

SC = Morris, H. M. (ed.), *Scientific Creationism,* San Diego: Creation-Life Pub., 1974.

SSt = Lammerts, W. E. (ed.), *Scientific Studies in Special Creation,* Nutley, N. J.: PRPC, 1971.

1
Approaching Genesis

Curiosity about our beginnings continues to haunt the human race. It will not call off the quest for its origins. One might have thought that 'future shock' would divert it and that, by adopting a 'prospective' attitude, modern man would no longer be interested in anything but the future. Far from it. Mircea Eliade has seen clearly that the enormous historiographical task that has been going on since the last century is another form of the old search: 'There is a veritable recuperation of the past, even of our primeval past' he writes, by which man 'protects himself against the pressure of contemporary History', and he is doing an *anamnesis* comparable to a return by psychoanalysis to the events of early childhood.[1] Futurology is mirrored by archeology, whose popularity remains unabated. And what is the most up-to-date way of explaining what happens to things? You consider their beginning, whereas Aristotle considered their end!

There we must see a wise method imposed by reality. Frequently, indeed, the *beginning* unlocks the *principle*, the *constitution* reveals the *nature*. The human race quite rightly feels that it cannot find its bearings for life today without having light shed on its origins.

Over a long period the biblical book of Genesis, and notably its opening chapters, provided successive generations with *the* undisputed reply. Augustine never tired of commenting on it,

[1] Mircea Eliade, *Aspects du mythe* (Paris: Gallimard, 1963), pp. 167ff.

devoting three books to it, quite apart from the relevant chapters in his *Confessions* and *The City of God.*[2] Luther described the opening of Genesis as 'certainly the foundation of the whole of Scripture'.[3] A vast number of believing Christians still turn to it as *the* Text. The position, however, has changed. It is now challenged by other visions of mankind's earliest days, and varying interpretations of the very text of Genesis abound.

We shall ignore the coarse disdain of amateur scientists like M. Homais, the pharmacist in Flaubert's *Madame Bovary*. One thing at least must be put right, the confusion of sincere readers who do not know how to read or to listen and whose excessive sensitivity and unease come out either in concessions made or in tension and defensiveness. We must consider how we are to approach Genesis.

Word of man, Word of God

How did we get these stories which begin 'In the beginning...'? We receive them as the testimonies and monuments of a culture which nourished our own and which has passed away. Indeed, that is true, and we shall bear it in mind. But in order to read them as they are intended to be read, we must see that they are first of all something else. We must hear them as the *beginning of a symphony* whose interpretative and illuminative power transcends all cultural diversity. In concrete terms, these pages come to us as the opening pages of the Bible, and the Bible has demonstrated sufficiently that it is not just any ancient book. The intelligence of the first part of the Bible asks us to respect in it the nature of the whole.

The uniqueness of the Bible, the Holy Scripture(s), is clear in its connection with Jesus Christ. Both Testaments, as Pascal put it so well, look to him. The Old Testament, from Genesis to the last of the prophets, bears witness to him (Lk. 24:27; Jn. 5:39). Throughout the Old Testament he is 'the One who is coming', whose coming God prepares in many ways. Then the relationship is reversed. Jesus Christ in his turn vouches for these witnesses, God's messengers. Unreservedly and unequivocally he bears witness to the Scriptures. He treats them

[2] *Cf.* Aimé Solignac, 'Exégèse et métaphysique. Genèse 1, 1–3 chez saint Augustin', *In Principio*, pp.155–161.
[3] Quoted by Richard Stauffer, 'L'Exégèse de Genèse 1, 1–3 chez Luther et Calvin', *In Principio*, p.245.

constantly as truth itself, the authority which settles all arguments, the Word of God which no-one may break (Jn. 10:35). He gives an exact quotation from the commentary of the narrator in Genesis 2:24 and takes it as the declaration of the Creator (Mt. 19:5). There is no doubt; for Christ, what Scripture says, God says.[4]

If we give the name 'inspiration' to that divine work by which the Bible was composed and which allows us to identify it with God's own utterance, then we must approach the opening chapters of Genesis as inspired texts, rich with the truth of God, clothed with the authority of God. We must also, in order to understand them better, make use of the harmony of the Scriptures. We must take advantage of the common inspiration, bringing other passages to illumine the difficulties. That we shall do. We shall trust the method of interpreting Scripture by Scripture, according to 'the analogy of faith'.

How could we reject that method if we claim to follow Christ? Those who know him know that they can follow him in his approach to the Bible and therefore in his approach to Genesis. We do not have to resort to allegory, a trap which Karl Barth did not manage to avoid, and to find the incarnation hidden in the account of creation;[5] the Bible teaches the order creation-fall-redemption and does not reverse it. Nor do we have to impose on the text a ready-made meaning; rather, knowing that *every* approach carries its own presuppositions (how naïve to think anyone could be totally free of them!), we must take the text as it presents itself, within the greater biblical whole. Admittedly this involves a risk. One must commit oneself in order to get the sense. Those, however, who dare not yet trust these chapters, we ask for the time being to join us in our venture; the power of the truth of the Bible's own words will perhaps pierce the defences of their scepticism or of their seemingly solid convictions. Let them accompany us a little way.

In the act of inspiration God spoke *through men*. Respect for God's action involves careful attention to its *manner*. The Bible

---

[4] See the study of this and of parallel passages in B. B. Warfield, *The Inspiration and Authority of the Bible* (Philadelphia: PRPC, 1948), pp.299–348.

[5] Karl Barth, along with those whom he influenced such as D. Bonhoeffer and W. Vischer, slips into allegory in a totally different way from early Fathers influenced by Plato, though in fact he sometimes reaches similar conclusions to theirs. Barth is concerned to exclude every relationship between God and men, even that of judgment, that is not *in Jesus Christ*. But, as in the ancient allegorists, his writings reveal a tendency towards a Platonic, static idea of eternity.

underlines that revelation occurred 'in various ways' (Heb. 1:1), as various as the men God raised up, and as their respective situations. Unswerving in our total trust, we must in our approach be adaptable to this variety, on pain of missing our goal. We follow God himself if we pay the most methodical and informed attention to the humanity of his Word, in every form that it may take.

There is nothing mechanical about inspiration. The God in whom 'we live and move and have our being', in order to move men, has no need to turn them into robots. His Word is as fully their word, expressed in their language. To someone like Ezekiel, God communicates his revelation in ecstatic visions, but the Chronicler is no less inspired as he compiles historical documents, or Luke as he compares eyewitness acounts, or the Preacher as he meditates through his mysterious meanderings. Conversely, the oracles of the LORD transmitted by Ezekiel are no less the words of Ezekiel, quite typical of his personality, than are the writings of the compilers; in the vision in which he transports the prophet, God does not short-circuit the mind of his creature, he makes it join in in fullest accord, both consciously and subconsciously. The various modes of inspiration, which include the re-use and the remoulding of ancient traditions and the reflection of the wisdom writer, and which are all the Lord's merciful accommodation to human situations, call for a philological study of Scripture. In order the better to dig out the message and teaching of the texts, we cannot have too much help from lexicographers, grammarians, experts in semantics, stylistics, history and historical background, even the human sciences in so far as they are sciences and not, by their ideology, *too* human.

☐ Especially when one prepares to read Genesis, one point of philology must be underlined, the importance of *figurative language*, or tropes in the broad sense. Human speech rarely remains at the zero point of plain prose, which communicates in the simplest and most direct manner, using words in their ordinary sense. The word acquires very varied effects by taking off from this lowest point by steps which one might number 1, 2, ... n. These are ways of speaking, turns of phrase which distort language to a greater or lesser degree – the listener, of course, must take this into account, if he is not to mistake the meaning in a comic, or sometimes tragic, way. Herod is a fox only metaphorically (Lk. 13:32), the troops of the kings of Canaan are equal in number to the sand on

the seashore only by very obvious hyperbole (Jos. 11:4) – we trust
that is plain to everyone! But the figures of speech are not all so
easily detected, nor are they all part of such small units of
discourse.[6] The adoption of a literary *genre* generally allows a
step to be taken away from ordinary expression, from the zero
point. Thus the reader will refuse to take 'literally' the seed and
the Sower (Mt. 13:4–9), not because of anything in individual
sentences, but because he knows he is reading a parable. The
indications of the literary genre of a text affect its overall reading
(by showing that the laws of *genre* have affected its writing).

For both *genre* and sentence, on both larger or smaller scale,
the following rule may be put forward: the more an author works
at the form, the more plausible it is that he is stepping away from
the zero point. To this a second rule may be immediately added:
the more the trope or *genre* is commonplace or stereotyped in the
author's historical setting, the easier it is for him to leave the
ordinary mode of expression. If he is inventing or innovating, he
must take more precautions, to prevent a derailment of the
message in the reader's mind, but he will do this frequently by
allusion to familiar procedures. In these conditions it is not
difficult to deduce that in order to measure the 'stylistic variation',
knowledge of the historical situation and the cultural setting play
a decisive part; one rarely obtains formal proof, but one comes
near to certainty when convergent pointers, of significance in
their context, accumulate. In this respect, the interpretation of
the Bible proceeds like that of other books, because of its humanity. ☐

What about the language of Genesis? What is the literary
genre of its opening chapters? Everyone will agree that the
biblical writers liked figures of speech, metaphors, symbols,
transpositions more than the modern unpoetic West. An English
writer, E. W. Bullinger, filled a large volume of more than a
thousand pages with the figures of speech he found in the Bible.[7]
But the debate on Genesis is far from over, clouded at times by
fears and passions. A considerable amount is at stake. You
mistreat the text in equal proportions by veering too far to the
right in excessive literalism and by veering too far to the left in

[6] Paul Ricoeur in *La Métaphore vive* (Paris: Seuil, 1975) demonstrates superbly that
metaphor lies not in a word but in phraseology and the exploitation of the resources of
language.
[7] E. W. Bullinger, *Figures of Speech Used in the Bible Explained and Illustrated* (London:
Eyre & Spottiswoode, 1898). See also Charles F. Pfeiffer, 'Figures of speech in human
language', *BETS* 2:4 (1959), pp.17–21, which emphasizes that Scripture makes liberal use
of a variety of figures of speech.

taking as symbolic what is not. At this preparatory stage it is too early to decide the issue; such a crucial question can be resolved only in the study of the text, which we hope to carry out with philological rigour and according to the analogy of faith. As a preliminary measure, however, it seems useful to outline the literary shape of the first three chapters, on which we shall be concentrating.

But first there remains one major question for our consideration, relating to principle and method.

The place of the sciences

If the sciences of language and of history come to the aid of the Bible reader, what are we to think of the natural sciences? Grouped together in the singular, they enjoy the prestigious title of 'Science'. They claim to reconstruct the most distant past. There is no avoiding their confrontation with the Bible, and especially with Genesis; the allegedly scientific vision of cosmogony and of human origins is today the standard alternative to the biblical revelation.

At the risk of caricaturing, we shall distinguish three principal ways of picturing the relationship of the Bible and Science. We shall give them the rather inelegant titles of *concordism, anti-scientism* and *fideism*. Concordism which was once very popular still has its supporters; they point with amazement to the harmony between Scripture and the discoveries of modern scientists, citing such and such a scientist who admits as much. The best anyone could do to summarize what is known about the origins of the world would be to copy out the first chapter of Genesis.[8] In their interpretation of the Bible, they strive to bring out points of agreement with accepted scientific theories.

The opposing attitude is probably best known today as 'Creationism', of which it must be admitted there are many forms. We propose to use the term *anti-scientism* for that strong element within Creationism which insists upon a heavily literalistic interpretation of Genesis. In doing so, we understand 'anti' in both senses of the Greek prefix *anti*, 'against' and 'in the place

---

[8] For example the geologist Albert de Lapparent, and others quoted by Daniel Vernet in his article 'Creation', *Nouveau Dictionnaire Biblique* (St-Légier-sur-Vevey: Emmaüs, 1961), pp.156ff. In his own colourful way, Pierre Chaunu, *La Violence de Dieu* (Paris: Laffont, 1978), pp.81ff., announces the perfect correspondence of Gamow's cosmogonic model and Gn. 1:1ff.

of'.[9] Its followers protest against the elevation of Science to a religion; in addition they build a substitute science, a scientific explanation of phenomena to *replace* current theories. This they do because they judge biblical revelation to be incompatible with present-day scientific opinions and because they find the latter ill founded.

The third attitude, fideism, thinks it can resolve the problem by suppressing it; it separates the realm of faith from that where the geologists, paleontologists and others are pursuing the research. Like Kipling's East and West, never the twain shall meet. Many people, Catholic and Protestant, follow this line, repeating: 'The Bible is not a textbook of Geology or Anthropology; its opening chapters are concerned with matters of faith and not with questions of cosmogony. They teach metaphysical or religious truth, not physical truth; they are doctrinal, not historical.'[10]

Notice the three-cornered battle: fideism rejects the element which is common to the first two attitudes, the conviction that revealed truth touches the area of science; *anti-scientism* rejects the element common to the other two positions, support for prevailing scientific theories; finally, the concordists are the only ones who find in the biblical text a sort of outline of modern cosmogony.

Which position should we take inside this triangle, assuming that we have to remain inside it? Each position has its share of truth and each lays itself open to criticism.

Concordism which is so disparaged today has the merit of assuming its responsibilities. Certain Christians exhibit 'discordism'; they cut the links between experimental religion and experimental science. They deliberately forget their paleontology while they are reading their Bible, and they forget

[9] Translator's note: In French, *'le scientisme'* means an attitude towards the entire world and the whole range of human experience which seeks to explain these completely in terms of the sciences; it has obvious affinities with nineteenth-century French Positivism. One who holds this position is *'un scientiste'*, a philosophical term which is *not* the equivalent of the English word 'scientist'. For a recent presentation of the Creationist case, see Nigel M. de S. Cameron, *Evolution and the Authority of the Bible* (Paternoster, 1983), especially pp.47f. and n.l. The author develops the thesis that the theory of evolution in any form is incompatible with an evangelical approach to Scripture, but he is by no means tied to a literalistic reading of Genesis.

[10] For an example of this kind of language, see J. de Fraine, *La Bible et l'origine de l'homme* (Desclée de Brouwer, 1961). Among the dialectical Protestant theologians, the emphasis falls on the distinction between faith and various world-views, *cf.* Barth, pp.340ff. (and his preface); Bonhoeffer, pp.34ff.; on the Catholic side, the distinction is rather between doctrine and history, *cf.* Renckens, pp.246f.

their Bible while they are classifying their fossils. That bears little resemblance to courage, nor to a passion for truth. But concordism looks for coherence, and in that it is faithful to the spirit of the Scriptures. Its respect for the conclusions of the scholars not only manifests the modesty of common sense but also accords with the healthiest theology. For the sciences work with God's first book, his 'General Revelation'. All facts arise from God and scientific truth belongs to his Truth. The intelligibility of the real world around us, without which the scientific enterprise would not be possible, is guaranteed by the creating Word (the Logos) and by the Law instituted by God. Historically, it was in the cradle of the Christian view of the world that modern science was born, as A. N. Whitehead has pointed out. Thus the believer is ready to prejudge favourably a 'scientific' conclusion.

But because of its principal proposition, concordism constantly runs the risk of asking too much from the texts, or at any rate of reading them in an anachronistic light, one which does not come from the Bible and which can, paradoxically, obscure its meaning. Badly equipped and badly trained for exegesis, the concordists have more than once projected the science of their own time on to the Word of God, superimposing a different and varying authority on that which should remain supreme. Whilst they were attaching their interpretation on to the end of accepted theories, they did not allow for their fragility, and in the world of Science there is much that is far from being scientific.

The language of science urgently needs demythologizing. *Anti-scientism* excels in this exercise. Its strength lies in its exemplary critical vigilance, whilst the great mass of people bow down before the sacred cow. What is the progress of science, but a perpetual groping in the dark? Every day readjustments are made, periodically there are major reversals. Without going into the personal dimension of the researcher, we should denounce as utterly illusory the notion of pure objectivity, in the sense of neutrality or autonomy. No science operates without presuppositions, guide-lines and organizing models which are above ordinary verification. Ideological choices readily interfere at this basic level; the case of Lyssenko (the biologist whose error Stalin imposed on all by terror) was merely the most outrageous example of a well-nigh universal disorder, which usually remains unnoticed. Now these choices, which are all the less obvious the commoner they become, are marked by the revolt of mankind against his Creator and by his spiritual sickness. With the frenzied 'present age', Science can catch the fever and ramble on deliriously; the believer who is set free from the tyranny of the *Zeitgeist* very wisely keeps his distance.[11]

Anti-scientism still rightly refuses to accord blind credulity to the scientific account of origins. The scientist is forced to extrapolate, because the facts which nourish his theories are mere crumbs. Planned experimentation, which in other fields is *the* method to test hypotheses, is impossible here in practice. 'Nearly a century ago Ernest Renan spoke of our "conjectural sciences". He was writing about normal history. What should we say about the hypotheses of paleontology on the origins of man?'[12]

But it is not sufficient to shake naïve assurances by criticism of method. In order to have the right to challenge beliefs held by the vast majority, one must show that their presuppositions lead to misunderstanding the facts. If possible, a better general theory must be elaborated. The exponents of anti-scientism do their best to do so. Have they succeeded? Observers who stand with them in the area of faith are dubious on this point: they appear to give in to the easy answers of a blatant Manicheism and underestimate the value of the scientific consensus reached in the world. They forget that the mutual criticisms of the specialists who are often each other's rivals protect them partly from unwarranted extrapolations. The agreement of thousands of researchers is reached neither by chance nor by conspiracy! In our eyes, the opponents of established opinions, the kamikaze pilots of the academic world, show their lack of weight at two decisive points: when they minimize the value of identical conclusions reached independently by divergent methods and of convergences between the researches of 'official' scientists, and when, without permitting discussion, they attribute to Genesis a meaning which other readers do not find there and which they themselves justify only on the *a priori* ground of literalism.

As for *fideism*, it is right to distinguish between the realms of faith and scientific research. It is true that reality comprises many parts, various aspects. Since God is in fact distinct from the world, the theme of our relationship to him, which is the

[11] Noel Weeks, however, minimizes the effect of common grace when he writes: 'Any view of creation that commands a consensus amongst unbelievers must be suspect' (p.14). Without joining in the epistemological debate, we note how vigorously Konrad Lorenz denounces the effect of cultural disorders on scientists and their ideas, *Les huit péchés capitaux de notre civilisation* (Paris: Flammarion, 1973), p.145, *cf.* p.138.

[12] Nicolas Corte, *Les Origines de l'homme* (Paris: Fayard, 1957), p.79.

chief object of revelation, does not coincide with cosmology. It is equally certain that the text of Genesis is forced if it is treated as the answer to the scientists of our time.

But distinguish is not the same as separate. We must expose the fallacies of the fideists. The Bible, they say, is not a handbook of science. Agreed. But that does not mean it will have *nothing* to say which touches the realm of the scientist. The fact that the primary purpose of Genesis is not to instruct us in geology does not exclude the possibility that it says something of relevance to the subject. In the last analysis one cannot make an absolute separation between physics and metaphysics, and religion has to do with everything, precisely because all realms are created by God and continue to depend on him. To oppose 'doctrine' and (factual) 'history' is to forget that biblical doctrine is first of all history. Faith rests on facts, objectively asserted. Noel Weeks is not wrong when he discovers in 'fideist' separation the influence of a philosophy that is foreign to the Bible, that of Kant with his division between knowledge and belief.[13]

Is there a passage between the rocks? Our remarks indicate a safe channel. The believer will not dodge the task of harmonizing his interpretation of Genesis with his extra-biblical knowledge about the beginning. But he will not be in a hurry to approve or condemn the views of the scientists; with equal vigilance he will guard against the twin excesses of veneration and execration. If his calling allows, he will turn his interests to the elaboration of a rigorous scientific account, with presuppositions that have been rectified or reformed. His first concern, however, will be to discern the meaning of the biblical text.

That will be our concern. All the more so because we consider that the difficulties of the confrontation between the Bible and the sciences are not insuperable – in large part we would say they have been created by the corresponding failures of both the theologians and the scientists to be sufficiently circumspect. We shall therefore devote our whole study to interpretation, the discernment of the meaning. To others we shall leave the task of harmonizing Genesis and science. We shall limit ourselves in that regard to a brief statement in an Appendix.

☐   Before abandoning the subject of the natural sciences and their proper place, we must still consider one particular extension of

---

[13] Weeks, p.13. Our allusion is to Kant's famous saying, 'I have abolished [*aufgehoben*] knowledge in order to establish belief.' It is encouraging to find a liberal like Westermann reacting against fideism (pp.2ff.).

the question: what is the proper place of the sciences *in interpretation?* This question can obviously not wait until the work of interpretation is completed. It concerns the procedure to follow and must be treated first. We can tackle it now since we have looked in general terms at the question of the place of scientific thought and defined beforehand the nature of the text to be interpreted.

Current positions always affect our reading of the Bible, whether by persuading or by causing reaction. But this *fact* is not a *necessity*. We can expect by striving for clarity of thought to make this influence negligible. *Ought* we? That is the question. Or is it right to take account of scientific conclusions, as far as they appear certain, in the interpretation of Scripture? Must we forget what the scientists have given us, when we read Genesis, in order to avoid all interference as we listen to the pure signal? Or must we on the contrary illuminate the text by 'natural' light, since that too comes from God, the ultimate author of facts?

The Bible must not be placed under any other authority! On that point we cannot compromise. If the Bible is the Word of God, no authority, even one at the apex of the scientific world, may impose his authority on the Bible in order to dictate how it is to be understood, even with the best of intentions. Even such great Christians as Gregory of Nyssa[14] have fallen into that trap. Even if the 'facts' invoked are of God – for scientific opinions grasp these facts in a fallible manner and cannot approach on the authority of God *speaking himself.*

Instead of an authority, however, a *ministerial*, servant-role appears possible. In fact, no interpretation can develop in a vacuum; all interpretation appeals to the services of prior knowledge. In order to understand a text one uses one's knowledge not only of the language but also of the reality encompassed by the word (the referent). Thus we grasp straightaway that the story of Jotham is a fable, when it makes the trees talk (Jdg. 9:7ff.) because we know very well that trees do not talk. Our knowledge about trees plays a *servant*-role; it helps us to discern the literary genre and hence the meaning. Can one not conceive of a similar service on the part of scientific knowledge? The knowledge derived from the observation of reality ('science') would help us to understand the language of the Bible better.

[14] *Cf.* Jean Rousselot, 'Grégoire de Nysse, avocat...de Moïse', *In Principio*, pp.95–113, esp. p.112. Gregory asked if it were legitimate and thought he could give a positive response. Kidner, to whom we are at many points so close, seems to us to incline in this direction (p.31).

The nub of the problem is this: how can we prevent the servant from surreptitiously turning into an authority? Abuse is easy. Under the pretext of making use of our prior knowledge of reality, we can impose it on the text to act as a silencer. This is how we would reason: we know very well that…, *therefore* God did not mean…and that is subjecting the text, his Word, to our supposed knowledge. And this is what we would say: we know that the genesis of the cosmos took millions of years, *therefore* the 'seven days' must be taken allegorically; and that is conferring an unacceptable authority on scientific opinions, which for the believer means cheating with God's revelation. You might as well say that the resurrection of Christ is a symbol because we 'know' that the dead do not come back to life!

For the ministry to retain its servant-role and the authority of Scripture to remain supreme, what rule should we follow? We suggest the following: we have the right to bring our prior knowledge of reality to bear only as far as we can presuppose it in the *human* author of the biblical text. Our knowledge helps us to understand Jotham, to discern the use of allegory, because we are sure that Jotham shared it; for he knew as well as we do that trees do not speak. If it were a little child, or perhaps an idiot, who might not know that much about trees, we could not interpret in the same way; we should say to ourselves, 'Perhaps he is speaking literally'. Our knowledge of trees would no longer play a part in the interpretation, because we should no longer be sure that the author of the word had shared our knowledge. But the biblical Word has two 'authors', God and the inspired writer. Have we the right to bring our knowledge to bear by attributing it to the divine author of the Bible? That would be too easy, a kind of elevation of science to the ultimate position of a holy dogma! But if we can attribute it to the human author, it comes into consideration as in the case of Jotham's fable. That rule follows from the humanity of Holy Scripture. In the act of inspiration God did not turn his spokesmen into robots; his Word became their word, under their signature and their responsibility. Thus we have no right to go over their heads in order to set forth a 'divine' meaning which they would never possibly have imagined – even if those men did not grasp the whole import of what they attested (1 Pet. 1:10ff.). God in his condescension has limited himself to their instrumentality; our interpretation must conform to the corresponding discipline.

In the case of the opening chapters of Genesis, it is not plausible that the human author knew what we are taught by astronomers, geologists and other scientists. Therefore we must curb the desire to make the scientific view play a part in the actual interpretation; the interpretation must cling solely to the text and its context. The inescapable comparison with the sciences of cosmic, biological and human origins will not come until after; this will no doubt have repercussions on the work of interpretation which is never completed, but they will be of a merely external nature. The sciences will stimulate the interpreter from without, driving him to verify his exegesis and test the evidence, or encouraging him by favourable convergences which bear witness to the common origin of the two Books of God. In order to submit ourselves to God in his sovereign declarations and in the condescension of his inspiration of men, we conclude that the place of the sciences in the reading of the Bible is this: they have neither authority, nor even a substantial ministerial role within the actual interpretation; they act as warnings and confirmations at a later stage. ☐

The pathway is free, therefore, and our calling clear: to study Genesis as God's Word and as human words, in harmony with the whole of Scripture and according to the characteristics of its language. It is time to consider those characteristics.

The two 'tablets' of creation

The revelation of origins, at least of universal origins, unfolds in the first three chapters of Genesis. Like our distinguished predecessors, we shall devote the majority of our work to them. From the fourth chapter the book is obviously telling the sequel, and there is a modification in the literary form. Our preliminary description can therefore be confined to the two tablets of creation.

Why 'tablets'? We use the word to recall the writing techniques used at the time of Genesis, and no doubt for Genesis itself;[15] it has furthermore the advantage of being neutral, of not prejudging the literary genre. Why 'two'? At the very first glance one can recognize two quite distinct groupings: 1:1 – 2:3(4) and 2:4 – 3:24. Structural analysis confirms this first impression. The framework of the seven days is sufficiently obvious for the first tablet. A recent study has shown that the second is made up of seven symmetrical paragraphs arranged in a V, which proves

---

[15] *Cf.* P. J. Wiseman, *New Discoveries in Babylonia about Genesis* (London: Marshall, Morgan and Scott, 1936).

2⁴ HERE IS THE GENEALOGY OF THE HEAVENS ANI

a On the day when the LORD (YHWH) God made earth and heavens, no shrub of the fields was yet, no herb of the fields had yet grown, for the LORD God had not made it rain on the earth, and there was no man to cultivate the ground: a flood arose from the earth and watered all the surface of the ground.

The LORD God modelled the man, dust (taken) from the ground, and he breathed into his nostrils the spirit of life, and the man became a living being.

The LORD God planted a garden in Eden towards the East, and he put there the man that he had modelled. And the LORD God made grow from the ground every tree desirable to behold and good to eat and the tree of life in the middle of the garden – and the tree of the knowledge of good-and-evil.

A river came out of Eden to water the garden and, from that point, it divided and became four heads. The name of the (number) one: Pishôn; it is the one that meanders through all the land of Havila where gold is found – the gold of that country is good; there is found bdellium and the onyx stone. The name of the second river: Gihôn; it is the one that meanders through all the land of Cush. The name of the third river: Hiddegal (Tigris); it is the one which goes to the east of Assyria. And the fourth river: the Euphrates.

The LORD God took the man and settled him in the garden of Eden to cultivate it and keep it. And he gave the man this order: Of every tree of the garden EATING you shall eat, but of the tree of the knowledge of good-and-evil you shall not eat, for, the day you eat of it, DYING you shall die!

b ¹⁸The LORD God said: It is not good that the man be alone; I shall make him a helper to be his companion. And the LORD God modelled from the ground all the beasts of the fields and all the birds of the heavens. He made them come towards the man to see how he would call them, and every name which the man gave for a living being, that was its name. The man gave names to all the livestock, to the birds of the heavens and to all the beasts of the fields, but for the man he found no helper to be a companion. The LORD God made a deep torpor fall on the man, who fell asleep, he took one of his ribs and closed up the flesh in its place. The LORD God constructed as a woman the rib that he had taken from the man, and he made her come towards the man. And the man said:

This woman, this time, bone of my bones and flesh of my flesh!
This woman, she shall be called woman, for from the man she has been taken.

That is why a man leaves his father and his mother and is joined to his wife and they become one single flesh.

They were both naked, the man and his wife, and they had no shame.

c 3¹Now the Snake was the most artful of all the beasts of the fields that the LORD God had made, and he said to the woman: 'It's really so that God said, "You shall not eat of all the trees of the garden"...!
The woman said to the Snake: 'Of the fruit of the trees of the garden we eat, but of the tree which is in the middle of the garden God said "You shall not eat of it and you shall not touch it, lest you die."' And the Snake said to the woman: 'DYING you shall not die! For God knows that the day you shall eat of it your eyes will open and you will be like gods, knowing good-and-evil'.

d ⁶The woman saw that the tree was good to eat, that it was intelligence; she took of its fruit and ate; she gave (some The eyes of both of them opened and they knew that they coverings.

And they heard the voice of the LORD God walking in the themselves from before the LORD God in the midst of the

' ²⁰And the man gave to his wife the name of Eve (Livia), for she it was who became the mother of every living person.

The LORD God made for the man and his wife tunics of animal skin and he clothed them with them.

The LORD God said: 'Now has the man become like one of us, with regard to the knowledge of good-and-evil; now, lest he stretch forth his hand and take also of the tree of life, and eat, and live for ever...'

And the LORD God drove him out of the garden of Eden, to cultivate the ground from which he had been taken. He threw the man out, and he stationed at the east of the garden of Eden the $k^e r\hat{u}\underline{b}\hat{i}m$, and the sword with its revolving flame to guard the way to the tree of life.

' ¹⁴The LORD God said to the Snake: 'Because you have done this, cursèd may you be amongst all the livestock and amongst all the beasts of the fields. On your belly shall you go, and the dust shall you eat, all the days of your life. I put enmity between you and the woman, between your seed and her seed: he will bruise you in the head and you shall bruise him in the heel.'

To the woman he said: 'MULTIPLYING I shall multiply your pain and your conception; in pain shall you bring forth sons. Towards your husband your desire (shall carry you), but he shall rule over you.'

To the man he said: 'Because you listened to the voice of your wife and ate of the tree concerning which I had given you this order, "You shall not eat of it", cursèd be the ground because of you, in pain shall you eat all the days of your life; brambles and thistles it will make grow towards you, and you shall eat the herb of the fields. In the sweat of your face shall you eat your bread, until you return to the ground since you were taken from it – for you are dust and you shall return to the dust.'

C' ⁹The LORD God called the man and said to him: 'Where are you?' He said: 'I heard your voice in the garden, I was afraid because I am naked, and I hid myself.' And (God) said: 'Who informed you that you are naked? Of the tree which I had forbidden you to eat, have you eaten?' The man said: 'The woman whom you put with me, she gave me of the tree and I ate.' The LORD God said to the woman: 'What have you done?' And the woman said: 'The Snake deceived me, and I ate.'

pleasant to the eyes, and that the tree was desirable to gain also to her husband with her, and he ate.
were naked; they sewed fig leaves and made themselves

garden in the breath of the day: the man and the woman hid trees of the garden.

they form a carefully composed unit;[16] the further references to
the two trees afford additional proof of this.

☐   Our only hesitation concerns the formula in 2:4a, literally: 'These
are the generations (*tôl^{e}dôt*, from the root 'to beget') of the heavens
and of the earth…' Is that a title or a conclusion? Does it belong to
the first or to the second tablet? It could be the conclusion of what
precedes, as in JB: 'Such were the origins of heaven and earth
when they were created'.[17] It can also introduce what follows,
acting as the title for the second section; the paragraphing of AV,
RV and NIV indicate this reading: 'This is the account of the
heavens and the earth when they were created' (NIV). RSV leaves
the matter open. The formula, 'These are the generations of…' is
found a further ten times in Genesis, apparently marking its
divisions: in 5:1 ('This is the book of the generations of Adam',
RSV); 6:9; 10:1; 11:10, 27; 25:12, 19; 36:1, 9; 37:2. Now, as Kidner
argues powerfully, it seems always to be used as a title preceding
the passage concerned.[18] Further, the word *tôl^{e}dôt* seems to focus
on descendants, those begotten, or at least on genealogy. E. J.
Young insists on this meaning, in keeping with its etymology; in
which case 2:4 speaks of what was engendered in a metaphorical
sense by the heavens and the earth.[19] The Wisdom of Solomon
1:14 and more notably Matthew 1:1 chose the Greek word *genesis*
to render this idea, in the second case to introduce a genealogy.
All these facts clearly tip the balance; we shall take 2:4a as the
title of 2:4b – 3:24.   ☐

Why in fact two tablets? According to the old documentary
theory established by higher critical methods in the last century
by Graf and Wellhausen, here we have two rival traditions
concerning the creation, which have little in common. The second
was supposedly the older, belonging to the 'Yahwist' document
(J) developed in the tenth century in the early years of the
monarchy. The first supposedly came from the 'priestly' document (P) in the time of the exile. This theory, with its negative

---

[16] Jerome T. Walsh, 'Genesis 2.4b – 3.24: a synchronic approach', *JBL* 96 (1977), pp.161–
177. Cassuto, p.94, also distinguishes the seven paragraphs. Symmetrical, or chiastic,
structure is quite common in the Bible.

[17] This is the current critical view, held also by evangelicals such as R. K. Harrison,
Introduction to the Old Testament (IVP, 1970).

[18] Kidner, pp.23f.; *cf.* Keil, pp.70ff. Other examples they give, Nu. 3:1; Ru. 4:18; 1 Ch. 1:29,
confirm the point. The vast majority of evangelicals adopt this position, and also a critic like
Chaine, p.31, supports it.

[19] Young I, pp.59f., with quotations from Skinner and Driver (n.45). Martin H. Woudstra
reaches the same conclusion in 'The toledot of the Book of Genesis and their redemptive-
historical significance', *CTJ* (1970), pp.184–189.

implications for the veracity of biblical statements, raises crucial objections on three levels: method, the use (or neglect) of data on the ancient Near East, and theology. We stand rather with the contemporary specialists who maintain the traditional positions, those suggested by the Bible itself which associate Genesis with the work of Israel's most powerful thinker, 'our Teacher' as the Jews call him, Moses.

☐   In any case, in their differences the two tablets complete each other. Far from standing as a rival of the first, the second, as Renckens recognizes, 'is not in fact a second creation narrative at all'.[20] It is interested above all in the emergence of evil, and the prominent Jerusalem scholar, U. Cassuto, stresses that the Torah's answer on this fundamental point 'flows from the continuity of the two sections'; we receive the answer only 'when we study the two sections as a single sequence'.[21] The great critic von Rad has rightly seen 'that the two creation stories are in many respects open to each other' and that exegesis must be carried out on both together.[22] As for what the two have in common, the formation of the man and the woman, their agreement is substantial,[23] as we shall have occasion to point out, and the differences concern the viewpoint and the method of exposition.   ☐

The *tôlᵉḏôṭ* of Genesis are basically traditions linked to genealogies, the ancestral stories, collected, approved and purified by the inspired writer of the book. The tablet 2:4 – 3:24 is the first of these stories or traditions. A patriarchal narrative, as it is often called, it is taken up by a Teacher who is very sure of his methods and of his aims. The first tablet resembles a panoramic prologue, the inspiration for the prologue of John's Gospel, a 'solemn overture',[24] a 'majestic gateway'.[25] It puts everything in place in the construction of the heavens and the earth, before the narration of the events of which the earth will be the theatre. The inversion from 'the heavens and the earth' to 'the earth and the heavens' in 2:4 symbolizes the change of perspective from one tablet to the other.[26]

The style of the prologue is amazing for its deliberate simplicity, its ascetic style. It shows not the slightest trace of rhetoric. Von Rad makes the excellent comment that this 'sober

---

[20] Renckens, p.157 (though he admits the theory of sources); *cf.* Barth, pp.239ff.
[21] Cassuto, p.92.   [22] Von Rad, p.41.
[23] I. Engnell has emphasized this and goes so far as to say that the second story is a variant of the first, quoted by Payne, p.28, n.5.
[24] Westermann *G*, p.129. (Westermann attributes it to the P source.)
[25] Michaëli, p.16.   [26] Barth drew attention to this, p.234.

monotony', this 'radical renunciation' manage to 'mediate aesthetically the impression of restrained power and lapidary greatness'.[27] If we leave aside hazardous guesses about the prehistory of the text (in which some would like to find traces of earlier documents), two main questions are raised by the tablet. What is the mode of revelation of this inspired word? What is its literary genre? It is better to take the second question first, for the form attained (the genre) must serve as a clue to the 'how' of the formation (the inspiration).

Is it prose or poetry? The choice is a gross oversimplification. Even Young who wishes to see in Genesis 1 only 'straightforward history',[28] recognizes without any sense of inconsistency that the chapter 'is written in exalted, semi-poetical language'.[29] It is clear that we do not find here the rhythms of Hebrew poetry, nor its more or less synonymous parallelism. The reader of the original, however, is sensitive to the rhythm of the sentences, he notices a number of alliterations and one phrase which is confined to poetry, 'beast of the field'.[30] Albright saw in the refrain '(God saw) that it was good' a cry of wonder, the sign of an antecedent poetic form.[31] The word 'hymn' comes to many writers. Whether it is a strophic hymn in prose or a hymn which is a unique blend of prose and poetry,[32] Paul Beauchamp, the most sensitive of analysts, wisely concludes: 'By the importance of repetition and of its corollary, silence, our text is indeed close to poetry, but its movement towards a solution places it in the order of prose.'[33] Following his lead we can say that the genre is composite. The *narrative* becomes at the same time a *classification*, like the orderly lists of priests and wise men. There are perhaps reminiscences of theophany (1:2) and one may recall the *cosmogonies* of other peoples (in the subject-matter rather than the form). The entire passage seems 'akin to the hymn', although the unuttered note of praise in the pure objectivity favoured by the writer remains only implied.[34]

In any case, the author has carefully calculated the whole

[27] Von Rad, p.62.

[28] Young I, p.105. *Cf.* Allan A. MacRae, 'The principles of interpreting Genesis 1 and 2', *BETS* 2:4 (1959), p.2: 'The passage is about as factual and literal as any section anywhere in the Bible'.

[29] *Ibid.*, p.82.   [30] In 1:24. See Cassuto, pp.10f.

[31] W. F. Albright, 'The refrain "And God saw ki-Tob" in Genesis', *Mélanges Robert*, pp.22–26.

[32] Westermann *C*, p.36; *G*, p.126.

[33] Beauchamp, p.384.   [34] *Ibid.*, pp.387ff.

passage. The regular flow of thought conceals a careful construction which uses symbolic numbers: 10, 3 and particularly 7. Ten times we find *'God said'*, and for Beauchamp that decalogue forms the framework of the text.[35] Of those ten words, three concern mankind (1:26, 28, 29) and seven the rest of the creatures.[36] The creative orders they include use the verb to be, 'let there be', three times for the creatures in the heavens, and seven different verbs for the world below.[37] The verb 'to make' also appears ten times, as does the formula 'according to its/ their kind'. There are three benedictions, and the verb 'create' is used at three points in the narrative, the third time thrice.[38] Above all we read seven times the completion formula 'and it was so', which Monsengwo Pasinya makes the key formula,[39] seven times also the approval 'and God saw that it was good', and seven times a further statement is added (God names or blesses). All these heptads, or groups of seven, are independent of that of the seven days, which we are setting aside for a special study. By counting the words, Cassuto finds several others.[40] Beyond any doubt, here we have no ordinary history, such as might be written in response to a simple request to be told what happened. Here we have the work of a Master whose thought is profound and expansive.

In what way did God inspire the author of such a passage? Two theories which have their supporters seem to us to run counter to the evidence. The idea that the sacred writer might have taken a pagan myth of origins in order to correct it and purify it in line with his monotheistic faith overlooks the perfection of the composition in its finest details; it gives undue weight to a number of resemblances which are incomplete, while neglecting the contrast which is very striking. In his classic work on the subject, Alexander Heidel declares that 'in the light of the differences, the resemblances fade away almost like the

---

[35] *Ibid.*, p.33.

[36] Cassuto, p.14.

[37] Beauchamp, pp.53f.

[38] You get 'create' seven times if you include 2:4a, but that half-verse is excluded in other calculations.

[39] L. Monsengwo Pasinya, 'The literary framework of Genesis 1', *Bib.* 57 (1976), p.231. The whole article (pp.225–241) is remarkable.

[40] Cassuto, p.14, points out that Gn. 1:1 contains seven words, 1:2 contains twice seven words and the seventh paragraph (2:1–3) seven times five. 'Earth' recurs thrice seven times, Elohim (God) seven times five times. We would add that the names of God occur seventy times in Gn. 1 – 4, a proof of their unity: forty times it is Elohim, twenty times Yahveh Elohim and ten times Yahveh.

stars before the sun'.[41] At the other extreme, orthodox Christians have imagined that we were dealing with a revelation transmitted from one century to the next, perhaps going right back to Adam, and recorded in writing by Moses.[42] But again the subtlety of the overall structures of the text make this theory improbable, and anyway how much information would survive after thousands of years of oral transmission, under conditions where life itself was precarious?[43] The text suggests nothing that points in that direction. Are we to think in terms of visions? Genesis gives us a 'restrospective Apocalypse', as Claude Tresmontant happily put it.[44] Now, we know that John's Apocalypse, the book of Revelation, combines visions with the highest literary achievements, but there is not a single comma in the Genesis text on which to hang a visionary hypothesis. Since the passage is constructed like the utterances of a Wisdom writer, the most prudent course is to suppose that God inspired this writer as he did the authors of Wisdom literature, not by short-circuiting him but, on the contrary, by directing and bearing along his meditation. The mode of revelation is that of Wisdom writing;[45] the Wisdom theologian who draws up his thoughts gives us 'knowledge in a most concentrated form',[46] matured in meditation on the finished works of God.[47] Is it necessary to recall that Moses, who was first 'instructed in all the wisdom of the Egyptians' (Acts 7:22), was filled with the Spirit of wisdom which he later passed on to Joshua (Dt. 34:9)?

Strangely enough, it is also the mastery of the wise man that we admire in the second tablet, which is so different in appearance and tone. How may we best characterize the differences? After the calm, majestic river, comes the stream which first of all skips along cheerfully and then suddenly plunges into dark ravines. The style is lively and picturesque; the pictures take

[41] Heidel, p.139. This conclusion is close to that of one of the two editors of the Atrahasis epic, A. R. Millard, 'A new Babylonian "Genesis" story', *TB* 18 (1967), pp.3–18. Amongst recent commentators, Westermann unfortunately insists on the idea of Genesis 1 as myth; without giving any reasons he ascribes to it the mythical function of actualizing primeval time (*C*, pp.10ff., 40ff.).

[42] Keil, pp.45f. Young I, pp.26f., seems to admit the idea of tradition, but because of its probable corruption it was accompanied with a revelation to Moses. Waltke (1975) holds to this view, p.331.

[43] Chaine, p.71. M. J. Lagrange, 'L'innocence et le péché', *RB* 6 (1897), p.377, considered the theory 'supremely unlikely'.

[44] Claude Tresmontant, *Etudes de métaphysique biblique* (Paris: Gabalda, 1955), p.143.

[45] See Payne, p.21.　　　[46] Von Rad, p.45.

[47] Westermann *C*, p.46, speaks of a 'drive towards a complete, objective, abstract comprehension of what is'.

shape spontaneously in the reader's mind. The LORD God takes on a human form: we see him mould clay, breathe into the man's nostrils, walk in the garden when the breeze gets up and make for the guilty couple better clothes than their improvised cloths. There is a dream-like garden with strange trees and a cunning animal who opens a conversation; you could believe you were in one of those artless legends, one of those timeless stories which are the fascination of folklore. To be sure, the second tablet is closer in language than the first to the myths of the nations. There you have the same opening, 'it was before...before...', the divine potter, the primeval age of gold, the woman emerging from a rib, the tree of life, the cunning snake.[48] In spite of the gravity of the themes dealt with, ought we to see in the early *tôlᵉ dôt*s the fruit of thinking that is in its cultural infancy? A closer, deeper study reveals rather the reverse. The author of Genesis, in (probably) taking over a patriarchal tradition, shows that he is anything but naïve; he works as an artist who is fully aware of his aims and means. 'This', writes von Rad, 'is anything but the bluntness and naïvety of an archaic narrator. It is, rather, the candor and lack of hesitation which is only the mark of a lofty and mature way of thinking.'[49]

The discipline of the structure which we have already pointed out[50] proves this, although the second tablet does not follow the same very elaborate geometrical structure as the first. It would be difficult to achieve spontaneously the art with which the dramatic tension is built up and then resolved. The dialogue between the woman and the snake is the work of an expert psychologist, as is the description of the attitudes after the fall. Commentators whom one could not accuse of partiality give a favourable verdict: here we have 'a religious and literary achievement of the highest order'.[51]

☐   One highly revealing feature is the play on words. They are too numerous not to arise from the literary technique. Jean de Fraine has devoted a complete article to several of them.[52] The most

---

[48] Of course, not all of these elements are found in every mythology, but each is found in one or several, particularly those from Mesopotamia. See the clear synthesis presented by Chaine, pp.61ff.; for a broad survey, *cf.* N. Corte, *op. cit.*, ch.1.

[49] Von Rad, p.24, *cf.* p.95.

[50] See above, p.30, esp. n.16 referring to Walsh.

[51] Robert Gordis, 'The knowledge of good and evil in the Old Testament and the Qumran scrolls', *JBL* 76 (1957), p.129.

[52] Jean de Fraine, 'Jeux de mots dans le récit de la chute', *Mélanges Robert*, pp.47–58, esp. pp.53ff. It seems to us that the author could have chosen even better examples.

obvious is the one which passes from 'naked' in 2:25 (*ᵃrûmmîm*, the plural of *'ārôm*) to 'cunning' in 3:1 (*'ārûm*), to which may be added 'cursed' in 3:14 (*'ārûr*).[53] A similar connection can be seen between 'tree' (*'ēṣ*) and 'pain' (*'eṣeḇ* and its derivative *'iṣṣāḇôn*) in 3:16ff.[54] There are also the various meanings of the same word, such as rib and side, on which the author plays with great skill. □

The theological richness of the teaching provides another reason to suppose a conscious distance between the writer and the language he uses. We hope to give the reader some feeling of this later in our work, but at this point we can quote von Rad who admits that the story of paradise and the fall is 'something unique'.[55] It is not simply that the tree of the knowledge of good and evil which is central to the biblical account is found nowhere else. The whole atmosphere differs profoundly from that of myth.[56] Again, along with several specialists, we can recognize that the way the story is treated places it with Wisdom writings.[57] It is a learned ingenuousness which here uses common language to set forth a unique message.

At this point the question presses on us: what are we to understand literally? The debate is by no means recent. Centuries ago Augustine declared:

> On this subject there are three main views. According to the first, some wish to understand paradise only in a material way. According to the second, others wish to take it only in a spiritual way. According to the third, others understand it both ways, taking some things materially and others spiritually. If I may briefly mention my own opinion, I prefer the third.[58]

□   The church's reading throughout history has been predominantly literal, even if one can quote an authority like Cajetan in the sixteenth century, who saw a parable in the formation of the woman from the rib and considered it childish to understand the punishment of the snake literally.[59] Lagrange exaggerates when he asserts: 'It has always been understood in the church that this story was very true but was not like any other, a story full of

[53] Cassuto, p.159.   [54] Cassuto, p.165; Young III, pp.123, 132.   [55] Von Rad, p.95.
[56] As von Rad recognizes, the narrative 'has very little in common with a real myth', p.95.
[57] See in particular Luis Alonso-Schökel on Wisdom and covenant motifs in Genesis, *Bib.* 43 (1962), pp.295–315.
[58] *De Gen. ad litt.* VIII, 1.
[59] M. J. Lagrange, *art. cit.*, pp.364, 367.

figures of speech, metaphors, symbols or popular language'.[60] But the dominant literalist trend has not always carried the day completely, even in the exegesis of its supporters. Such an unbending literalist as E. J. Young warns against too literal an interpretation of 3:21 and stresses that it would be ridiculous to picture God sewing the clothes with his fingers.[61] No commentator who has received the story as the Word of God has been satisfied with a completely flat literalistic reading. He has had to admit the presence of anthropomorphisms and he has added a symbolic meaning to the elements that he supposedly took literally. Conversely, the authors at the opposite extreme who have ranked the story in the same category as myths, to be taken symbolically, have admitted the originality of the biblical text. Paul Ricoeur is the signal example.[62] In our view this indicates that we must set the Genesis narrative apart and not treat its content as that of myths, which are attempts of the human imagination to give formal expression to the meaning and the struggles of existence.[63] □

One point ought to be established. The alternative of all or nothing rests on purely arbitrary grounds. The use of figurative language by no means determines the main question, that of the connection of the narrative with events that are located and dated from the beginning. The acknowledgment of symbolic elements hardly weighs at all in favour of a symbolic interpretation of the whole. Conversely, those who favour the literal historicity of the content have no reason to demand the same literalness of the language. Scripture, as has been pointed out by the evangelical scholar J. A. Thompson and by Fr. A.-M. Dubarle, abounds in examples of mixed genre.[64] It frequently recounts the passage of history in the categories of parable or allegory, and expresses the facts it recalls in images and symbols. Thus Jesus himself summarizes centuries of history in the parable of the wicked tenants (Mt. 21:33–41) and elsewhere refers to history by speaking in a figurative manner.[65] Before him the prophets had recalled past facts and predicted the future with a welter of images. Ezekiel paints vast allegorical frescoes; Ezekiel 16 says figuratively what Ezekiel 22 says liter-

[60] *Ibid.,* p.361.   [61] Young III, p.149.   [62] Ricoeur, pp.183ff.

[63] Dubarle thus summarizes the conclusions of the critical scholar, Martin Noth: 'The author of chapters 2 – 3 has not followed any of the ancient Near East creation narratives, but has simply used detailed images to express what was his own creation', p.51, n.

[64] Thompson, p.17; Dubarle, p.51, n.2.

[65] Dubarle instances the parables of Mt. 13 with their historical range and the allegory of Jn. 10.

ally, and Ezekiel 23 does likewise for the historical events of chapter 20.[66] And what else is the book of Revelation? The majority of commentators see in it not only 'ideas' but 'what must soon take place' (Rev. 1:1). Now Revelation is very fond of taking over items from Genesis and using them symbolically. These examples do not prove that this is the case in the second tablet, but at least they prove that we could not exclude the possibility. It is a possibility that it is wise to consider.

The decision concerning the first three chapters of the Bible can be taken only in the light of the rest of God's revealed Word, with the help of all the information or suggestions it supplies. As we pass to more detailed study, we shall take care not to forget that.

[66] Dubarle adds Ezk. 19:10–14; Thompson adds 2 Sa. 12:1–4; Is. 5 and also Jdg. 9:8–15 and 2 Ki. 14:9.

2
The week of creation

Nobody reading the panoramic prologue of Genesis can miss the structural fact which gives the text its most obvious arrangement: the framework of the seven days. The division of the paragraphs corresponds to that of a week, whose days are carefully numbered. Even if this organization had been imposed on an older narrative of eight works of God – which we do not consider to be the case[1] – the proofs we have given of the author's careful structuring of his material would be enough to warn us not to suppose that the sevenfold shape is either imaginary or incidental.

Since on the seventh day God 'finished' and rested (*šābāt*), and since he blessed and sanctified that time of rest, it is impossible to miss the connection between the week of Genesis and the institution of the sabbath (*šabbât*) in the time of Moses. Indeed, the decalogue in Exodus refers back to the creation account (Ex. 20:11). Certainly Genesis nowhere calls the sabbath a primeval law; as Renckens points out, 'there is no text which says explicitly that *man* was from the beginning under an obligation to observe a day of rest'.[2] Its institution is found only from Exodus onwards (Ex. 16, particularly v.29: 'The LORD has given you the sabbath'). It is a provision made for Israel, with perhaps a reference of a

[1] The opinion that an earlier version contained only the eight works which were subsequently compressed into six days is very common: *e.g.* von Rad, pp.62f.; Payne, p.18. Beauchamp, who supports the structure of ten words, shows that this is superficial. We should add that the addition of an extra work at days 3 and 6 is in no way a sign of difficulties on the part of the author; it is a subtlety pregnant with meaning.

[2] Renckens, p.100.

critical nature to the Mesopotamian *šabattu*.[3] But the celebration of God's creation as a work of six days followed by a day of sacred rest is undoubtedly intended as an allusion to the sabbath.

What is the meaning of the allusion? And how are we to compare the assertion of the seven days with the billions of years, at the lowest estimate, which current scientific theory attributes to the origin of the universe? It is impossible to avoid these questions, which revolve around the central question, that of interpretation: how are we to understand Genesis when it enumerates the days of the divine handiwork?

The authors who like us put their faith in the text and who wish to model their attitude towards it on that of Jesus Christ, receiving it as a reliable revelation, do not reply with a single voice. Interpretations differ. If we put aside suggestions that are too marginal or lightweight, like that of the days of visions,[4] there remain four rival theories in the arena. These four interpretations which enjoy considerable support amongst the Christian public (if not amongst the specialists) vary sufficiently from one another to necessitate a choice between them.

Were we to classify these four positions in order of decreasing tension between them and the conclusions of geology and paleontology, we should have to start with the literal interpretation which takes the days as 24-hour days, for it leads to a total rejection of the usual dating of the cosmos and its associated theories. The reconstruction theory would come next; that takes the days as days in which God restored the earth after it had been ruined by the fall of the devil. So it allows the original creation (Gn. 1:1 only) all the time anyone wants. But the plan corresponds poorly with the scientific reconstruction of the past. Third would come the concordist theory which sees the days as ages or geological eras. It agrees more closely with the views of the scientists, which is precisely its aim. As for the fourth, it

---

[3] In spite of the similarity of the words, many reject this connection because the *shabattu* or *shapattu* of the Babylonians and Assyrians, the fourteenth and twenty-eighth days of the month, were unlucky days, inauspicious for any kind of undertaking. Cassuto, however, pp.65ff., quotes a text where the *shabattu* is also the 'day of rest of the heart'. Both sabbath and *shabattu* divide the lunar month, another point in common. The similarities are sufficient to admit a conscious reference to the *shabattu* on the part of Moses, but in guise of a counter-motif which reversed the meaning of inactivity.

[4] This was the theory of the Jesuit priest, Hummelauer, criticized by M. J. Lagrange, 'Hexameron (Genese 1 a 2,4)', *RB* 5 (1896), pp.391f. It was defended by P. J. Wiseman, *Creation Revealed in Six Days* (London: Marshall, Morgan and Scott, 1948); but we agree with F. F. Bruce, B. Ramm (p.222) and Kidner (p.54) that it is impossible to make the word 'made' mean 'made known'.

takes its place without any difficulty, since it views the framework of the days as a logical and literary device; the point of conflict disappears. We shall not, however, follow that order; so as to maintain the course we have set with regard to the role of science in biblical interpretation, we shall avoid a classification which would make the Bible's relationship with science the decisive factor. Exegesis must rather free itself from excessive concern in that direction. We shall discuss the four notions in order of increasing probabilities. From the thesis which has the weakest foundations we shall progress towards the one which seems to us to take greatest account of the data as a whole.

The reconstruction theory

The renowned Scottish preacher and theologian, Thomas Chalmers (1780–1847), was the first major proponent of the view that we shall examine first. It seems that he was seeking to reconcile Genesis with the new discoveries about the age of the earth.[5] His ideas made headway throughout the nineteenth century. The Swiss theologian Augustin Gretillat followed them. Most notably the lawyer C. I. Scofield incorporated them in his annotated Bible, thus assuring them enormous diffusion. As late as 1970 A. C. Cunstance strove to defend them.[6]

According to this theory, the six days are not, as had been believed, days of creation, but days of reconstruction. God restored the original edifice after the creation suffered a terrible catastrophe. What was this disaster? The action occurred between the first and second verses of Genesis 1, in the mysterious gap which lies between them; hence the common label, 'the gap theory'. According to the majority of the theory's supporters, one should in fact translate, 'and the earth *became* without form and void', and, since the expression (*tōhû wābōhû*) elsewhere designates the effect of destruction (Is. 34:11, *cf.* 45:18 with *tōhû*; Je. 4:23), one must suppose that a catastrophe occurred. Besides, the argument goes, the presence of darkness, the symbol of evil, clearly shows that evil came into the world. Some exponents would also adduce the death of animals, which preceded the appearance of mankind on earth. How did the evil arise, if it were not by the revolt of Satan, which can be read

---

[5] John C. Whitcomb, 'The ruin reconstruction theory of Genesis 1.2', *SSt* 32; *cf.* Ramm, p.196, for certain precursors and followers.

[6] Quoted by Waltke (1975), pp.136ff.

between the lines in Isaiah 14:3–23 and Ezekiel 28:11–19?

The advantages of the hypothesis could well be simply superficial. Invented in order to please the scientists, it has had considerable difficulty satisfying them. What evidence have they found of the three supposed phases with their radical discontinuity? The explanation of 'evil' in nature would be more attractive, but *nowhere* does the Bible establish any connection between the fall of Satan and alleged cosmological effects.[7] It would be necessary to decide whether the Bible sees animal death as an 'evil'. It seems to us that this is not the case, and the speeches of God in the book of Job exalt the terrifying beauty of the beasts of prey as God's work (Jb. 38:39ff.; 39:26ff. and the description of Leviathan in Jb. 41).

☐ For reasons of biblical theology we must assert the fall of Satan, but Scripture's reticence on this fact should warn us against giving it a key position in our system. The time of that fall has not been revealed. It is a misuse of Scripture to appeal to the two prophetic passages (Is. 14; Ezk. 28) in order to make them the foundations of the doctrine. The first expressly concerns the king of Babylon and nothing requires us to look further than him.[8] The second is directed against the prince of Tyre, and if behind his fall another can be sensed, it is rather the fall of mankind.[9]

The fact that elsewhere chaos is the result of a catastrophe does not mean that this is so in Genesis 1:2. What has received form returns into formlessness only as a result of some misfortune. But this is very obviously not the case for the unformed which has yet to be formed! The reconstructionists overlook this obvious point. As for the darkness of Genesis 1:2, it is not necessarily a symbol of evil; here it could simply be the state of readiness for the appearance of light. Thus the grounds for the theory vanish into thin air.

In particular the hypothesis raises two insurmountable diffi-

---

[7] Rev. 12:12 is the only text which speaks of 'woe' for the earth and sea, but that is after the defeat of Satan and the ascension of Christ; v.17 makes clear that the reference is to the persecution of Christians.

[8] Waltke (1975) recognizes this, p.143.

[9] With the ancient versions we should read Ezk. 28:14: 'I set you with a towering cherub...' and 28:16: 'the guardian cherub banished you' (so NEB). God is here speaking to a man. Verses 1–10 recall the sin of Adam, for the prince of Tyre has grown proud as a man, and he will receive the punishment of man by returning to the dust. John L. Mackenzie, 'Mythological allusions in Ez 28. 12–18', *JBL* 75 (1956), pp.322–327, has shown, contrary to certain allegations, that no known pagan myth is sufficiently close to Ezk. 28 to justify the idea of a heavenly character in this passage; the closest text is Gn. 2 – 3. We agree with Ramm, pp.205f.

culties. The translation 'And the earth became' takes inadmissible liberties with the Hebrew grammar. The only admissible translation is 'And [or better, Now] the earth was...', by analogy with constructions that are totally similar in Jonah 3:3 ('Now Nineveh was...') and, nearer home, Genesis 3:1 ('Now the snake was...').[10] Only in defiance of philology may the pseudo-translation 'the earth became' act as the basis of the theory. Further, the theory requires that the verb 'make', even in 2:2f. and in Exodus 20:11, be given the meaning 'remake'. There is no justification for such violence to the language. Hebrew offers the means of expressing the notion of remaking and repairing, but the text does not show the slightest trace of it. □

The verdict on the whole theory must be 'quite impossible'.[11] It draws no support from the text, but rather brings its own framework, digging its own imaginary gap between the two verses in order to set it up. We could in truth have set it aside immediately, as we did the theory of visions. But its example provides a valuable warning. It puts us on our guard against an interpretation which adds ingeniously to Scripture by exploiting silences and arranging things with the very best of motives, without submitting to the discipline of philology. As Bacon put it, the human imagination has no need of wings, rather it needs lead weights to bring it down to earth.

The concordist interpretation

The idea that the days of Genesis represent the interminable eras and periods of which the scientists speak was also launched in the nineteenth century. Ramm mentions as its first proponents Hugh Miller (1869), J. Dana and J. W. Dawson.[12] It seemed plausible to many excellent minds. In France it was taken up by the scientist Henri Devaux and today it is argued by Daniel Vernet, who has written plenty on the relations between the Bible and science.[13] With some hesitation that penetrating, careful exegete Derek Kidner gives it his approval.[14]

[10] In order to fit the reconstructionist view, the text would have to read *watt^e hî hā'āreṣ*. Hebrew scholars are in total agreement, *e.g.* Ramm, p.202; Whitcomb, pp.33f.; Waltke (1975), pp.138–140.

[11] Von Rad, p.48.   [12] Ramm, p.211.

[13] *Cf.* his article 'Création' in the French publication, *Nouveau Dictionnaire Biblique* (St-Légier-sur-Vevey: Emmaüs, 1961), and the relevant passages in *La Bible et la Science* (Guebwiller: Ligue pour la lecture de la Bible, 1978²).

[14] Kidner, pp.55ff.

The heart of the argument concentrates on the meaning of the word *yôm*, day. The term is not always restricted to the 24-hour rotations of the earth. It can be used for an indefinite or considerable length of time. In this respect Kidner cites Psalm 90:4, 'For a thousand years in thy sight are but as yesterday when it is past', and the expression 'in that day' for the coming messianic age (Is. 4:2; there is no shortage of examples). The text of Genesis provides a very valuable indication that this must be the case with the seven 'days'. Indeed, the seventh day does not conclude with the formula, 'there was evening and there was morning', from which one must with Augustine deduce its permanence;[15] in the same sense F. Delitzsch spoke of its 'infinite perspective'.[16] If the seventh day extends across thousands of years of history, the six others can cover the millions of centuries of cosmogony. When you thus give yourself all the time you wish, you are amazed at the correspondence with the geological diagram. The Bible was ahead of the scientists. It may even have been ahead with the priority of light, certainly with the succession from inorganic to organic, the location of the earliest animal life in the sea, and its placing of mankind not in the centre but at the conclusion.

The concordist theory deserved a large share of the favour it enjoyed. It brings a responsible attitude to both revelation received and knowledge acquired. It honours the call to a synthesis implied by the summons of truth. It suffers, however, from a number of small failings and comes up against one enormous difficulty.

First of all we must make clearer distinctions. The metaphorical use of a word like 'day' is a function of style which must not be confused with the presence of a broad meaning amongst the usual meanings of the word; and if this broad meaning exists, it is not yet certain that it fits the context. True, *yôm* is not always used in its most precise sense in the Old Testament, but the reader is given a false impression if he is led to believe that *yôm* in Hebrew behaves very differently from 'day' in English. We are familiar with the loosest usage when we speak of the 'day' when Britain ruled the waves, or when the human race will colonize other planets. The context makes the sense clear. Now, as anyone who reads the passage in English fully realizes, the numbering of the days and more particularly the mention of the evenings and the mornings[17]

[15] *Confessions* XIII, xxxvi, 51.   [16] Kidner, p.53.   [17] Payne, p.8.

diminish the possibility of such a loose usage here. Inevitably the mind turns to clearly defined days in the ordinary sense, days of twenty-four hours. Concordists suggest in that case that the evenings and mornings could represent phases of slowing down and then of intense activity in the creation of the cosmos. But have they noticed that they have suddenly shifted their ground? Here they are abandoning their enquiry into the meaning of *yôm* in order to suppose a figurative style, which is quite a different matter. It is possible to treat the terminology of the week as figurative language, but at that moment 'day' has its ordinary meaning and *with that meaning* plays a figurative role. In the same way, in 'Herod, that fox' (Lk. 13:31f.) the fox does not vaguely indicate any animal, but is used metaphorically. The concordists seem less than clear on this point. Thus, in Psalm 90:4 which they quote, 'day' has its most commonplace meaning, but it is used in a comparison and that is what brings out the relativity of human time for God (as also in 2 Pet. 3:8); it is not the vague sense of the phrase 'in that day'. If we opted definitely for figurative language, we should have to take the whole framework of the week in those terms, ask if the progression is to be taken literally, and if the referent of the figure is the series of geological periods. The last possibility would seem unlikely. Kidner does not dare attribute to the author the conscious awareness of what his exegesis claims to discover.[18]   □

Next, the agreement with the scientific view is not as easy and complete as at first appears. If we may pass over the problem of the unequal duration of the day-eras, there are noticeable differences in the order of the details. In the Bible, trees (Day 3) precede marine organisms (Day 5), and birds (Day 5) precede insects (Day 6); scientists think the opposite.[19]

But the biggest disagreement stares you straight in the face: the creation of the sun and stars on the fourth day, after the earth and its vegetation, even after the trees. On this reef the concordist boat is wrecked. The usual explanation, that at that particular epoch God dispersed a thick covering of cloud and *revealed* the luminaries for the first time, looks like an admission of failure. Once again, in order to get out of a difficulty, people would like to change the meaning of a word which is simple and well known. The geocentric viewpoint of the narrative gives no

[18] Kidner, p.57.
[19] Morris develops this point, *SC*, pp.227f.

authority to turn 'make' into 'reveal'.[20] Genesis has a perfectly
good word for 'appear' when it needs to use it (1:9). We join many
writers in rejecting the proposed 'solution'.[21] Quite apart from
the gratuitous nature of the 'cloud' hypothesis, the theory of
day-eras does violence to the text with regard to the fourth day.

The literal interpretation

The two interpretations we have just examined sought primarily
to supplant the literalist reading of the prologue of Genesis.
This is the reading that enjoys the support of the majority
throughout church history, notably that of the Reformers.
Competent, authoritative commentators have followed it, such
as C. F. Keil in the nineteenth century and E. J. Young in this
century. Mention may also be made of the Australian, Noel
Weeks, and of the scientists associated with the Creation
Research Society (with J. C. Whitcomb filling the theological
role).

They are all agreed that the days are to be taken in the
ordinary sense and that the narrative aims to give us the
chronology of the work of creation. It is quite simply history. Not
that any human eyewitness could supply the information, but
God provided for that by revelation. The first days without the
sun present no difficulty for those who know the power of God.
He could produce light from a source other than the sun.[22] As for
the different order of the appearance of the creatures in the
second 'tablet' (Gn. 2), either the second narrative is not
chronological,[23] or else it concerns simply a local appearance (in
Eden),[24] or else in 2:19 one should read: 'The LORD God *had
formed* from the ground every beast...'[25]

Defenders of the literal interpretation argue that the text
contains no indication of figurative language.[26] They constantly

[20] In order to illustrate the negligence of certain authors in their exegesis, we can quote
Pearce, p.90, who adopts the concordist explanation of v.14 and adds that the existence of the
luminaries is indicated two verses later by the Hebrew perfect, which conveys completion
rather than action. But there is no Hebrew perfect in v.16 (nor in vv.15 and 17, that of v.15
being consecutive, with the value therefore of imperfect), nor is it clear, anyway, how a
perfect tense would prove his theory.

[21] J. C. Whitcomb, 'The creation of the heavens and the earth', *SSt*, p.24; Ramm, p.221,
n.66 (with a quotation from S. R. Driver); Thompson, p.20; M. G. Kline, p.153.

[22] Young I, p.95. [23] *Ibid.*, pp.73ff. [24] *Ibid.*, p.61.

[25] MacRae, *art. cit.* (p.32, n.28 above), suggests that $w^e y\bar{a}sar$ should be read instead of
wayyiser; this is not impossible with the consonants of the text that we have, but it seems
unlikely within the movement of the sentence and of the narrative.

[26] Young I, p.47; Weeks, p.17.

hint that the Word is emptied of its power when it is not taken literally,[27] and that the other side is giving in to the pressure of the intellectual climate, to the spirit and mind of an apostate world.[28] They challenge concepts currently accepted by scientists. Weeks vigorously rejects their authority and questions their presuppositions. Others construct an alternative system which they call 'creationism', with a young earth and a prodigious flood which plays a key part in explaining geological phenomena and fossils. The functions of this flood would justify the name 'neo-catastrophism' (see our Appendix). Finally, the advocates of a literal reading stress that both Old and New Testament texts confirm that the first chapter of the Bible must be read literally. Weeks lays weight on Exodus 20:11 (the sabbath commandment), Matthew 19:4 (Jesus' comment on the man and the woman) and 2 Peter 3:5 (the reminder that the earth was formed out of water).[29]

☐   The last argument deserves our attention first; the principles of our approach to Genesis require that we give it priority in our enquiry. What do we ascertain? The last two passages referred to (Mt. 19 and 2 Pet.) have nothing to do with the debate. It is not at all obvious that they imply a literal reading, particularly in the case of Jesus' reference, and in any case they at no point refer to the days and to the 'week' whose meaning we are trying to determine. There remains the Exodus verse, which might appear to be evidence of considerable weight. Indeed, the language of the decalogue can scarcely pass for figurative language, and the reason given for the divine commandment seems to found the institution of the sabbath on the week of creation – it would be a reversal of the order if the days of Genesis were made to be a literary reflection of the Israelite week.[30]

But does Exodus inevitably demand the literal reading? The question can at least be raised. The verse in the decalogue makes no commentary on Genesis and does not ask questions about its interpretation; quite simply, it sends us back to the first 'tablet' (or to the oral teaching which we know only through this written passage). So it leaves us to face the task of interpreting. The

---

[27] Young I, p.56, adds a pejorative adverb, 'merely figurative', and on p.65 speaks of the same text being 'dismissed as figurative'. The quotation from his p.105 that we made in the previous chapter seems to contrast figurative with 'trustworthy'.

[28] *Ibid.,* pp.53, 100ff. We take Young as our witness because he is the ablest and best of the literalists. The attacks made in the publications of the Creation Research Society are much more violent, *e.g.* Morris, *SC*, pp.243ff.

[29] Weeks, pp.18f.   [30] *Ibid.,* p.18.

problem is not settled in advance. In the repetition of the sabbath law, using the same argument, the same book (Ex. 31:17) makes bold use of figurative language, when it says that on the seventh day God 'was refreshed'. This free use of clear anthropomorphism suggests that the presentation of the divine work as a week of work was also, following Renckens, understood as such.[31] Exodus 23:12 states the commandment without adding anything. The second version of the decalogue (Dt. 5:12–15) replaces the reference to creation with the memory of Israel's slavery in Egypt, a memory which should move the Israelites to compassion for their servants. This justification of the sabbath does not contradict that of Exodus 20, but the fact that it could replace it warns us against the temptation to forge too close a link between the work of the Creator and the weekly rhythm of human life. Would any 'literalist' have dared make such a substitution? When everything is taken into account, we consider that Exodus 20:11 demands, for the validity of its argument, only this: the development of creation ought to be able to act as an archetype for the work of mankind followed by his rest; the possibility remains that the days may be an anthropomorphic figure. The debate is still open.   □

The rejection of all the theories accepted by the scientists requires considerable bravado. It may be said that the work of many neo-catastrophist writers shows courage, not ignorance. Nevertheless, current opinions, built on the studies of thousands of research scientists who keep a very close eye on one another, continue to look very probable. Anyone rejecting them is taking an immense step. One must be absolutely sure of one's ground, especially since the neo-catastrophic hypothesis raises formidable objections. One must be sure that the text *demands* the literal interpretation. It must not be adopted out of loyalty to the past, out of sheer habit, or from a reflex hardening before the possible threat of apostasy. Might that in fact be the case?

□   The literal interpretation can always fall back on miracle; it brings in God's omnipotence when needed, for example in the case of the light in the first days. In these circumstances it is significant that E. J. Young shows, in spite of himself, a little hesitation on two occasions. Without there being anything in the text to suggest it, he allows a sort of progressive formation of the heavenly bodies during the first three days.[32] Again, concerning these same days, Young recognizes that their length is not clearly defined and he

---

[31] Renckens, pp.98ff.   [32] Young I, pp.95f.

dares to use the word 'figurative' with regard to them.[33] Literalism cannot stand as an absolute rule.   □

Accusations and insinuations of compromise with modern unbelief are greatly to be regretted when the question is one of interpretation. Who knows all his own motives? Who would dare claim to be totally untouched by any secular influence, even at a subconscious level? But when a fellow-Christian says he submits to the Word of God and finds in it indications of figurative language, though his arguments might be refuted, his faith should not be called into question. Christian charity, after all, should outdo academic courtesy! It is also essential to get rid of the deep-seated feeling once and for all that figurative language would be inferior to literal language, somewhat less worthy of God. Such an idea has no biblical support. Revelation is as seriously maltreated when, for example, its symbols pass unrecognized, as when symbols are seen where they do not exist.

Whether or not one opts for a literal interpretation depends finally on possible indications of non-literal language. Claus Westermann, who has no apologetic interests in the question, believes he sees such indications, since from examining the text he concludes that the days 'have something of the character of a parable'.[34] If these indications vanish under close scrutiny, the literal reading will compel recognition. If, however, they are sufficiently clear, they will justify a fourth interpretation, which we shall call 'literary'.

The literary interpretation

□ The fourth interpretation, which has also been called 'historico-artistic',[35] or the framework theory, is not, as is too often imagined, an innovation of the modern age. Augustine, who thought that everything had been created 'at once' (*cf.* Ecclus. 18:1), constructed a brilliant and startling interpretation of the days in *De Genesi ad litteram*. In his view, their temporal character is not physical but ideal; they are a 'sextuple confrontation of the angelic nature with the *order* of creation'.[36] In the Middle Ages, Gersonides (1288–1344) considered that the days 'indicate the prior order

---

[33] *Ibid.,* p.104.

[34] Westermann *G*, p.126, 'haben etwas wie Gleichnischarakter'. We refer to Westermann because, as a liberal, he does not identify his position with that of the biblical writer and cannot be suspected of wishing to reconcile the Bible with modern science.

[35] By Ceuppens, *Genèse I–III* (Desclée de Brouwer, 1946), pp.72ff.

[36] Aimé Solignac, *In Principio*, p.168.

between beings in logical and natural terms, but not in chronological terms'.[37] Rightly or wrongly, Ceuppens attributes this view to Thomas Aquinas.[38] Nearer our own day the great Dominican scholar, M. J. Lagrange, writes without hesitation: 'the author's intention is crystal clear ... his procedure is one of logic: it is a literary form'.[39] For several decades quite a number of theologians in the evangelical churches have been advocating the same opinion. The pioneer, around 1930, was probably A. Noordtzij of the University of Utrecht,[40] and since World War II the main proponents have been N. H. Ridderbos of Amsterdam, B. Ramm of California, M. G. Kline of New England, D. F. Payne of Britain and J. A. Thompson of Australia. There is no questioning their competence or, generally speaking, their respect for Scripture. ☐

The literary interpretation takes the form of the week attributed to the work of creation to be an artistic arrangement, a modest example of anthropomorphism that is not to be taken literally. The author's intention is not to supply us with a chronology of origins. It is possible that the logical order he has chosen coincides broadly with the actual sequence of the facts of cosmogony; but that does not interest him. He wishes to bring out certain themes and provide a theology of the sabbath. The text is composed as the author meditates on the finished work, so that we may understand how the creation is related to God and what is its significance for mankind.

This hypothesis overcomes a number of problems that plagued the commentators. It recognizes ordinary days but takes them in the context of one large figurative whole; the differences in order between the two 'tablets' no longer cause difficulties, neither does the delay in the creation of the stars, nor does the confrontation with the scientific vision of the most distant past. So great is the advantage, and for some the relief, that it could constitute a temptation. We must not espouse the theory on the grounds of its convenience but only if the text leads us in that direction.

To put it plainly, both the genre and the style of the Genesis 1 prologue, as our introductory chapter saw them, provide strong grounds for presuming in favour of the literary interpretation. We discerned a composite literary genre, skilfully composed. We

[37] Charles Touati, 'La lumière de l'intellect, création du premier jour. L'exégèse de Genèse 1. 1–3 chez Gersonide', *In Principio,* p.38.
[38] Ceuppens, p.74.   [39] Lagrange (1896), pp.395f.
[40] Mentioned in Young I, pp.44f.

admired its author as a wise man, supremely able in the art of arranging material and very fond of manipulating numbers, particularly the number seven. From such a writer the plain, straightforward meaning, as in two-dimensional prose, would be most surprising when he is setting out the pattern of seven days. From such a writer you would expect the sort of method which is discerned by the 'artistic' interpretation.

Immediately we pass to the study of the days themselves, we find once again that the author keeps closely to his most careful style. He shows the same geometrical mastery and thus suggests that other thoughts overshadowed in his mind any concern for chronology. Two centuries ago Herder recognized the powerful symmetry between the two triads of days: Day 1 corresponds to Day 4, Day 2 to Day 5, Day 3 to Day 6. Corresponding to the light (1) are the luminaries (4); to the creation of the expanse of the sky and the separation of the waters (2) correspond the birds and the fish (5); and to the appearance of the dry land and of vegetation (3) correspond the land animals including mankind together with the gift of food (6).[41] Medieval tradition had recognized the broad pattern, since it distinguished the work of *separation* (Days 1–3) from the work of *adornment* (Days 4–6).[42] It would be better to speak first of *spaces* demarcated by divine acts of separation, then of their corresponding *peopling*. It can also be stressed that only the creatures of the second series are mobile (some speak of the immobile creatures for Days 1–3 and of mobile creatures for the rest).[43] The duality of habitations and inhabitants reappears in Isaiah 45:18.[44] It is tempting to play on the plausible nuances of *tōhû* and *bōhû* in the second verse and find there a negative foretoken of the two themes: indeed, the separating work of the first three days deals with the trackless, shapeless desert and the work of the three following days fills the *bōhû*, the void.[45] At any rate the thought behind the two is most carefully distinguished at the conclusion, in 2:1: 'Thus *the heavens and the earth* were finished [Days 1–3], and *all the host*

[41] Young I, pp.70ff., tries to undermine the case by arguing that the fish (5) swim in the seas (3), and that the birds are related to the earth (v.22). But the birds are also linked with the expanse of the sky (v.20), and Day 2 established the waters below; the importance of Day 3 is the emergence of the dry land. Young's argument appears strained.

[42] *Ornatus* may well come from a misreading of *ṣābâ* (army) in 2:1 as *ṣᵉbî* (adornment) by the translators of the Septuagint and of the Latin versions; see Renckens, pp.54f.; Young I, p.72, n.66; Beauchamp, p.39.

[43] Young I, p.72, and in particular Weeks, p.18, mention the duality kingdoms/suzerains; but if the great luminaries and mankind dominate, this is not suggested for any animal.

[44] Payne, p.18.   [45] Lagrange (1896), p.382; Waltke (1976), p.29.

of them [*i.e.* the great crowds of all that filled the heavens and the earth]'. Let us notice a further point of composition. The presence of two works in parallel manner on the third and sixth days, far from betraying a difficulty for the author, is in our opinion, as in Barth's,[46] a mark of his skill. The second work in some respect anticipates what is to follow, prevents the series of three closing in on itself and thus consolidates the structure of the week. Thus the vegetation on Day 3, although an element of the immobile environment, is already, at the same time, one of the first inhabitants; in the text the power of reproduction relates it to the animals and thus it announces the second series. On Day 6, mankind created in the image of God is the creature who will enjoy the sabbath rest. As we shall see, his privilege of bearing the divine image has basically the same meaning as the ceasing from work on the seventh day. Thus between the final two days there is no separation. The structure of our hymn-narrative leaves nothing to chance; it is the fruit of mature meditation.

The reader who is in sympathy with that meditation no longer stumbles at the 'problem' of the fourth day with its 'delayed' creation of the stars. He has no need to construct the problematic theory of days like solar days but without the sun, of which the text gives not the slightest hint. If the principle which directs the distribution of the works is their classification into two categories, the places and their occupants, then the creation of the luminaries is in its proper, logical position. Chronology has no place here.

☐ Paul Beauchamp discerns a further structural reason for attributing the peopling of the heavenly expanse to the fourth day: the author wanted to make it the centre of his *structure*.[47] In a span of seven days the fourth is central; but here we notice that it corresponds on the one hand to the first day (by the themes of light and of the heaven), and on the other, by anticipation, to the seventh day. The luminaries will serve as signs for the religious *festivals* (such is the meaning of v.14b), among which figures the sabbath.[48] It is therefore the pivot on which the whole structure turns. Beauchamp also observes that the creative command is the fifth

---

[46] Barth, p.144. For Day 6, Beauchamp, p.385, emphasizes also the technique of packing the framework full, thus indicating the approach of the conclusion.

[47] Beauchamp, pp.67f.

[48] With JB and with Michaëli, p.24, we consider that here *môⁿⁱᵈim* has its most frequent meaning, *i.e.* festivals, sacred times, and not simply the seasons; the sun and the moon act as signs for the liturgical calendar as well as for the ordinary calendar of days and years.

word out of ten, and that the total number of words for Days 1–4 is 207 and for Days 5–6 it is 206; the fourth is also central for the *six* days of work.[49] What is the meaning of this prominence within the overall structure? The inspired writer reminds mankind, in spite of the glory he confers on him, that there is a whole realm beyond his grasp – mankind lives under heaven, and the text 'encloses the greatness of mankind within exact limits'.[50]

But could this extremely careful construction of the narrative not coincide with the chronological reality of the divine work, as certain literalists attempt to plead?[51] Of course, you can always *imagine* anything. But, in the face of what the author shows of his method, there is no reason to suppose it. The hypothesis of the literary procedure gives sufficient explanation of the form of the text; anything further would be superfluous. Occam's razor, the principle of economy which argued against the multiplication of hypotheses, removes ideas of this kind. The suggestion betrays the *a priori* desire to find literal language.

E. J. Young himself points out the frequency in ancient Near Eastern texts of the pattern 6 + 1 (and most often six days plus one).[52] He does not seem aware of the implication of the fact, for it moves away from literalism. The more it appears that the biblical writer used a stereotype from his cultural milieu in presenting creation in the form of a week, the less likely is it that he limited himself to transcribing a chronological sequence. Meredith G. Kline underlines the parallel of the heptads in the book of Revelation, which are also artificial patterns that do not teach a literal succession in time.[53]

The same scholar, who is not afraid to leave the beaten track, has thrown into the arena a new argument of considerable force. Young admits that it is 'one of the strongest'.[54] Kline draws attention to the preamble to the second tablet, in Genesis 2:5, which explains the absence of grass or shrubs (whether locally or

---

[49] Beauchamp notes that Day 4 finishes the first half (counting the number of words), by the government of the stars, just as Day 6 finishes the second half by the government of mankind. We notice that the total of words (207 + 206 = 413) is a multiple of 7 (7 × 59); by adding 7 × 3 for 1:1–2 and 7 × 5 for 2:1–3, we get 7 × 63 for the first tablet. We make no particular claim, however, to any expertise in biblical numerology!

[50] Beauchamp, p.45; *cf.* pp.94, 113ff.

[51] Weeks, pp.17f. Weeks does not appear to be acquainted with all the works that we have used and seems to have an inadequate notion of structural subtlety.

[52] Young I, p.79. He quotes the Gilgamesh Epic, Tablet XI (lines 127–130, 142–146, 215–218), *Enuma elish* V (lines 16f.), Ugaritic literature (*Keret* I iii, lines 2–4, 10–15; *Aqhat* II ii, lines 32–39; and *Baal* II vi, lines 24–32). *Cf.* Loretz, p.44.

[53] Kline, p.157. [54] Young I, p.58.

1 ¹ IN THE BEGINNING GOD CREATED

²Now the earth was waste and void, darkness (covered) the face of the

I ³And God said: Be light! And was light.
⁴And God saw the light, that good; and God separated the light from the darkness.
⁵And God called the light 'day', and the darkness, he called 'night'. And (it) was evening, and (it) was morning – *day one*.

II ⁶And God said: Be an expanse in the middle of the waters, and let it be a separation between the waters and the waters!
⁷And God made the expanse and he separated the waters which go on the lower side in relation to the expanse, from the waters which are on the upper side in relation to the expanse; and (it) was so.
⁸And God called the expanse 'heavens'. And (it) was evening, and (it) was morning – *day second*.

III ⁹And God said: Let be gathered the waters on the lower side of the heavens in one single place, and let be seen the dry! And (it) was so.
¹⁰And God called 'earth' the dry, and the gathering of waters he called (it) 'seas'. And God saw that good.

¹¹And God said: Let the earth green with verdure, with herb which sow its seed, and with fruit trees which make fruit according to their kinds bearing their seed, on the earth! And (it) was so.
¹²And the earth brought forth verdure, herb which sows its seed according to its kind, and trees which make fruit bearing their seed according t their kinds. And God saw that good.
¹³And (it) was evening, and (it) was morning – *day third*.

VII 2¹AND THE HEAVENS AND THE EARTH WERE FINISHED, AND
²And God finished *the seventh day* his work which he had done, he 'idled' the seventh day and he hallowed it for he 'idled' then from all the work

THE HEAVENS AND THE EARTH

abyss, and the Spirit of God hovered over the face of the waters.

IV [14]And God said: Be luminaries in the expanse of the heavens, to separate the day from the night, and let them serve as signs, both for festivals and for the days and years! [15]And let them serve as luminaries in the expanse of the heavens to give light on the earth; and (it) was so. [16]And God made the two great luminaries, the great luminary for the government of the day and the little luminary for the government of the night, and the stars. [17]And God placed them in the expanse of the heavens, to give light on the earth [18]and to govern the day and the night, and to separate the light from the darkness. [19]And God saw that good. And (it) was evening, and (it) was morning – *day fourth.*

V [20]And God said: Let the waters teem with a teeming of living beings, and let the birds fly over the earth, over the face of the expanse of the heavens! [21]And God created the great sea monsters, and all the living beings that move, with which the waters teemed, according to their kinds, and all the winged birds according to their kinds. And God saw that good.
[22]And God blessed them in these terms: Be fruitful, multiply, and fill the waters in the seas, and let the birds multiply in the earth.
[23]And (it) was evening, and (it) was morning – *day fifth.*

VI [24]And God said: Let the earth bring forth living beings according to their kinds, livestock, tiny creatures and wild beasts according to their kinds! And (it) was so.
[25]And God made the wild beasts according to their kinds and the livestock according to their kinds, and all the tiny creatures of the ground according to their kinds. And God saw that good. [26]And God said: Let us make the man as our image, like our resemblance, and let them rule over the fish of the sea, over the birds of the heavens, over the livestock and over all the earth, and over the tiny creatures which move on the earth.
[27]AND GOD CREATED THE MAN AS HIS IMAGE/AS THE IMAGE OF GOD HE CREATED HIM/MALE AND FEMALE HE CREATED THEM.
[28]And God blessed them and said to them: Be fruitful, multiply, fill the earth and subdue it, and rule over the fish of the sea, over the birds of the heavens, and over every beast which moves on the earth!
[29]And God said: Behold, I give you every herb which sows its seed on the face of the earth, and every tree with a fruit of tree that sows its seed, that will serve for you as food; [30]and to every wild beast, to every bird of the heavens, and to all that moves over the earth and which has the breath of life, every growth of herb for food; and (it) was so.
[31]And God saw all that he had made, and behold: good exceedingly. And (it) was evening and (it) was morning – *day sixth.*

ALL THEIR HOST.
the seventh day from all the work that he had done. [3]And God blessed that he had done by way of creation.

universally is of little importance) by the absence of rain and of human irrigation: 'there was no...for (*kî*) the LORD God had not caused it to rain, and there was no man to till the ground'. That explanation presupposes the normal activity of the laws of nature for the growth of plants (an operation of divine providence),[55] and a sufficient length of time for the absence of rain to be able to constitute the cause of the absence of plants. That does not fit the hypothesis of a literal week for the creation of the whole cosmos. If the dry land did not emerge until Tuesday and if vegetation has existed only from that day, an explanation is not going to be given the following Friday that there is no vegetation because there is no rain! Such reasoning would be against reason. Now the inspired author of Genesis, who revised the *tôlᵉdôt* and constructed the prologue, the wise man (whom we are bold enough to name as Moses) would not have preserved a contradiction in 2:5. If he repeated the explanation given, it is because he did not understand the days of the first chapter literally. It is a necessary implication that in Genesis 2:5 Scripture supplies the proof that the week of the Genesis prologue is not literal; this proof has not been refuted.[56]   □

The other confirmatory clue, provided by the first tablet itself, is the omission of the formula for the evening and the morning on the seventh day. It is deliberate. There can be no doubt about that in a text that has been composed with such exact calculation. What is its significance? The most simple and natural conclusion is that drawn by Augustine: the day was never finished. As far as the author is concerned, it is still continuing. God's rest signifies the completion of creation and the conditions for history to proceed, since mankind may act on the basis of laws that have been permanently established.[57]

□   E. J. Young questions the view that Hebrews 4:3–5, which is sometimes referred to in this debate, upholds the idea of an eternal seventh day.[58] This notoriously difficult passage in any case gives no support to the literal reading of Genesis 1. Young, however, overlooks a pertinent saying of Jesus. Accused of

---

[55] Kline, pp.147ff.

[56] Young I, pp.58–65, tries to criticize it, but he strangely avoids it: he asserts that Day 3 did not enjoy the present operation of divine providence, and that Gn. 2:5 'may rather be fitted into the sixth day'; but at no point does he explain how, in this scheme of things, the explanation of the biblical writer is possible. His reply misses the main point.

[57] Westermann *G*, pp.57f. To the authors already mentioned we can add von Rad, who holds that the seventh day is still continuing (p.60). Keil (pp.67f.), Young I (pp.77f.) and Weeks (p.18) deny this, but without explaining the omission of 'evening and morning'. Weeks criticizes his old teacher, Professor John Murray, on this point, in his n.17.

[58] Young I, pp.77f., n.73.

breaking the sabbath law because he has healed the paralytic, Jesus pleads that he is working as his Father is still working (Jn. 5:17), following the principle 'Whatever the Father does, that the Son does likewise' (Jn. 5:19). Jesus' reasoning is sound only if the Father acts *during his sabbath*; only on that condition has the Son the right to act similarly on the sabbath. Jesus stresses, 'My Father worketh *even until now*' (RV); God's sabbath, which marks the end of creation but does not tie God's hands, is therefore co-extensive with history. Our Lord himself did not see the seventh day of Genesis as a literal day.

The consequence is crucial for the interpretation of Exodus 20:11. If the sabbath at creation and the sabbath of the Mosaic law have no common measure in their length, the analogy put forward by Exodus 20:11 and 31:17 must be a loose one; it is not a strict correspondence. But in fact the analogy remains valid if the six days represent the great logical articulations of the divine work. In its sixfold development, which was a reality though not in the sense understood by the literalists, the creation is indeed the archetype of human work.   □

The use of the anthropomorphic figure of the week for the logic of creation and of its completion allowed the author to outline a theology of the sabbath. That was the theme closest to his heart. The narrative has two peaks, mankind and the sabbath.[59] This would be better expressed by saying that the creation of mankind crowns the work, but the sabbath is its supreme goal.[60] Now, what is the meaning of the sabbath that was given to Israel? It relativizes the works of mankind, the contents of the six working days. It protects mankind from total absorption by the task of subduing the earth, it anticipates the distortion which makes work the sum and purpose of human life, and it informs mankind that he will not fulfil his humanity in his relation to the world which he is transforming but only when he raises his eyes above, in the blessed, holy hour of communion with the Creator. With this meaning it would be no exaggeration to state that the sabbath sums up the difference between the biblical and the Marxist visions. The essence of mankind is not work!

What is the basis of the subordination of work to this 'chief end' of mankind, 'to glorify God and to enjoy him for ever' (The

[59] Beauchamp, p.59. In both cases there is a threefold, rhythmical formulation.

[60] Paul K. Jewett, *The Lord's Day* (Grand Rapids: Eerdmans, 1971), p.157. Loretz, p.82, also says that the end of the creation is rest in communion with God.

Shorter Catechism)? It is nothing other than his creation in the image of God. And as long as he is in his image, mankind is firstly related to God. But what is also meant by the presentation of the divine work at the beginning as a workman's week, as an archetype of the human week, except that mankind is to live according to the image of his Creator? So we see linking together the meaning of the sabbath and the theme of the image of God, which are in a profound manner interdependent; and this link is achieved by the process of the literary composition. The form of the days, employed with consummate skill, tells mankind that he will imitate God on earth, which very calling forbids him to identify with his earthly work. It refers him back to his most essential relationship, that with God. That is the message of the sabbath.

Since God's rest envelops the whole of history, it would no doubt be possible to find another link between that rest and mankind's privilege as the divine image-bearer: mankind exercises that privilege in his deliberate, free activity. Now, such free activity presupposes a stable world, a completed creation, since all deliberation would become pointless in an unpredictable world of continual new creative activity. We are not certain, however, that the writer gave thought to this aspect. It is more likely that in seizing upon this vast image of the week he transmitted this further thought: God in the act of creation also creates time. By creating the days, the evenings and the mornings, he initiates the fundamental rhythm of the life of mankind. Bonhoeffer makes the point with great insight, and brings out the way that technology is undermining this divine pattern, to mankind's great detriment.[61] (The pursuit of sin also seeks frequently to abolish this pattern, in its general effort to abolish divine ordinances; a 'dissolute' life dissolves the difference between day and night, between light and darkness.) The initiation of the rhythms of life is implied in the archetypal role played by the pattern of the divine work.

If God creates time, he creates *with* time, as Augustine stresses, and even *in* time, as Luther[62] and Karl Barth[63] dare to assert. The presentation of the seven days at least suggests so. Beauchamp, taking the analysis further, shows that the first tablet gives second place to spatial separation, priority being

---

[61] Bonhoeffer, pp.24f.: 'It is the great rhythm, the natural dialectic of creation.'
[62] Quoted by Stauffer, *In Principio*, p.248.   [63] Barth, pp.67f.

given to the division of time,[64] that same time which Israel will learn from God to value as the fabric of history. Since God creates in time, time will not suffer from a negative coefficient, as it does generally in mythical and ancient thought. Redemption, too, will be able to function within time, instead of being (as elsewhere) a deliverance *from* time. Other consequences begin to emerge. Once we grasp that God creates in time and not in a single instant, we can understand that God is involved when he creates, that he *enters* into his work; and similarly we can understand from the finishing of that creation and from its completed time-span that God is *not absorbed into* what he creates. He remains sovereignly free, holding his creation before him and delighting in it with the joy of the seventh day.

These suggestions deserve reflection for their own sake, but they also help us to discern the sense of the biblical presentation and to bring our discussion to a close. What are we to conclude? The theological treasures of the framework of the Genesis days come most clearly to light by means of the 'literary' interpretation. The writer has given us a masterly elaboration of a fitting, restrained anthropomorphic vision, in order to convey a whole complex of deeply meditated ideas. Of that we have no doubt; though whether it is the content or the form that calls forth the greater admiration, we cannot tell.

[64] Beauchamp, pp.112, 371.

3
Being, order and life

.

Skilful though the architect of the Genesis prologues may appear to us, we must not allow ourselves to be dazzled by the mere framework, nor even the message of that framework. Two steps can help us to perceive the central meaning: first, to note carefully the things that are actually said, and, second, to make comparisons with other accounts of origins and thus bring out what is peculiar to the biblical account. We shall attempt to combine the two, considering the results of our enquiry into Genesis 1:1 – 2:3 under three headings: being, order and life.

'Thou didst create all things, and by thy will they existed' (Rev. 4:11)

There is a danger of the obvious passing unnoticed: the beginning of Genesis proclaims first of all *creation*. The one God has created everything. At the time it was formulated, the proposition was anything but commonplace. It stands in stark contrast to the myths of Israel's pagan neighbours. Pagan cosmogonies are at once theogony and theomachy; in other words, they tell how the gods were born and how they quarrel, the birth of the universe coinciding with their battles, love affairs and reproduction. The Bible is the only exception,[1] for even the Greeks, when they made the divine impersonal, did not set it free from the world.[2] Tresmontant saw clearly that the first verse of Genesis breaks

[1] H. and H. A. Frankfort, *Before Philosophy* (Penguin, 1963), pp.237ff.
[2] *Ibid.*, pp.248ff. The authors emphasize the rational quest for the impersonal principle,

60

with all the mythologies of the ancient East: 'Just as Abraham left his family and the land of his ancestors, so with its very first step the metaphysics of the Bible leaves behind the metaphysics of the pagan world.'[3] And Karl Barth brings the charge that the notion of a creation myth 'contains a *contradictio in adjecto*' – a contradiction between the essence of myth and the concept of creation that is being associated with it – because 'in the actual meaning given to it and to be gathered from it, myth is always monistic'.[4] For creation to take place, in fact, God must be free and distinct from the world, and that is the case only with the God of Genesis. If in the first tablet there are allusions to Mesopotamian cosmogony, these are highly discreet features and their purpose is *polemical*.[5]

The verb which we translate 'create' (*bārâ*) carries very considerable force in Hebrew. The Old Testament uses it most sparingly and, in that form, exclusively of the God of Israel. Never is any material mentioned. The creative act appears supremely effortless and its result sometimes miraculous (Ex. 34:10), frequently new (Pss. 51:10; 104:30; Is. 48:7; 65:17; Je. 31:22).[6] For God it is a matter of 'doing' – for that ordinary verb is used as a parallel for *bārâ*, and Genesis 2:3 speaks of 'all his work which he had done in creation'[7] – but 'done' in a unique sense, reserved for God, from which arises complete newness.

☐   Alliteration links the verb to the first word of the Bible, *bᵉ rēšît*, 'in the beginning'. The first three consonants (Hebrew was written, of course, without any vowels) are the same as those of the verb *bārâ*, the second word. Young makes the bold suggestion that the two concepts are connected.[8] But this raises two highly controversial issues. Should the opening word be translated 'in the beginning' or 'in a beginning'? Or else should we rather take the first verse as temporally subordinate to the second or to the third verse? The New English Bible has followed this course: 'In the

---

but are obliged to recognize that gods and men come very close to being confused with one another, *cf.* Pindar's 6th Nemean Ode: 'From one race only come both men and gods'.

[3] Tresmontant, *op. cit.* (see above, p.34, n. 44), p.40.   [4] Barth, pp.84f.

[5] There has been enormous exaggeration of similarities which could be fortuitous. Heidel has brought the matter back into perspective and more recently Gerhard F. Hasel has discussed the question in a well-documented article, 'The polemic nature of the Genesis cosmology', *EQ* 46 (1974), pp.81–102.

[6] There have been many studies of the word *bārâ*; Renckens provides a useful summary, pp.87f.

[7] For the translation of this difficult phrase we follow Beauchamp, pp.82f.: the principal verb has really the sense of an adverb, as in Jdg. 13:19; Ps. 126:2ff.; Joel 2:20f. The contraction in JB is close: 'all his work of creating'.   [8] Young I, p.6.

beginning of creation, when God made heaven and earth, the earth was without form and void...'.

Those who advocate such a rendering rest their case on the following literal reading, defended by certain scholars since Ibn Ezra: 'In the beginning of "God created the heaven and the earth"...' (grammatically similar to Ho. 1:2, but with another word for 'beginning').[9] This is what we must compare with the traditional reading.

The *only* difficulty in the translation 'In the beginning God created' rests in the absence of the article 'beginning' (*rēšît*). It would be tempting to supply it, because it would be marked only by a vowel and the Hebrew manuscripts omitted vowels. It would nevertheless be imprudent, for the traditional synagogue reading for the first verse of the Bible is most unlikely to have changed during the course of the centuries.[10] But its omission need not disturb the reader; Isaiah 46:10 uses *rē'šît* similarly without an article to refer to the absolute beginning. It is a fact that temporal phrases of this sort regularly occur without the article.[11] The accentuation suggests that in the synagogue, despite the absence of the article, the reading corresponded to the understanding 'In the beginning'.[12] All the ancient versions, the Septuagint, the Vulgate, Aquila, Theodotion, Symmachus, the Targum of Onqelos, interpreted it in this way, as of course do most modern translations. The apostle John confirms it when he echoes the prologue of Genesis in that of his Gospel (Jn. 1:1).

Along with many scholars who have studied the problem in detail, Heidel, Young, Westermann, Hasel, Waltke, and great commentators who have been brief but penetrating like Cassuto

[9] *Rē'šît* is considered as constructed from the proposition 'God created', a most rare situation, but one that cannot be excluded *a priori*. Some would like to read the infinitive *b^e rō'* instead of *bārâ*, but in this verse the Massoretic pointing carries considerable authority; who could have forgotten the reading of the very first verse of the Bible?

[10] We maintain this point of view although several ancient transcriptions have, in fact, added the vowel.

[11] Heidel, p.92, proves it. Gerhard F. Hasel, 'Recent translations of Genesis 1.1. A critical look', *BT* 22 (1971), pp.158f., approves it.

[12] The Massoretes attributed a disjunctive accent to it, which removes the possibility of understanding 'the beginning *of*'. André Caquot, 'Brèves remarques exégétiques sur Genèse 1.1–2', *In Principio*, p.13, retorts that *rē'šît* has always, even in the construct state, a disjunctive accent at the start of a verse, and he quotes Je. 26:1; 27:1; 49:34. He could have added Nu. 15:20, and Je. 49:35 has such an accent at the end of the verse. On the other hand he has overlooked three passages with *rē'šît* at the start where the accent is *conjunctive*: Dt. 18:4; Ps. 111:10; Pr. 4:7. Thus the rule he lays down is supported by four passages (three of them from Jeremiah) and contradicted by three others. In the construction proposed as a model, Ho. 1:2 (with *t^e hillat*), the accent is conjunctive.

and von Rad,[13] we have no hesitation in retaining the reading of
the ancient versions. There is no question of its superiority to that
of Ibn Ezra and his followers. It avoids ascribing quite a difficult
construction to the text, and is incomparably more suitable for
the first verse of the Bible, the opening of a majestic passage. 'In
the beginning God created...' acts as a title, as Beauchamp and
others have seen.[14] The two 'tablets' of our study begin by following
the same pattern: first a comprehensive formulation, which
functions as a kind of title by introducing what follows (1:1 and
2:4a); then a description of the initial or prior state, in terms that
are essentially negative (1:2 and 2:4b ff., comparable to the
beginning of the *Enuma elish*); finally comes the beginning of the
narrative proper (1:3 and 2:7).[15] At the end of the first 'tablet', 2:1
corresponds to 1:1 by also summarizing the contents of the chapter;
2:2–3 adds as an epilogue material concerning the seventh day.[16] □

If the beginning mentioned in the opening verse is to be taken
in an absolute sense, and if 'create' is a verb of such force, are we
to speak of creation out of nothing, *ex nihilo*? Calvin, who was
one of the best Hebraists of his day, thought that it was to be
deduced from *bārâ*.[17] This has often given rise to amusement.[18]
But in our own time such a prestigious specialist as von Rad has
declared that his proposal is right: the verb *bārâ* 'contains ... the
idea of *creatio ex nihilo*, since it is never connected with any
statement of the material'.[19] Without the idea being expressed
clearly, we can say that the usage of the verb points in the
direction of the notion of being produced out of non-being, which
has become the classical Jewish and Christian position. But how
then are we to understand the *tōhû* and *bōhû*, and the darkness
and the deep, of the second verse?

□   Although they sail under the flags of great theologians, we must
rule out two explanations that are decidedly inadequate. Since
darkness symbolizes evil, some have tried to see in the elements
of Genesis 1:2 an adverse reality, a hostile power, over which God
triumphed by creation; after all, does not Scripture call *tōhû* idols
(1 Sa. 12:21)? It is 'non-being', but a non-being of substance,
capable of effective aggression. Karl Barth in particular has
developed this thought with characteristic vigour. In his view, this

---

[13] Heidel, pp.92ff.; Young I, pp.1–5; Westermann *G*, pp.107ff., 130ff.; Hasel, *art. cit.*,
pp.154–167; Waltke (1975), pp.222ff.; Cassuto, pp.19f.; von Rad, pp.46f.
[14] Beauchamp, p.153; before him, Barth, p.100.
[15] Waltke (1975), pp.225f.   [16] *Ibid.*, p.228.   [17] Calvin, p.70.
[18] Stauffer, *In Principio*, p.260.   [19] Von Rad, p.47.

substantial, hostile non-being exists not *before* but *by virtue of* God's denial and exclusion of it; the creative Yes implies a No, and that No implies the negative which God denies.[20] Defeated beforehand, non-being nevertheless leaves its shadow hovering over creation; it is there as darkness and as sea.[21] In spite of the great care and dexterity of the language used (and a lot depends on the figurative style), this interpretation introduces a dualism which is profoundly foreign to Genesis; the text contains not the slightest hint of any battle whatsoever. The idea that God's denial produces the negative is a mere play on words, and the idea that this negative should have a prior existence – in eternity – plunges the narrative back into polytheism. Young brings out from the text the fact that God names the night, which would not be the case if the night arose from a negative principle.[22]

The second explanation goes back at least to Augustine and was championed by Thomas Aquinas, the Reformers and the majority of orthodox theologians including Derek Kidner.[23] According to this view, the *tōhû* and *bōhû* describe the fruit of the first creative act, that of the first verse. In the beginning God created the heavens and the earth as a shapeless mass, as undifferentiated matter, in their 'seminal' form, so to speak. This interpretation, which is diametrically opposed to the previous one, does not run into the same kind of difficulty. The objection is rather of a philological order: 'the heavens and the earth' is a formula which always designates the totality of the universe in its order and beauty. To apply the phrase to a confused mass is to make it mean its opposite.[24] Further, the analysis of the passage's structure has shown us the function of the first verse as a title;

[20] Barth, pp.101–110, also *CD* III 3 section 50, 'God and Nothingness'. Bonhoeffer anticipated Barth in these developments by a number of years; he spoke of the 'nothing' (*das Nichts*) as something already negated by God, which 'God only affirms to the extent that he has overcome it'. But, unlike Barth, he wrote: 'The void contains no anxiety for the first creation. On the contrary, it is itself the eternal song praising the Creator who created the world out of nothing' (p.15). In both Barth and Bonhoeffer the deepest motif is the desire to find Christology in creation, and to make creation a primary victory of redemption over evil: 'That word from the darkness upon the deep was the first reference to the Passion of Jesus Christ' (p.21). Although he does not belong to the same theological family, Waltke (1975) is close to them: 'The darkness and the deep are not at first called "good", but they were later when they became part of the cosmos.... A good God...could not create...evil, disorder, darkness. And besides, that evil could not have remained eternally outside God, for it would have limited divine sovereignty' (pp.338f.).

[21] Barth, pp.117f., 141ff., 147ff.

[22] Young I, p.21, n.13 (following Ridderbos); *cf.* Ps. 104:19 quoted by J. C. Whitcomb, *SSt*, p.36.

[23] *Cf.* Barth, p.100; Stauffer, *In Principio*, pp.253f., 260f.; Kidner, p.44.

[24] Waltke (1975), pp.218f.; Beauchamp, p.157.

this the Augustinian explanation fails to recognize. If we add that creation was achieved by the word (Ps. 33:6) and that the first word is not heard until verse 3, we shall firmly exclude the possibility that verse 2 speaks of what was created according to verse 1.

We are left with two other proposals, which it is difficult to choose between. The first takes 'the enormous aquatic heap, undifferentiated and amorphous, at the heart of a dark void'[25] as the raw material of the creative action. The text says nothing about its origin, but its overall thrust suggests that the author, if asked, would have replied (though in fact he did not say it) that this material was created by God in the first place.[26] Rabbi Gamaliel II (*c.* AD 95) defended this solution.[27]

The second is more audacious. It boils down to treating the theme of chaos as a 'conventional narrative procedure' and saying, with Renckens, 'this *tohu-bohu* is in reality nothing more or less than a very concrete way of saying: "absolutely nothing whatever"'.[28] Is total non-being conceivable? It is at any rate a limiting marginal concept: we aim at it rather than grasp it, striving with the help of negative images such as darkness, shapelessness and emptiness. Being free of mythological implications,[29] the terms of Genesis 1:2 can suggest the notion of nothing. *Tōhû*-and-*bōhû* is a 'rhetorical device which consists in reinforcing a word by a term with the same meaning which rhymes with it'.[30] The first word, which is more common, recalls by its etymology the desert, uninhabitable and trackless (*cf.* Dt. 32:10, *etc.*), and several times it serves to convey the idea of non-being (Jb. 26:7, *etc.*).[31] Beauchamp says that it 'suggests the horror of certain wastelands'.[32] *Bōhû* which reinforces it (as in Is. 34:11 and Je. 4:23)

[25] Caquot's words, *In Principio*, p.18.

[26] Herbert Junker, 'Die theologische Behandlung des Chaosvorstellung in der biblischen Schöpfungsgeschichte', *Mélanges Robert*, p.37, agreeing with Eichrodt.

[27] According to Georges Vadja, 'Notice sommaire sur l'interprétation de Genèse 1.1–3 dans le judaïsme post-biblique', *In Principio*, pp.29f.

[28] Renckens, p.84.

[29] Tiamat, the monster goddess of the *Enuma elish*, has often been mentioned in connection with the *t^ehôm* (the deep) of Gn. 1:2 and even (by A. Jeremias) in connection with the *tōhû*. Heidel, pp.98ff., and Young I, pp.28f., have refuted this. Gustave Jéquier, *Considérations sur les religions égyptiennes* (Neuchâtel: à la Baconnière, 1946), pp.154ff., sees a striking correspondence with the dog-headed monkeys that represent primeval chaos in the religion of Hermopolis magna, Upper Egypt. Westermann *G*, pp.142f., emphasizes the great distance between the Genesis passage and the whole of mythology.

[30] Caquot, *In Principio*, p.15. Arabic grammarians call this figure of speech *'itba'*.

[31] *Ibid.*, pp.15f. See further 1 Sa. 12:21; Is. 24:10; 40:17, 23; 41:29; 44:9, all referred to by Caquot.

[32] Beauchamp, p.162.

suggests an Arabic verb, 'to be empty'. Two ancient translations, those of Aquila and of Theodotion, translated the phrase as 'empty and nothing'.[33] If the earth in verse 2 were just nothing, the text would indicate by its obscure images that creation was *ex nihilo*.

We feel very strongly the attraction of Renckens' solution. It has the added advantage of giving verse 2 the same negative function as in the first sentences of the cosmogonies ('It was before... nothing yet existed...'). But one serious objection arises. Among the elements of the verse, the darkness and the water will in actual fact serve as the raw material for the Creator. God will name them, thus assuring us of their positive reality. 2 Peter 3:5 speaks of the earth 'formed out of water and by means of water'; the latter concept removes the idea of non-being, even if the water is subsequently the destructive agent of the flood, that partial 'de-creation'. Therefore Gamaliel's interpretation emerges as preferable.   □

Von Rad's opinion seems wise: 'The theological thought of ch. 1 moves not so much between the poles of nothingness and creation as between the poles of chaos and cosmos',[34] the former being involved obliquely in the latter. Thus the text is interested directly in the gift of *form*, rather than in the gift of *being*. (Why? We may surmise one of the reasons: that it is as a gift of form that the universe is *intelligible* to us, and that we can *imitate* it in *our* six days.) But this interest is not exclusive. In choosing terms that have echoes of non-being, the writer suggests also the notion of being. Within the chapter as a whole Beauchamp is sensitive to an 'impression of the absence of the subject created',[35] as if to say that the creature has being only from God. He points out also that the form of the creative command is 'Let there be!'(for the celestial creation), and that it can be linked with the divine name YHWH, derived from the verb to be (Ex. 3:13–15).[36] I AM commands and bestows being! The Genesis prologue limits itself to suggesting this thought (thus warning us against the pitfalls connected wih contemplation of being 'in general', which easily forgets the complete, concrete relationship of Creator/creature), but it does not allow us to disregard it.

God alone gives form and gives being, owing nothing to any-

[33] Rousselot, *In Principio*, p.107.   [34] Von Rad, p.49.   [35] Beauchamp, p.373.
[36] *Ibid.*, pp.270f. Beauchamp appears to follow F. M. Cross in interpreting the name YHWH as causative (the One who brings into being – the hosts of heaven). Ex. 3 makes us hesitant, but the etymology of the word and the meaning given in Ex. 3 do not necessarily have to coincide.

thing. This is the passage's great doctrine. But a dual theme is joined on to it. God does this *with* Word and Spirit. We must interpret this dual qualification in order to survey completely what the text says about the creative act.

God creates by a word. It is important to weigh both aspects of the fact. It is *sufficient* for God to speak for the acts of separation and peopling to occur. But it is significant that God *did* it. It pleased him, in order to create, to break the silence. What is meant by the instrumentality of the word (revealed, of course, with the help of an anthropomorphism)? First of all, it means the absolute authority of the One who speaks; nothing resists his command, everything bows to his decrees. In the *Enuma elish,* when Marduk by his word alone destroys then restores the cloth of a garment, he demonstrates his supremacy amongst the gods; he it is who is sovereign.[37] The refrain, 'And it was so', celebrates in the first tablet of Genesis the perfect mastery that God possesses over every event. The same significance can be attributed to the frequency of the 'etymological figure', also called the 'internal accusative': let the earth (literally) 'green with greenery' and with plants 'seeding seeds' (1:11, 12, 29); let the waters 'swarm with swarms' and let the 'winged creatures take wing' (1:20). The execution of the command follows infallibly on the word. The instrumentality of the word, by replacing that of the hand or of the tool, proclaims the absolute liberty of the Creator, the radical difference that distinguishes his 'making' from all the 'making' done by mankind.

We ought not to deduce from the power of the divine word that 'for the Hebrew mind' the word of God as such always produces what it utters. That hasty and superficial conclusion confuses the various sorts of divine word with the creative word. The creative command obtains what it defines – even though 'God said' and 'God made' are not merely synonyms.[38] It is a different case with the precept, or with the diagnosis that God may make on his creatures. In Genesis 1 another kind of word is distinguished from the creative 'fiat': the word which *names* the creatures. It expresses the right of the Master, but nothing implies that it would confer life or being.

Furthermore, the theme of the fulfilment of the sovereign word does not permit the exclusion of another meaning. When

[37] *Enuma elish* IV, lines 19ff.; the theme of the word that decides recurs frequently: III, lines 48, 62ff., 120ff.; IV, lines 7ff.; VII, lines 151ff. The texts can be found in Heidel.

[38] Pasinya, *op. cit.* (see p.33, n.39), pp.229, 236, 240.

we read Genesis, we cannot overlook Egyptian parallels. According to Jéquier, two gods are associated in very ancient cosmogonic texts: 'Hor represents the thought which conceives, Thot the word which executes';[39] later, in the eighth century, Memphite theology made these two gods the heart and the tongue of Ptah, the divine craftsman who fashioned the world.[40] This conception is less interested in the power than in the wisdom (the heart) required to make things. Now, the idea of divine wisdom, revealed by the word, could well be the unnoticed counterpoint of the idea of authority at the start of Genesis.[41] Creation by the word is not only a creation without tools or effort, it is a creation by which God shows his 'heart', demonstrates his intelligence and inaugurates the communication of himself which he will make by speaking to mankind. Creation by the word is the attestation of the divine Lordship, of his majestic eminence and is also the expression of the divine will to express himself and to be for the creature, in which Karl Barth rightly sees 'the mystery of grace'.[42]

All too easily the Spirit might pass unnoticed. Certain writers have refused to recognize him and at the end of verse 2 translate 'a mighty wind that swept over the surface of the waters' (NEB). This minority interpretation[43] has lost all credibility since the formal refutations by Young and by Beauchamp.[44] *Everywhere* else in the Old Testament the phrase used here (*rûaḥ ᵉlōhîm*) indicates the Spirit of God (or a spirit from God); strong reasons would be needed to give another meaning to such an established formula. The idea that the qualification 'of God' can simply denote the superlative (a 'mighty' wind) does not stand up to scrutiny; with the qualifying 'of God', the reference to the holy is never absent.[45] And lastly the associated verb is applicable to a bird and not to a storm. Its meaning is determined with the help of the other biblical usage, for the eagle hovering over its young (a single verse, Dt. 32:11), and several occurrences in Ugaritic literature. It does not signify 'to brood', but it conveys precisely 'the quivering of the bird which allows it to hang motionless in

[39] G. Jéquier, *op. cit.*, p.132.   [40] *Ibid.*, p.134.

[41] Beauchamp, p.152, n.4, risks the suggestions that the *rē'sit̠* of Gn. 1:1 is not unrelated to that of Pr. 8:22.

[42] Barth, p.116.

[43] Von Rad opts for 'storm of God', pp.47f. *Cf.* Speiser, p.5.

[44] Young I, pp.39ff.; Beauchamp, pp.168ff.

[45] Beauchamp, p.170.

the air',[46] to hover like a kestrel. The test, then, speaks definitely of the Spirit of God, compared with a bird; when Jesus was baptized in Jordan, the descent of the Spirit like a dove, over the water, recalled Genesis and suggested the initiation of a new creation.

What, then, is the Spirit doing in the second verse of the Bible? He does not seem, as in Psalm 33:6, to be the bearer of the word.[47] Even less would he be 'condemned to complete impotence' above the *tōhû-bōhû*, as Karl Barth claims.[48] The word 'spirit' (breath) in the Old Testament constantly makes us think of power, and Calvin once again demonstrates his exegetical insight: 'the world…was an undigested mass; he now teaches that the power of the Spirit was necessary in order to sustain it'.[49]

☐   M. G. Kline interprets the eagle in the Song of Moses (Dt. 32:11) as an image for the cloud of the exodus, which hovered above the camp of Israel and symbolized the presence of the LORD; since Genesis uses the same verb, it would suggest that this was the original theophany.[50] Kline's position is amazingly close to that of Paul Beauchamp, with which he appears not to be familiar, who also detects reminiscences of theophany.[51] Beauchamp's close and well-nigh exhaustive analysis show that the hovering flight is at first a gyrating movement; the Spirit circles like the wind (Ps. 104:3f.), like Wisdom (Pr. 8:30f.), and like the wind-borne Glory beheld by Ezekiel (Ezk. 1). But the movement advances towards a goal, like the flight of a vulture over its prey. The flight of the Spirit prepares the creative intervention, and in the same moment bears witness that 'God existed before he had spoken' and signifies 'God's presence, at large and moving towards its goal'.[52] Contrary to Job 37 and Psalm 104, the seven-day cycle does not localize the Creator: 'our passage makes up for this omission. God comes, he arises in his *rûah*, which is neither in heaven nor on earth, but, like the Wisdom of Proverbs 8:22–31, between one and the other. Thus, the God of the seven days is

[46] J. Bonnet, *Les symboles traditionnels de la Sagesse* (Roanne: Horvath, 1971), p.53. *Cf.* Caquot, *In Principio*, pp.19f. (Je. 23:9 uses the qal of the verb for 'quiver'.)

[47] Renckens, p.56, lacks rigour at this point. *Cf.* Beauchamp, p.178, n.44.

[48] Barth, p.107.   [49] Calvin, p.74.

[50] Meredith G. Kline, 'Creation in the image of the Glory Spirit', *WTJ* 39 (1976–1977), pp.250–272).

[51] Beauchamp, pp.186–228 in particular. 'But the aspect of power is completely absorbed by that of wisdom', p.227.

[52] *Ibid.*, pp.174–181.

localized in the same way as the God of Ezekiel, by an impalpable vehicle'.[53] Further, in Beauchamp's estimation, the function of the Spirit 'balances the principle of separation by being placed at the opposite pole';[54] if the Word brings about diversity, the Spirit unifies.[55]   □

It seems that we can understand the Spirit which hovered as the bearer of the free, quivering presence of God by which he draws near, while yet remaining distinct from the elements of the universe.[56] The text implies without actually stating it that the Spirit will share in the very creation, complementing the Word, and that creation is a kind of theophany in the sense of being a revelation of God.

Concerning the instrumentality of the word, we brought in the theme of wisdom; concerning the Spirit we have quoted Proverbs 8. A line could be traced from the prologue of Genesis, through Proverbs 8, ending at the prologue of John's Gospel. That Gospel reveals to us the creating Word who is also Wisdom in person. The first page of the Bible is not so explicit, but the part played alongside God by his Word, which distinguishes and communicates, and by his Spirit, which is a living presence, suggests that the writer's monotheism is not as simple as might appear. With his immense audacity, Karl Barth declares that the Church Fathers were right to have heard 'echoing' here 'the whole mystery of the Trinity'.[57] And in his punctilious exegesis Beauchamp finds in the mention of the Spirit 'valid support for the attempts made by Christians in the early centuries to see in the first chapter of Genesis the distant dawn of a trinitarian revelation'.[58]

'God is not a God of disorder' (1 Cor. 14:33)

The God of the Bible calls himself 'the God of peace', and one can expect peace to reign over his first created work. But what is 'peace', *šālôm*, in the Bible? To the excited Corinthians the apostle Paul mentions one of its major components: 'God is not a God of disorder but of peace' (1 Cor. 14:33, NEB). Now the emphasis on the order of the creation is the one most loudly heard in the

[53] *Ibid.*, p.185.   [54] *Ibid.*, p.186.   [55] *Ibid.*, p.341.
[56] Bonhoeffer, p.18, notes this. Origen commented on the word 'over': 'The Spirit does not come *into* all following their baptism' (quoted by Pierre Nautin, 'Genèse 1.1–2, de Justin à Origène, *In Principio*, p.92).
[57] Barth, p.116.   [58] Beauchamp, p.341.

opening of Genesis. It is not for nothing that the throng of creatures is there called literally an *army* (2:1), and that army, as Beauchamp puts it, 'does not fight, it parades'.[59] The phrase is used commonly for the celestial creation, the angels and the stars (the LORD is the LORD of those armies); they are models of perfect obedience and of regular motion. 'Army of the earth' is found only in Genesis 2:1, doubtless by assimilation with the common phrase and in order to record that, when they were created, earth's living creatures followed as perfect an order as the order of the heavens. In all its usages, the word translated 'army' or 'host' designates a diverse totality that is properly arranged, organized and differentiated. The heavens and the earth and their inhabitants constitute a *cosmos*.

The *separations* of the first days serve the cause of order. They trace clear lines that drive away any confusion. They permit classification by categories. The repetition of the formula 'according to its/their kind' reinforces the theme, though the etymology of the term used, *mîn*, is still under discussion (resemblance, reproduction, number?),[60] and it would be better to avoid translating it as 'species' in order not to identify it too quickly with the category so described by Linnaeus (1707–78) and now in common scientific use; but the sense of the repeated formula leaves no doubt; God's creating work orders the world of living creatures. Everything is in its place, everything prepared for. God assigns to the luminaries their exact function; he designates for mankind and the animals what they may have for food. This enthusiasm for order and separations does not arise from the author's own temperament. It finds expression elsewhere, for it is the God of the Bible who desires order. The cosmology of the wisdom writers celebrates the decree of God: he imposed a limit on the sea, that image of indiscipline (Jb. 38:10f.; Ps. 104:9; Pr. 8:29). The Law makes a careful separation between clean and unclean animals, itself comparing that separation with that of Israel, set apart amongst the nations (Lv. 20:24–26). It even goes so far as to proscribe ploughing with an ox and an ass together, sowing the same field with two different kinds of seed and wearing hybrid cloths, such as a mixture of wool and linen (Lv. 19:19; Dt. 22:9–11). As Goldstain recalls, the synagogue prayer which closes each Sabbath and is called by this very

---

[59] *Ibid.*, p.377. For his study of the word ṣābâ, see pp.247–267, *cf.* p.64.
[60] *Ibid.*, pp.240f.

name, *Abdala* (separation), brings together all the biblical aspects of the theme: 'Praise be to thee, O Lord our God, King of the world, who dost distinguish the sacred from the profane, the light from the darkness, Israel from all other nations and the seventh day from the days of work. Praise be to thee, O Lord, who dost distinguish the sacred from the profane.'[61]

The prohibitions which we recall (Lv. 19; Dt. 22) are perhaps directed against pagan practices of magical intent. When we study non-biblical religions, we constantly discover a fascination with intermixture and a kind of longing for a universal dissolution of differences. Techniques are applied to break up categories, in the hope of releasing spiritual power. The orgy seeks to rejuvenate the world by plunging it back into the creative chaos. The mystic, whom the Romantic wants to imitate, claims to descend or to rise 'beyond the good and evil' and all earthly distinctions. The modern-day dialectic which manages to integrate the negative and to synthesize good and evil is another manifestation of the rejection of the separations of Genesis. What lies behind this desire to cross boundaries and this vast effort to confuse everything, is described in its contemporary form by none better than the French philosopher, Jean Brun.[62] In all this there is no doubt that we should see the anarchic revolt of mankind who wishes himself to be free of all law – having neither God nor master. Not only is it moral law but also natural law which must appear intolerable to our God-defying liberty. *Liber*, from which comes the word 'liberty', was the Roman god of chaos! Together with revolt goes resentment against being, as it is given and shaped: the desperate will not to be oneself. There is also weariness of definition and dissatisfaction with the finite; what is there to hope for, then, shut up within categories?

Beneath this dissatisfaction, if one digs still deeper, what a surprise awaits us! There we find the yearning for the infinite Unity of the Creator. The individual man or woman will indeed never be satisfied on this side of that limit. We are made for the limitless God who is revealed in the Bible – but only in a communion which respects order and not confusion. So we finally arrive at the tragic paradox: fury against God's order feeds on

---

[61] Goldstain, p.73.

[62] *Le retour de Dionysos* (Paris: Les Bergers et les Mages, ²1976); *La nudité humaine* (Paris: Fayard, 1973); *Les vagabonds de l'Occident* (Paris: Desclée, 1976); *A la recherche du paradis perdu* (Lausanne: PBU, 1979).

the desire for God. Once the knowledge of God is lost, the sense of God wanders among created things, and not finding him, seeks for his substitute in their dissolution. Once the knowledge of God is lost, mankind accuses finitude of causing his disorder, whereas that disorder is the fruit of disobedience. Once the communion is lost, mankind wants to replace it with confusion.

There is a triangular connection between creation, order and the word. The word brings forth clear differentiations, and an ordered world refers us back to a God who speaks – without him the order of the world would be denounced as artificial and illusory. The idea of creation would be difficult to conceive without both order and word, since it posits the radical distinction between the Creator and the creature which is reflected in distinctions between the creatures, and since, like the word, it implies a relationship within the distance. Beauchamp was aware of this: 'The word is closest to the sense of otherness which is inherent in the concept of creation....Every word, even if it does not contain a commandment as is the case here, is volitional. It chooses and sets in order.'[63] In any case, the creator God of Genesis shows himself throughout the Bible as a God who speaks. His word, as opposed to the silence of the mystics and the din of pagan worship, is a word in the proper sense, an orderly discourse with the same firmness in what it defines as the work of the six days:

> For thus says the LORD,
> who created the heavens
>   (he is God!),
> who formed the earth and made it
>   (he established it;
> he did not create it a chaos,
>   he formed it to be inhabited!):
> 'I am the LORD, and there is no other.
> I did not speak in secret,
>   in a land of darkness;
> I did not say to the offspring of Jacob,
>   'Seek me in chaos.'
> I the LORD speak the truth,
>   I declare what is right.'   (Is. 45:18f.)

---

[63] Beauchamp, p.119.

If at the culminating point of revelation the Son himself takes the name 'the Word', in a pre-eminent and foundational sense (Jn. 1; 1 Jn. 1; Rev. 19), it is the very opposite of a blurring of that clarity; on no account is it allowed to make the Word of God a subjective event with indistinct, elusive limits. We know rather that the God who is light has within himself no darkness (1 Jn. 1:5). The carefully ordered distinction which is seen in his words and his works also characterizes the eternal life of the LORD – in him there is distinction and no separation. We come back once again to the mystery of the Trinity, the foundation of every foundation.

Perfect order does not require only unblurred edges, but also, because of the link between all the elements in the whole, a *hierarchy*. The use of a scale of values brings separated categories together in harmony. The first tablet of Genesis also records order from that point of view. The night, named by God, is not bad; but only of the light is it said that God saw that it was good: it was better. If the various creatures are *good* – and Westermann asserts that the word also means *beautiful*[64] – in their entirety, at the end of the sixth day they are *very good*.[65] God does not stop at appreciation, for three times he adds his *blessing*. Finally, at the two peaks of the narrative, we find the highest value assigned: with the glorious favour bestowed on mankind in being in the image of God, and with the sanctification of the seventh day. The benedictions, however, and what has to do with the human race, bring us into contact with aspects of creation other than its order, for order is not everything.

'It is the Spirit that gives life' (Jn. 6:63)

Peace in the biblical sense implies good order. Primarily, however, it implies fullness (its root is a verb 'to fill'), and then prosperity, well-being, health. People wish one another *šālôm* as a common daily greeting. This meaning of peace is not absent in Genesis. The living God fills his creation with *life*.

The inhabitants with which God peoples the regions are not all living. No word suggests that the stars have life. In spite of their motion, they are treated as the parts of a functional

---

[64] Westermann *C*, p.63.

[65] Cassuto, p.60, brings out the point that the sixth adjective has the article, whilst the other ordinals do not have it; that distinction is reserved for the day of completion.

mechanism.[66] But this arrangement which contributes to the geometry of the whole[67] does not prevent the 'fullness' of the waters, of the air and of the earth from consisting of living creatures.

What is life? Bonhoeffer writes: 'The living differs from the dead by the fact that it can itself create life.'[68] For modern science that capacity to reproduce remains a decisive criterion for marking the boundary of life – it is on this issue that the life of viruses is disputed.[69] It is indeed that reproduction of every living creature 'according to its kind' that is brought out in the text of Genesis 1. Just as the goodness of the creatures reflects that of the Creator, it is reasonable to think that this power of living things reflects the very power to create that God has.

In the landscape of creation, two stages stand out on the pathway of life. With the vegetable kingdom there emerges the notion of *nature* (the word is directly connected with the Latin *natus*, 'born'). The earth is a mother since she produces vegetation, the plants which broadcast their seeds and those which nurture them inside a fruit. Nature is certainly not divinized. The concept is 'bounded by the term *creature*'.[70] Nevertheless it has its place in the vision and it responds to the Creator's will to unite the different parts of the universe *in life*. In the case of the animal kingdom swarming with life, God is not just content to make and to affirm, he *blesses*. Why the blessing for creatures that are already good? It seems to be added when the creature possesses a semi-autonomous function, as it were, a wide open space in front of it. For the animal that can move, life turns into an adventure. By blessing it, God adds his favour to the very movement of what he has created. With the birds and the fish, life is proclaimed as a reality of the *subjects* within the vast kingdom of the Lord.

'The living creatures converge towards the man.'[71] He will

[66] It is often emphasized that 'sun' and 'moon' are not named and that this implies a deliberate devaluing, a polemic against the worship of the stars. Beauchamp, p.102, sensibly notes that sun and moon were also common nouns, and that the text is seeking to denote simply their kind and their function as luminaries.

[67] To the points already made about structure we may also add that the following pattern links the two triads of days together (*cf.* Beauchamp, p.66):

HEAVENS	HEAVENS	HEAVENS		
		EARTH	EARTH	EARTH

[68] Bonhoeffer, pp.30f.

[69] Paul A. Zimmermann, 'The spontaneous generation of life', *SSt*, p.318. It is the cell that is attacked that reproduces the virus, a parasitic particle.

[70] Von Rad, p.53, *cf.* p.64.   [71] Beauchamp, p.45.

feed from the fruit of the earth, with a special relationship between mankind and the tree (Gn. 1:29f.) – the man is like the tree of the animal kingdom, by his vertical stance and by his calling to a long life-span.[72] He will have dominion over all the animals. And if the various animals that walk on the earth receive no particular blessing, it is without doubt because the blessing of humanity spills over on to them, so close is their association (*cf.* vv.29f.). Mankind is, in point of fact, the supreme living creature. This can be seen on reflection. Bonhoeffer goes so far as to say that life remains basically dead as long as it lacks liberty.[73] For life suggests liberty. More than that, it cannot be conceived of except in reference to liberty. Life is really unthinkable as long as it is not achieved in the freedom of a living being! The current approach seeks to define man in terms of the animal world, and succeeds in understanding neither mankind nor the animals. The metaphysical enigma of animal life, which puzzles anyone who really thinks, is clarified only when it is discovered to be the preparation, the sketch and the image of human life. Schiller had observed this, when he called living nature 'an apparent liberty'; Buytendijk who quotes him comments that true transcendence of nature belongs only to the consciousness of mankind, 'but the expansive vigour of life is in a certain sense the *image* of that transcendence, it is an apparent transcendence.... Indeed, a bird is not really free, even when it soars into the sky and needlessly sings its heart out. It is the image of liberty, a liberty in appearance.'[74] Further on, the same author shows that there is no scientific explanation why the sexes are differentiated in the animal realm.[75] Now, this fact involves a necessity which is intelligible *for humanity*, the necessity of the complementary difference for full communion between two incarnate liberties. This will be understood *first and foremost in terms of mankind* for the living creatures which are lower than ourselves. Mankind is the supreme living creature, as is brought out by the convergent features of the Genesis narrative.

☐   In the rest of Scripture, the Spirit is so often associated with life that the question presses, Is there also a connection here? The phrase 'Spirit (or breath) of life' is typical of biblical language

---

[72] Barth, p.155.   [73] Bonhoeffer, pp.33f.

[74] Taken from the French translation, *La Femme, ses modes d'être, de paraître, d'exister* (Paris: Desclée de Brouwer, 1967), p.85.

[75] *Ibid.,* pp.91ff. The theories of amphimixis and of rejuvenation are inadequate.

from Genesis onwards. It is God's in-breathing that gives life to the man. The apostle Paul takes this up (Rom. 8:2). That very free commentary on Genesis, Psalm 104, pictures the Spirit giving life to all living things (Ps. 104:29f.) and Job 33:4 applies this to mankind in particular. Jesus underlines, 'It is the Spirit that gives life' (Jn. 6:63), and the book of Revelation finally symbolizes the Spirit by a river of life (Rev. 22:1ff.). If the function of the Spirit of God in the second verse of Genesis is 'to balance the principle of separation', is it not from him that would arise the living fullness of creation? It is difficult to resist the conclusion that, as order comes from the Word, life is born of the Spirit.

The Genesis text, however, remains astonishingly reticent. Why not state clearly the role of the Spirit? Perhaps the author was struggling to avoid any hint of pantheism; the emphasis falls on the lordship of the One, who rules alone without confusion with his creation. Perhaps too the author wished to hold back the Spirit for the special relation he has with mankind. In a detailed study, D. J. A. Clines suggests that the 'us' of v.26, the plural that has so exercised the exegetes, is best understood of God speaking to his Spirit, the only one with whom he could converse, so far as the context is concerned.[76] The Spirit was at work particularly in the creation of mankind. The second tablet of Genesis (2:7) represents the special privilege of mankind as the communication of a 'breath'. The term employed ($n^e šāmâ$) is a near synonym of $rûah$ in 1:2, but its usage is less common. The term $n^e šāmâ$ is used rarely for God and avoids any notion of emanation. It is used for mankind and not for animals, and designates the spirit of mankind created to correspond to the Spirit of God.[77]   □

Mankind! Despite the raising of the heavens above his head, he, the living creature endowed with a spirit, appears clearly as the one for whom the whole work has been made. If the sabbath was made for mankind, and not mankind for the Mosaic sabbath (Mk. 2:27), even the sabbath rest of God has been 'made' in order that human history may unfold. What is the work of the six days, said Gregory of Nyssa, other than the building of the palace, until the entry into the place prepared of the prince beloved by the Father?[78] Or rather, the construction of the

[76] D. J. A. Clines, 'The image of God in man', *TB* 19 (1968), pp.68f.

[77] T. C. Mitchell, *VT* 11,2 (1961), pp.177–188, defends the special meaning of $n^e šāmâ$. One single text, Gn. 7:22, might possibly use the word of animals. Jos. 11:14 excludes the animals. In Pr. 20:27 it is the lamp of the LORD. *Cf.* Payne, p.24, n.8.

[78] According to Goldstain, p.52.

sanctuary – a word such as 'luminary' recalls the tabernacle[79] –
until the Image of God comes to inhabit it?

The apostle Paul, having stressed that in God we have life,
movement (which is not so very far from order) and being, moves
on to mankind's situation: 'We are his offspring' (Acts 17:28).
We must now do the same.

---

[79] Goldstain, p.80, quoting Ex. 35:8, *etc.* He is wrong, however, in saying this usage is
exclusive (see Pss. 74:16; 90:8; Pr. 15:30).

4
The image of God

'Man is neither angel nor beast...'[1] This brief but famous frag-
ment from Pascal's *Pensées* could provide us with a starting-
point to classify many philosophies of man, both ancient and
modern. The advocates of idealism see man as an angel, sometimes even a god, accidentally encumbered with material
appendages. The proponents of materialism find him no
different from the beasts except in the degree of complexity of
his nervous system and brain; naked ape or trousered ape, he is
merely the most highly evolved of the primates. For many
thinkers seeking a middle way, and perhaps for popular common
sense, man is basically a mixture of angel and beast, combining
in himself somehow or other a celestial principle with animal
matter. For the Bible, man is neither angel nor beast, nor even a
little of both;[2] the prologue of Genesis defines him as a creature
made *as the image of God*. The perspective and vision are totally
different.

No commentator can skip over the formula set out in such
bold relief at the climax of the narrative. The Doctors of the
church felt that it was decisive, the most concise summary of
biblical anthropology, from its original viewpoint. They strove
to translate its language, which was itself an image. Their
labour bore a great variety of fruits; the history of the interpret-

---

[1] *Pensées*, Lafuma edition, *Everyman's Library* (London: Dent, 1960), p.68, no.257.

[2] O. Loretz, p.55, falls into this trap: 'Man is a mixture of the earthly and of the divine'.
This is precisely not the viewpoint of the Bible, even if it teaches a dual composition of the
human being – man's spirit is not divine!

ation of 'the image of God', of which many people have recently given good résumés,[3] reveals wide divergences. It would be possible, however, to bring them together and reconcile them; the propositions are less incompatible than at first appears. That is why we shall be content to give a quick review without hurrying to choose between them.

☐   If we set aside a proposal such as that which credits the author of Genesis with belief in a bodily God (we are sufficiently well acquainted with the biblical writer, a subtle theologian, to make any refutation superfluous), four principal types emerge from the multitude of attempts.

1. The interpretation held by the majority throughout church history – in many eras the *only* interpretation – refers the image to our *spirituality.* Mankind shares in the spirit as does God himself: that is the implicit point of the comparison. In the created spirit, the ancient writers make *reason* the 'hegemonic', or predominant, part. From Irenaeus and Clement of Alexandria onwards, many distinguish between the image and the likeness as between the natural and the supernatural; the image is that metaphysical quality which makes mankind distinctively mankind, and the likeness means that growth in conformity to God produced by grace.[4] No exegete defends this distinction any longer,[5] but the interpretation referring to spirituality, which goes back at least as far as Philo and the hellenistic Wisdom of Solomon ('Yet God did make man imperishable, he made him in the image of his own nature', Wisdom 2:23, JB), has had notable advocates in recent times, for example H. H. Rowley.[6]

2. The second interpretation is combined with the first in the book of Ecclesiasticus (17:3–5). It is attested in ancient Judaism,[7] the Socinians of the sixteenth century identified themselves with it, and several modern scholars subscribe to it, among them E. Jacob and H. Gross. It understands the image in terms of *dominion.* As God reigns over the entire universe, mankind, his representative, will rule the earth. Genesis develops the theme of

[3] Loretz, part 1; Westermann G, pp.203–214; D. J. A. Clines, *art. cit., TB* 19 (1968), pp.54–61.

[4] *Cf.* T. Camelot, 'La théologie de l'image de Dieu', *RSPT* 40 (1956), pp.460ff.

[5] C. Spicq, *Dieu et l'homme selon le Nouveau Testament* (Paris: Cerf, 1961), pp.180f., seems to do so still, but in fact he is simply bringing out a very slight difference between the two notions: likeness 'signifies a more or less exact parity', image 'adds the idea of origin and of the imitation of an example'.

[6] Quoted by Clines, p.59.

[7] Spicq, p.179, refers to 4 Esdras 8:44; later he indicates that it is one of the two tendencies in the pre-rabbinic exegesis of Gn. 1:26, p.182, n.2.

the authority given to mankind in the immediate context of the declaration concerning the image; furthermore, the effigy of himself that a king had erected in a city he had conquered or recently built signified his power, *represented* it. Is not mankind, then, the image of God in so far as he represents him and governs in his name?

3. Luther, who refused to distinguish 'between 'image' and 'likeness' and wished to bring out the gravity of the effects of sin, offered a third suggestion: the image is basically what certain scholars had called the likeness (when they distinguished it from the image). It is the *original righteousness*, the moral exellence, that was lost at the fall. Mankind was created in the image of God, as good and holy and pure as God himself. Redemption restores this shattered image (Col. 3:10; *cf.* Eph. 4:24). On the whole Protestants have followed Luther in this, with a few variations.[8] Luther himself was obliged to distinguish a 'private' image that had been lost from a 'public' image that had been preserved.[9]

4. Karl Barth has championed a fourth proposal, with characteristic boldness. Since, immediately after the assertion, 'God created man in his own image', Genesis specifies 'male and female he created them', Barth concludes that creation in the image of God refers to human *sexuality*! Not that the image consists of sexuality (summaries that have been made simplify Barth's thought to the point of distortion), for man does not possess the image.[10] Rather, it should be understood that the difference male/ female calls mankind to a personal, face-to-face relationship, as God himself exists in face-to-face relationship (hence the divine plural, 'let us make'). The image of God is fulfilled, ultimately, only in Christ's face-to-face relationship with the church. Goldstain quotes a rabbinic anticipation of Barth's ideas: '"In our image, according to our likeness" means that man cannot come into existence without woman, nor woman without man, nor either of them without the *Chekina*, the glory of God'.[11] That is, however, less than explicit and is not to be equated with Barth's interpretation.

Mediating solutions or partial combinations can be imagined.

[8] Calvin's interpretation is quite complex; it has been emphasized that the metaphor of the mirror is important in his thinking on this; *cf.* G. C. Berkouwer, *Man: the image of God* (Grand Rapids: Eerdmans, 1962), pp.110f.

[9] Emil Brunner, *The Christian Doctrine of Creation and Redemption* (*Dogmatics* 2) (London: Lutterworth, 1952), p.76.

[10] Barth, pp.197, 211ff. For the whole discussion, see pp.183–206.

[11] *Bereshit-Rabba* VIII, 9, in Goldstain, p.101.

For that reason, we forgo examination of the four interpretations we have described. We prefer to allow ourselves to be guided by the text, by its echoes in Genesis 2 and all references elsewhere in Scripture, in order to discover the meaning of the creation of man in the image of God.

☐

Mankind, only an image

We must take a step backwards. Too little notice has been taken of the critical suggestion implied by the term 'image', the function of 'likeness', according to some scholars, being to weaken the first term.[12] An image *is only an image*. It exists only by derivation. It is not the original, nor is it anything without the original. Mankind's being an image stresses the radical nature of his dependence. As Calvin observed, by the expression Scripture is 'suggesting that man was blessed, not because of his own good actions, but by participation in God'.[13]

One may well imagine images that are exact replicas, but the verb 'create' excludes that idea from Genesis. Mankind remains infinitely lower than his Creator; he is mere creature and nothing more. From its very first page the Bible excludes the pagan theme of the divinization of man and all the dreams of hidden divinity and self-creation. It does not follow Babylonian mythology with its humanity moulded with divine blood.[14] The spirit conferred on mankind does not emanate as if it were a portion of the Spirit of God. Zechariah 12:1 uses for the creation of the spirit of man within him the same verb 'to form' as Genesis 2 uses for the body, the verb that describes the work of the potter. From this point of view Scripture places mankind firmly alongside the world, before the LORD.

The two 'tablets' of the beginning each teach in their own way the solidarity of mankind with the animals. Mankind arrives on the sixth day, as do all the various animals, and God appoints their food to all at the same time.[15] In the paradise narrative, God models or fashions from the ground both the man and the animals that will pass by before him (2:7, 19). Without going as far as St Francis of Assisi in calling the beasts our brothers, the

---

[12] L. Köhler, K. L. Schmidt, mentioned by Berkouwer, p.70 n.9.

[13] *Institutes* II. ii. 1.

[14] The blood of the god Kingu, Heidel, p.78. The Atrahasis Epic included this theme, with the commentary, 'So let God and man be mingled together in the clay' (Millard, *art. cit., TB* 18 (1967), p.9).

[15] Barth, pp.177, 180f.

Bible informs mankind of his links with the animal kingdom.

The first chapter of Genesis does not mention the clay, the material from which the human being is made. But by calling him Adam (*'ādām*) it indicates his connection with the earth: *'ªdāmâ*. Adam is the 'earthling' and his name is fitting since God gave it to him (Gn. 5:2). Beneath the sky which overhangs the earth, beneath the luminaries which govern the divisions of time, his very name is for man a solemn reminder: 'God is in heaven, and you upon earth' (Ec. 5:2). It is sometimes claimed that in our own language the word 'human' traces its etymology back to the Latin *humus* – which is also the root of the word 'humility'!

Mankind alone in God's image

Humility precedes glory. If the announcement, 'God created man in his own image' does not conceal but rather underlines his creaturely dependence, its principal aim is incontrovertibly to exalt mankind. Or, rather, it seeks to extol the magnanimity of the Creator, who has created him to come so close to the divine condition (Ps. 8:6). To be created in the image of God is the privilege of the human race and is shared by none of the animals mentioned in Genesis. The rest of Scripture does not seem to attribute it even to the angels, even though they are 'greater in might and power' (2 Pet. 2:11).[16] Mankind is in the image of God, and he alone; this singular honour marks him out as God's choice creature.

The carefully constructed narrative indicates in various ways that the creation of the image-bearer is the supreme moment of the work of the six days. Not only does it come at the finish, but the verb 'create' which the writer uses so sparingly appears three times. It is preceded by a divine deliberation, 'Let us make...' which adds to the solemnity of the account and marks, as it were, God's own commitment to this work.

We have already mentioned Clines' suggestion concerning the mysterious plural, 'Let us make man in *our* image'. It has caused so much ink to flow that we should pause a moment in our exploration to consider it. How are we to understand it? A piece of left-over polytheism is absolutely impossible in such a

[16] It was the identification of image with spirituality or holiness that led older writers, like Calvin, to attribute the image to the angels. We prefer to follow Kuyper and Bavinck in opting for the contrary view, see Berkouwer, *op. cit.*, pp.85ff.

carefully written text; the author is not the kind of man to make a blunder! It would be difficult to understand it to mean that God was addressing the assembled angels, of whom there is not a single word. If the word referred to them, it would invite them to *share* in the creation. Now, the Bible nowhere suggests such a thing, and only a novelist would have the imagination to suggest that the angels, invited to create, declined the offer in order to let God act alone![17] In any case, God did not consult with anyone else (Is. 40:14).[18]

So what can 'us' and 'our' mean in the case of God? The royal plural has no certain attestation in Hebrew. Ezra 4:18, which is written in Aramaic, could easily refer to the whole Persian government. The plural of deliberation or exhortation, when an individual addresses himself, is the only plural to appear occasionally (like the English, 'Let's have a look'). David says of himself, 'let us fall' (2 Sa. 24:14) and the lover in the Song of Songs, 'Let us make' or 'We will make' ornaments of gold (Song 1:11). In Genesis 1:26 such a plural could be acknowledged; it fits the context.[19] But let us notice what it supposes theologically: it supposes an inner distinction in God which is comparable to that in the inner life of a man, between himself and his mind. What right have we to imagine that there is a similar distinction in God? The answer to that, from the text, is the mention of the Spirit. That is why we consider we should stand by Clines' view: God addresses himself, but this he can do only because he has a Spirit who is both one with him and distinct from him at the same time. Here are the first glimmerings of a trinitarian revelation. They illumine all the more brightly the announcement of the creation of mankind.

In the divine words and in the rhythmical announcement of the completion of the work, it is the word 'image', repeated, that draws our attention. Two ways of understanding it are put forward. Either the 'image' would refer to the shape of God (man being made in the image, according to the divine prototype), or else it would refer to the created effigy itself (man being made in the image, in order to be the effigy of God). *Selem* generally refers to a concrete image, a statue, often an idol (*e.g.* Nu. 33:52). Twice in the Psalter it concerns a more or less spectral shape, the image in a dream that vanishes (Pss. 39:6; 73:20). It would be difficult for it to be used for the model, the form of the

[17] The rabbinic explanation, see Clines, *art. cit.*, *TB* 19 (1968), pp.66f.
[18] Kidner, p.51. [19] This is Cassuto's preference, for example, p.55.

original; it is rather the image made *according to* the original.[20]
The second word, $d^e m\hat{u}t$, 'likeness', is made of more abstract
elements, but does not throw doubt on our interpretation; it
specifies the nature of the image, one which resembles and has
analogical features which are not, however, identical.[21] This
image 'represents' God in both senses of the word.

☐   If the *ṣelem* refers to the copy and not to the model, is the current
translation 'created *in* (after) the image of God' appropriate? It
suggests that the word 'image' has in view the form of God, the
divine master according to whom mankind has been fashioned.
Barth lays massive emphasis on this.[22] Now, such a meaning is
not within the range of *ṣelem*. The preposition b^e ought rather to
be rendered 'as': 'He created him *as* the image of God', in order
that man *may be* the image of God.[23] The preposition k^e, used with
the word 'likeness', can have the same meaning: the k^e of essence
or of truth, since the two prepositions change places with each
other in Genesis 5:3. So 1:26 can be read: 'Let us make man as our
image, as our (concrete) likeness'. The apostle Paul seems to have
read the preposition b^e in this way, since he declares that man is
the image of God (1 Cor. 11:7).   ☐

If man *is* the image, the emphasis falls on his *situation*. The
metaphor of the *ṣelem* does not speak firstly of the nature of the
human creature (although a secondary interest in it cannot be
excluded). It defines our *constitutive relationships*. Mankind
belongs to the visible world, as befits an image. But in particular
we are defined in relationship to God. Mankind is to be the
created representation of his Creator, and here on earth, as it
were, the image of the divine Glory (1 Cor. 11:7; 2 Cor. 3:18),[24]
that Glory which mankind both reflects and beholds.

The theme of beholding is also suggested by the term 'image'.

---

[20] Clines, *art. cit.*, pp.73ff.   [21] *Ibid.*, pp.90ff.   [22] Barth, pp.197f.

[23] The b^e in that case is the b^e of essence, as the grammarians call it, the classic example of
which is in Ex. 6:3: 'I appeared … *as* God Almighty'. Clines, pp.75–80, makes a brilliant case
for the possibility of understanding it in this way, along with other modern authorities. He
shows in particular that any other turn of phrase would have failed to render the thought of
the writer, *e.g.* the preposition l^e would have suggested the transformation of a creature that
already existed (pp.76f.), and he cites grammatical parallels (p.77): Nu. 18:26; Dt. 1:13.
Among the authors who opt for the b^e of essence, he mentions K. L. Schmidt, E. Jacob, Von
Rad, J. Jervell and H. Gross. Spicq, p.181, n.2, seems to follow Jervell in his footnote but not
in his text. Loretz, p.62, n.66, leaves the possibility open. Opposed to it are James Barr, 'The
image of God in the book of Genesis. A study of terminology', *BJRL* 51 (1968–1969), pp.16f.;
and Westermann *G*, p.201.

[24] Kline, *art. cit.* (*WTJ* 39, 1976–1977) insists on this, but we cannot allow that the divine
model for the creation of mankind should be the theophanic Glory-Spirit. At this point Kline
strains the language of the text.

W. Vischer introduces it in another very beautiful metaphor:
'Man is the eye of the whole body of creation which God will
cause to see His glory'.[25] Vischer's thought is a legitimate extension of the language of Genesis 1. Westermann provides proof of
this. Many ancient Near Eastern texts link the idea of the
'analogical face-to-face encounter' with the formation by a god
of a being as his image.[26] Mankind, it could be said, represents
God for God and not only for the world.

This definition of humanity, mankind as the image of God,
illuminates the harmony of biblical truth. If mankind is the
image, does not the prohibition of making images of God appear
in a new light?[27] God himself has placed his image in his cosmic
sanctuary, and he wishes due homage to be paid to it by the
service of mankind, the neighbour created in his image. And
Christ joins the first and great commandment with the second
which 'is like it' – 'You shall love the LORD your God...you shall
love your neighbour...'; surely the logic behind that is the likeness between God and his image. The same logic is appealed to
by James, when he is indignant that with the same mouth 'we
bless the Lord and Father and we curse men, who are made in
the likeness of God' (Jas. 3:9). It appears also to lie behind John's
argument about loving your brother (1 Jn. 4:20).

We can go even further. There is perhaps a *polemical* thrust to
the Genesis declaration, not only against idols of wood, stone or
metal, but also against the limitation to *certain* men of the
privilege of the image of God; it is all mankind and everyman,
not the king, whom God has made in his image.[28]

☐　　In Mesopotamia the theme of the image occasionally comes into
　　the language of the court: 'The father of the king, my lord, was the
　　very image (*ṣalam*) of Bel, and the king, my lord, is likewise the
　　very image of Bel' says a cuneiform text.[29] In Egypt, parallels
　　abound, with several terms translated 'image'; Erik Hornung has
　　made a most valuable systematic study of these.[30] When it is a
　　question of the divine image, the majority of these terms are used
　　only for the king. Their usage is frequent from the first inter-
　　mediate period (2140–2040 BC) until the time of the Ptolemies. One
　　term, *znn,* is used for all men in the two most democratic periods,

[25] Quoted by Barth, p.194.　　　[26] Westermann *C*, pp.58f. (quoting from V. Maag).
[27] Berkouwer, *op. cit.,* p.78; Loretz, pp.106ff.
[28] Clines, *art. cit.,* p.94.　　　[29] Quoted by Clines, *art. cit.,* p.83.
[30] E. Hornung, *Der Mensch als 'Bild Gottes' in Ägypten,* in the appendix to Loretz,
pp.123–156.

namely the first intermediate period, with *The Instruction for King Merikarē*, and the religious revolution of Akhenaten (1364–1347); but these periods were exceptions to the general rule.   □

Thus the Genesis prologue could have been a reaction against the ideology of the pharaoh as the 'image of God', 'the living image of Amon' (as the name Tutankhamun can be rendered, for example), against the arrogation by a few of the privilege of mankind as such.

Images were supposed to share in the powers of the beings they represented. In Egypt, on the inscriptions on tombs, the letter f which was shaped like a snake has been decapitated to prevent it from biting the dead.[31] Even if the Old Testament is free of confusion between the sign and the things signified (which it is), and even if it distinguishes perfectly between the properties of an image and those of the original, the special mention of the likeness (*d^{e}mût*) makes us ask questions about its implications for the nature of mankind and of his privileged position.

The first chapter of Genesis certainly does not specify the attributes by which mankind resembles God. We can only suppose that the transcendence of God, his use of speech and the presence of his spirit will be reflected in the human creature. Conversely, the second chapter shows us as it were mankind in close-up and directs its interest to the composition of his nature. Perhaps it uses in a purified form the imagery of the Egyptians, who 'used to depict the god *Khnum* sitting before the potter's wheel and making human beings, and next to him his consort *Heket* putting to the noses of the created people the sign of life ('*nḥ*)'.[32] What is important in Genesis 2 is the divine in-breathing which distinguishes the man; there is no question of this in the case of the animals who, like the man, are moulded from the dust of the ground. The gift of the *n^{e}šāmâ* acts as an equivalent to the formula 'in the image of God'. This fact, together with the specific reference of the word *n^{e}šāmâ* (which is not used in the case of the animals), plus the role of the seat of conscience, 'the lamp of the Lord' (Pr. 20:27), which has devolved upon it, allows us to understand Genesis. It wishes to affirm the *duality* of the constitution of mankind. For that is our nature.

The rest of Scripture confirms this. The duality of soul/spirit and of body which is peculiar to human nature belongs to the

[31] *Ibid.*, p.154.   [32] Cassuto, p.106.

propositions of biblical anthropology. From 1930 to about 1960 it was fashionable amongst theologians to deny this. Under the influence of J. Pedersen in Old Testament studies and Rudolf Bultmann in New Testament studies, and out of an aversion to nineteenth-century idealism, a whole host of authors repeated continually that for 'the Hebrew mind' mankind was a unity, nothing more than a psychosomatic unity, and that mankind does not possess a body, rather he is a body, and so on. They were, of course, right to underline the Bible's view of the unity of the human person and in that regard to reject the long-standing confusion between Christianity and a kind of popular Platonism. But, caught by academic fashion, they moved too quickly to the rejection of every kind of duality and every kind of structural composition. This rejection was supported only by flimsy, methodologically dubious material, but they did not take the time to examine it. In the end a healthy reaction occurred. R. H. Gundry's work on the concept of body has restored what nearly every generation of Christians has understood on the matter.[33] Duality stands out unambiguously in the New Testament, just as it does in the Judaism of that era. Furthermore, it is pre-supposed by the doctrine of the intermediate state, of the survival of the soul/spirit without the body in the period between death and the final resurrection. But even in the Old Testament, despite the haziness of the concepts and the different meanings that words can have, it would be wrong to suppose that it was absent. The idea of an inner life is often expressed, with the help, amongst other things, of the concept of the heart. The word is used metaphorically, of course, for the *heart* in the sense of the inner being is peculiar to mankind. Edmond Jacob pointed out that 'the animal has no heart', which could not be said of the literal physical organ![34] The heart and the spirit are often associated, and there is an undeniable reference in Genesis 2:7 to the spirit which, in the man, is joined to the body. We recognize, therefore, that the interpretation of 'the image of God' as spirituality is part of the truth. Genesis 1 has in view

[33] Robert H. Gundry, *Soma in Biblical Theology with Emphasis on Pauline Anthropology* (Cambridge: CUP, 1976). See also a brief but excellent piece by John Murray, 'The nature of man' in *Collected Writings of John Murray* 2 (Edinburgh: Banner of Truth, 1977), pp.14–22.

[34] E. Jacob, 'Homme' in J.–J. von Allmen (ed.), *Vocabulaire biblique* (Paris: Delachaux & Niestlé, ²1956), p.125. Even Karl Barth, who was scarcely a monist when it came to anthropology, allowed himself to be swept along by the current and missed the metaphor; he writes: 'To the body there belongs also the heart, and therefore what we call the human personality' (p.245). And what are we to make of circumcision of the heart?

first of all the situation of mankind, but the uniqueness of his nature is implied there and is then brought out distinctly in the second tablet.

Nevertheless, mankind is not an amalgam of angel and of beast! The spirit of man is not angelical but terrestrial, formed for the existence that is appropriate to such a creature. In the order of God's creation, the inner nature and the outer nature contribute together to the value of humanity, and in the corruption of sin they are affected together, the soul firstly. It is acceptable to say concerning the union of the components that mankind is spiritual even in his instincts (Maurice Merleau-Ponty). Taking a theme already used by Ovid, Augustine stressed that our upright stance was the sign and the means of spirituality. Aquinas agreed with this; in Calvin's view, in it 'glows' the image of God.[35] If mankind is the image of a Creator who is really distinct from the world, it is fitting that his being is really distinct from the visible realm of which he too is a part; hence his duality. But both spirit and body come equally from God and equally are creaturely, and it is in the visible world that God wants his image; hence mankind's unity.

A concrete image which represents its archetype, stands face to face with him, and resembles him by nature – we have examples of this every day. What else is a son to his father? In all the Babylonian and Egyptian texts we have mentioned, the idea of sonship repeats that of the image. In the New Testament, the Son bears also the title of Image (Col. 1:15), Image and Son in a pre-eminent sense, in eternal equality, as the principle in God of all creation and of all revelation.[36] Nearer the prologue of Genesis, the book of the *tôlᵉdôt* of Adam, having recalled the creation of man 'in the likeness of God' (Gn. 5:1), records that Adam begot his son 'as his own likeness, as his image' (Gn. 5:3). Is that not the obvious key to the language of Genesis 1:26f.?[37] God created man as a sort of earthly son, who represents him and responds to him.

At the end of its genealogy of Jesus, the third Gospel dares to call Adam 'the son of God' (Lk. 3:38) and Paul dares take up for his own use the line of the pagan poet, 'For we are indeed his offspring' (Acts 17:28). Why does Genesis not state it clearly? Doubtless it wanted to keep as far away as possible any panthe-

---

[35] Ovid, *Metamorphoses* I, 11. 85f; Augustine, *De Gen. contra Manich* I. 28; Aquinas quoted in Loretz, pp.18f.; Calvin, *Institutes* I. xv. 3.

[36] *Cf.* Camelot, *art. cit.*, pp.445ff. [37] Thus Loretz, pp.62f. and others.

istic temptation. 'Son' rather than 'image' could have suggested that mankind possessed divinity, the idea that had to be banned.[38] In particular we would say that Scripture wished to reserve the word 'son' for the closer, indissoluble relationship of communion that God established with us in Jesus Christ, the Son who became the new man. In the Son we become sons, an act of grace which fulfils and transcends our primeval quasi-sonship.

Mankind the image of God: purpose and person

If we have understood the text of Genesis correctly, mankind was created as the living image of God, in a quasi-filial relationship with him and, like him, endowed with the spirit. Two phrases, however, still require commentary. The man was created in this manner for a purpose and for a person: on the one hand, in order to subdue the earth;[39] on the other hand, the man was made to be with the woman, and the woman with the man.

The command to subdue the earth, with the authority it implies, does not seem to belong to the definition of the image, even in 'some portion, though very small', as Calvin put it.[40] It is rather the consequence of that, as several writers have observed.[41] Psalm 8, which sings of the paradox of the smallness of man and the glory of his position, can be read in this light. As the quasi-son of the King, mankind will bring his princedom into submission (*cf.* 1 Ki. 5:4 and Ps. 110:2 for the use of the verb). This royal title in no way authorizes tyranny; the reign of the created image could only be that of a deputy. Mankind is a vassal prince who will follow the directives of the Sovereign and will give an account to him. Further, the king acted as the mediator of blessing for his country; so will mankind for the earth. Like a shepherd will he rule the animals, with a view to their own welfare as well as to his own.[42]

It is not by brute force that mankind will assure his mastery, precisely because that mastery distinguishes him from the brute beasts. As the imitator of God in the six days of the week, the

[38] Renckens, p.118.

[39] The *waw* of Gn. 1:26, 'and let them have dominion', has a final force, *cf.* Clines, *art. cit.,* p.96.

[40] Calvin, p.94.

[41] Von Rad, p.57; Loretz, p.72. Beauchamp, pp.34f., interprets the images as the means of the dominion, but we consider that the text is interested in the creation of mankind as an image for its own sake, hence the repetition in 1:27. The dominion is no longer mentioned when the theme of the image is repeated in 5:1.

[42] Westermann *C*, pp.50–54.

viceroy of creation will deploy the power of the word and of the spirit. So he is presented in the second tablet. What relationship does the man establish with the animals? He *names* them. Thus he indicates the right that he has over them, as the pharaoh will show his suzerainty over his vassal by changing his name from Eliakim to Jehoiakim (2 Ki. 23:34) and Nebuchadnezzar will show his over Mattaniah whose name was changed to Zedekiah (2 Ki. 24:17). But the bestowal of names undoubtedly reveals at the same time the insight of knowledge. The man must in fact study the character of the animals which pass before him, in order to see whether any one of the birds or animals can bring him the company he desires. The name he gives summarizes his conclusion, and if the text adds, 'and whatever the man called every living creature, that was its name' (Gn. 2:19), can that be only to confirm his authority? Does it not wish to praise his precision and his judgment? The picturesque, almost humorous, scene suggests a rudimentary kind of science, the means of man's domination over nature. The French philosopher Condillac (1715–80) held that science was simply an advanced state of language. Language in any case is the form and condition of science, and in language the act of naming is the first and indispensable operation.[43] By naming, the man demonstrates his power of distinguishing things immediately, and makes thought about the real world possible by the mental combination of symbols instead of the impossible manipulation of objects. We may therefore see in Genesis 2:19f. the first exercise of human intelligence, justification for which may be found in the ancient traditions about the incomparable wisdom of the first man.[44]

The clause, 'male and female he created them' (Gn. 1:27), to follow the blunt Hebrew expression, is not developed to the same length as the theme of domination. But it recurs in Genesis 5:2, and the second tablet gives considerable attention to the question of the sexes. Its important is such that we shall have to consider it separately.

☐   Karl Barth, who went much further on this point than W. Vischer and D. Bonhoeffer who are quoted as his precursors,[45] made the

[43] *Ibid.*, p.85, Westermann finds in Gn. 2 the two essential functions of language, naming and calling – in v.23. We would say that conferring a name corresponds to defining, and that v.23, expressing a judgment, conveys the idea of significance.

[44] Robert Gordis, *art. cit.* (*JBL* 76, 1957), insists most vigorously on this theme, pp.125–129. Ezk. 28, which partially classifies the Prince of Tyre with Adam (see p.42, n.9, above), attributes to him originally immense wisdom (vv.3ff., 17): *cf.* Jb. 15:7f.

[45] W. Vischer sees the analogy in the face-to-face companionship. For Bonhoeffer, sexuality, by directing man towards the other person, qualifies his liberty as creaturely, the emphasis

formula concerning the sexes the key to the doctrine of the image of God, and that obliges us to make a few remarks at this point.

It is impossible to differ from Barth when he observes, following the text, that 'in the case of man the differentiation of sex is the only differentiation'.[46] No other distinction, racial, ethnic or social, belongs to his essence. Mankind is the only living creature lacking the formula 'according to their kind' (which has a distributive sense); the reason is that he does not divide into different species like the feathered tribe or the cattle. 'With Adam commanding the whole animal kingdom,' comments Beauchamp, 'it is a case of the unique one placed above the many.'[47] The importance of the duality 'male and female' is beyond all doubt. But nonetheless is it the explanation of the-being-in-the-image-of-God? Nothing indicates this. One could quite as well imagine that the sentence contains a contrast: as the image of God, *although* male and female! Karl Barth's hypothesis is not only arbitrary, it also lacks clarity at times and forces him to an impossible exegesis of the passage in which Paul calls the man (as opposed to the woman) the image of God (1 Cor. 11:7).[48] We cannot therefore subscribe to his views. ☐

The addition 'male and female he created them' should above all assure us that our sexuality is the work of God and that it is not incompatible with the privilege of the image of God. History proves that this precision was not superfluous. Emil Brunner could celebrate 'the immense double statement, of a lapidary simplicity, so simple indeed that we hardly realize that with it a vast world of myth and Gnostic speculation, of cynicism and asceticism, of the deification of sexuality and fear of sex disappears'.[49] Genesis excludes in particular the myth of the primitive androgyne, recalled in Plato's *Symposium*. By a strange loss of sight, Gregory of Nyssa thought he saw it in the Bible and made the fall the origin of sexuality.[50] A modern thinker like Berdyaev allowed himself to fall into that trap.[51]

---

falling on liberty as 'being-free-for', pp.38, 60f. Barth acknowledges their contribution, pp.194f.

[46] Barth, p.186.

[47] Beauchamp, p.246, *cf.* p.47. See pp.242–244 for the distributing sense of 'according to its kind'.

[48] Barth, p.203, wants to see in this the New Adam with his church. 1 Cor. 11 does not support this interpretation.

[49] From *Der Mensch im Widerspruch,* p.357, quoted in von Rad, p.58.

[50] *Cf.* Camelot, pp.458ff.

[51] Nicolas Berdyaev, *The Meaning of the Creative Act,* 1915 (E. T. London: Gollancz, 1955), ch.8.

But the biblical text moves to the plural in order to leave no doubt: 'he created *them*'. The duality of the sexes implies the plurality of the persons.

Being immediately associated with the proclamation of creation as the image of God, the phrase undoubtedly intends to teach also that both man and woman participate equally in the privilege.[52] This too was by no means unnecessary: one remembers that Aristotle considered woman to be of a different nature, inferior to man.

Finally, since sexuality is the means of reproduction, and the writer was obviously aware of the fact and records the blessing, 'Be fruitful', we may ask if he has not a further thought. Might there be in procreation – that mysterious gift granted to the man and the woman, of bringing into the world a being who is the image of God – a reflection of divine creation? The word 'procreation' suggests the idea. The man and the woman are images of God separately, and they are also the image of God together, procreating as he created. Eve was amazed at this mystery (Gn. 4:1). In Genesis 5 the begetting of Seth, who is the image and likeness of his father, follows immediately on the reminder of creation in the divine likeness, male and female. These clues are thought-provoking, and there is without doubt still plenty to explore on the meaning of the sexual differentiation that was created in the beginning.

Before pursuing our quest any further, there remains one question to resolve. What became of the 'image' in the flow of history, after the fall? Several Fathers said that it had been tainted or changed, or, more rarely, 'lost'.[53] The Reformers, because they did not wish to soften their denunciation of sin and its slavery, spoke more strongly; the image, they said, was wiped out, destroyed. One may fully sympathize with their motive and yet question the accuracy of such language.

When the image of God is defined in terms of original righteousness, its loss, whether partial or total, is a necessary conclusion. But we have not seen that meaning emerge from the text. A single argument weighs in its favour; people refer to the passage where the apostle Paul speaks of the new self 'renewed in knowledge after the image of its creator' (Col. 3:10). But with this verse we are a long way from proof. The fact that the new creation in Jesus Christ is made according to the image of the

[52] Payne, p.24; Loretz, p.67.   [53] Camelot, pp.459, 464f.

Creator does not permit us to decide what of the first creation-as-image survives in the state of sin. The subtle distinctions between the lost image and another image that is not lost, whether they are called private and public, existential and essential, special and general, material and formal, in no way recommend the theory of destruction or deletion.[54]

With D. J. A. Clines and John Murray, a Reformed theologian who was always most sensitive to the demands of exegesis,[55] we consider that the Scriptures do not teach the disappearance of the creational privilege. All the indisputable references to the declaration of Genesis 1:26f. appear to suppose the permanence of the-being-as-image-of-God (Gn. 9:6; 1 Cor. 11:7; Jas. 3:9). If mankind no longer possessed this privilege, why would it be scandalous to take away his life, or to curse him at the same time as one is blessing the Lord?

Of the image we must say what we say of humanity; for mankind *is* the image of God, the 'earthling' image. The death entailed by sin is not a disappearance of the subject, it is not even a subtraction of being. It is the unique, unthinkable contradiction: nature set against itself, humanity become inhumanity. No category designed for being is adequate to express the perversion of being. We must state both that after his revolt mankind remains mankind, and also that mankind has radically changed, that he is but a grisly shadow of himself. Mankind remains the image of God, inviolable and responsible, but has become a contradictory image, one might say a caricature, a witness against himself.

In Jesus Christ, who is both the Son of God and the Image of God, we are restored to our humanity, as true images of our Creator, and more than images; we become God's sons in his Son, by the bond of a new covenant.

---

[54] For these distinctions and a critique of them, see Berkouwer, *op. cit.*, pp.39ff. Berkouwer himself remains quite ambiguous on this question throughout his book.

[55] Clines, *art. cit.*, pp.99f.; J. Murray, *op. cit.*, pp.40f.

5
Man and woman

What was missing in God's creation when his judgment fell: 'It is not good...' (Gn. 2:18)? What prevented him from feasting his eyes on his work and declaring it 'very good' (Gn. 1:31)? The world was suffering from an absence: the absence of woman. The narrative of the *tôl^e dôt* of the universe gives no less importance to the distinction of the sexes than does the prologue. The divine deliberation, which in the first tablet solemnly announced the creation of humanity, here precedes the forming of the second sex, *i.e.* the introduction of sexuality. (The word 'sex' implies the differentiation of the two, signifying etymologically the dividing of humanity.) The emphasis in the text encourages us to reflect further on this fundamental ordering of our race; we shall concentrate this time on the development of Genesis 2.

The text achieves a balance between restraint and openness which is quite admirable. By implication it denounces the sexual obsession of the Syrian and Canaanite nature cults, involving male and female prostitution. By the same token it exposes the alienation and frenzied escape into the erotic in our own age. This eroticism is often nothing other than despair, scarcely disguised by the false frigidity of the sexologists, although it is also the search for a reality that is not artificial, for an opening up of existence, for a way out of the banality of life. The openness of the Bible is equally opposed to Victorian prudery and unhealthy repressions. It gives the proper balance, sets the limits on the place that sex may occupy and discloses its meaning.

From solitude to greeting

'It is not good that the man should be alone' (Gn. 2:18). The remark amazes us. It is the only negative assessment in the creation narrative, and it is emphatically negative.[1] By this divine reason of the creation of the woman, Scripture could not underline better the degree to which solitude contradicts the calling of humanity. From the very beginning, the human being is a *Mitsein*, a being-with; human life attains its full realization only in community. No man is an island, and everyone must discover himself to be his neighbour's neighbour. At the final completion of the operations of the grace of God, the multitude in the City of God multiplies the victory of the first couple over human solitude (Rev. 21 – 22). In the final paradise, as in the first, mankind will for ever be no longer alone.

Community does not abolish personal individuality, which is more sharply marked in the Bible than in any other ancient culture.[2] Or rather, the Bible is its very foundation. Just as the most natural mirror we have is the eye that beholds us, so it is our encounter with another which allows our inner life to become aware of itself. The Genesis narrative says this in its own way. When did mankind use the first person singular for the first time? It was certainly not while he was forming his first zoological knowledge and discovering his superiority over the animals. The self does not establish its identity over against the non-self of the impersonal universe. The self, the 'I', discovers itself in greeting another. In the 'joyful welcome' which he addresses to his companion (Gn. 2:23), to use Herder's expression, he recognizes his own self.[3] The individual finds himself only beyond himself, in salutation.

Dare we point out that, as with mankind, so it is with God, whose image he is? The oneness of the LORD is not loneliness, since he deliberates with himself, with his Spirit. This he wished to show in the course of his creation. He was not satisfied with proving his mastery and with displaying the glory of his knowledge and wisdom in the beautiful construction of the world; he raised up before himself another who was like him, similar and face-to-face, mankind his image. Here lies the truth of the

---

[1] Cassuto, pp.126f., declares that *lô' tôb* is stronger than *'ên tôb* would have been; it is not only the absence of something good, but a painful deficiency.

[2] H. and H. A. Frankfort, *Before Philosophy* (Penguin, 1963), pp.241, 245.

[3] Quoted by Westermann *C*, p.75.

Barthian proposition that we had to criticize; if we cannot find exegetical grounds for explaining 'the image of God' by the phrase 'male and female', our thoughts should turn to the undoubted analogy between the non-solitude of God and the communal structure of humanity.

Can we go a step further? Might there be more here than analogy? Would the being-with of mankind be *necessary* for him to be able to respond to God as a quasi-son to his Father? This we have the right to suppose. If the calling of mankind is to be with his God, it is fitting that his earthly existence should already be characterized by being-with; otherwise the relationship with God would be, as it were, laminated on to his nature, and he would risk becoming lost instead of fulfilled in it. It is not good for mankind to be alone on the earth, because it would be fatal for him to be alone, without God, amongst the creatures. Immediately we can see the perversity of the androgyne myth; by conferring on the same individual the attributes of both sexes, it expresses the ideal of self-sufficient solitude, it rejects the duty towards one's neighbour that God has inscribed within mankind, and thereby it rejects the duty towards the Creator that neighbour-love both reflects and honours.[4]

Why, however, should there be the differences between the man and the woman, and not simply the distinction between one person and another? Sexuality is certainly not necessary to being-with. True enough, but it necessitates being-with. The fact that the first company given by God to man in order to break his solitude was of the other sex reminds us that God does not institute an abstract otherness. He gives a *neighbour* and not merely an 'other'. He gives a concretely qualified presence, in the order he has decreed and not in abstraction. And the 'neighbourship' which is defined within God's order by sexual differentiation is of a most radical nature; every human individual, being either masculine or feminine, must abandon the illusion of being alone. The constitution of each of us is a summons to community. Genesis throws light on this privileged relationship.

---

[4] One wonders whether the myth of the Virgin-Mother does not have a similar aim, a claim to self-sufficiency in procreation. The miracle of the conception of Jesus in the Virgin Mary has the opposite meaning: it requires a creative act of the Spirit of God, coming on Mary just as he hovered over the primeval waters (Lk. 1:35). It is not the sufficiency of the virgin that is indicated by the sign announced in Is. 7:14, but the radical insufficiency of all humanity, in need of the help of God; that meaning is brought out in Mary's song, the *Magnificat*.

The relationship of the man and of the woman

In the paragraph that constitutes Genesis 2, with its anthropomorphisms that Karl Barth considered 'more powerful than
anywhere else in the two accounts of creation', he draws
attention to 'four things' which man evidently knows and which
could become the four pillars of the relationship between man
and woman. Woman, taken from man, is close to him, not
foreign; man had to be, as it were, robbed of himself by a kind of
death; in that he found his wholeness and the restoration of his
harmony; and he must recognize in woman a being that is
independent of himself.[5] Our commentary will in part follow
paths that are parallel to this interesting perspective.

The emphasis of the passage is on the similarity of the man
and the woman, on their close kinship and on their possession of
an identical essence. The addition of 'male and female' in 1:27
already suggested the equal humanity of the two sexes. The
construction of the narrative highlights in this case the qualitative difference between the man and the woman on the one hand
and all other living creatures on the other. 'This', cries the man
– in his delight 'he names three times "this", the beautiful
creature whose presence astonishes and charms him'[6] – 'shall
be called *'iššâ* because she was taken out of *'îš*' (2:23). The play
on words, which comes over only partially in the English 'man'
and 'woman', is intended to express the common nature the two
share.[7] 'Bone of my bones and flesh of my flesh' affirms the
family tie (as in Gn. 29:14; Jdg. 9:2; 2 Sa. 5:1; 19:12f.); again it is
the same meaning. The man underlines what he has in common
with the woman.

The removal of the rib and its conversion 'into a woman'
(literally, v.22) illustrate the same essential truth. Ought we to
take this element of the narrative literally, since the apostle
Paul declares that 'woman was made from (*ek*) man' (1 Cor. 11:8,
12)? The Creator, obviously, was able to do as he liked; in his
sovereign wisdom he could have chosen a method which would
make us, in our ignorance, smile. But the presence of one or
several word-plays casts doubt on any literal intention on the

[5] Barth, pp.295f.

[6] M. J. Lagrange, *art. cit., RB* 6 (1897), p.349. The first 'this' could also refer to 'times'
(*pa'am*), but the subtle insight brought out by Lagrange is undoubtedly there in the text.

[7] Attempts at reproducing the word-play have not been successful. In Hebrew, *'iššâ* is not
etymologically the feminine of *'îš*, as it might seem; the text is making a deliberate play on
words.

author's part; they reveal an author who is in no way naïve, but who uses naïve language for calculated effects. Paul's *ek* does not require a literal interpretation of Genesis on this point. There are different kinds of causality, and that which the apostle has in mind may be exemplary or final.[8] It could perfectly well be said that the woman is 'from' (*ek*) the man if he played the part of a prototype and if God created the woman because of the need the man had of her. Such a conclusion emerges by itself from Genesis 2, even if the text does not reveal the detailed method of the divine procedure. The author plays on the double meaning for rib, which also means 'side' and therefore '*alter ego*'. The Arabs apparently use the expression, 'He is my rib' to mean 'He is my close friend'.[9] We use a similar turn of phrase when referring to one's 'better half'. If Paul does not require a literal reading, and if the word for rib/side is rich in symbolism, we have the right to consider the hypothesis of figurative language.

Certain other clues favour it. A second word-play may be involved in the word rib/side. In Sumerian, *ti* means both 'rib' and 'life'. Now the name Eve comes from the word for 'life' (Gn. 3:20). The image of the rib removed and transformed had also the great advantage of throwing into relief the traditional phrase, 'bone of my bones and flesh of my flesh'. And there are no end of possibilities of allied symbolical inferences which have given ingenious commentators a field day. One fairly misogynous rabbinic commentator puts these words into God's mouth: 'Where shall I make her from? Not from the head, lest she stand too proudly; nor from the eyes, lest she be excessively curious; nor from the ears, for she would risk being indiscreet; nor from the nape of the neck, which would only encourage pride...' and so it goes on. The rib is selected in order to make the woman modest – but the dreaded faults will appear all the same.[10] The old commentator Matthew Henry, who seems to follow Thomas Aquinas, is in much closer agreement with the spirit of Genesis: God did not make the woman 'out of his head to rule over him, nor out of his feet to be trampled upon by him, but out of his side to be equal with him, under his arm to be

---

[8] J. de Fraine, *La Bible et l'origine de l'homme* (Paris: Desclée de Brouwer, 1961), p.65. We should make clear that we are translating the Greek of 1 Cor. 11:8 literally; it has only the verb 'to be' in the present and the preposition *ek*; in v.12 the verb is understood.

[9] *Ibid.*, p.58, n.1.

[10] Quoted by Goldstain, p.124, referring to *Bereshit Rabba* 18.

protected, and near his heart to be beloved'.[11] More subtly, Augustine understood that the man is the strength of the woman (from him comes the *bone*), whilst the woman softens the man (in the place of the rib, God closes up the *flesh*).[12] There is no question of attributing *all* these meanings to the inspired author's intention; but he no doubt had several of them in mind, which increases the probability that the writing is figurative.[13] As the image is chosen with admirable suitability, in its development it corresponds with that of the teaching communicated. (Since other scriptural references do not settle the issue, however, we refuse to be dogmatic about it; if someone insists on the literal meaning, we have no objection, but let him make sure he also sees the symbolic richness of the account!)

The emphasis on the co-humanity relativizes the differentiation as such. 'Male and female' will never be anything more than a second truth about man and woman. History shows an ever-recurring tendency to imprison woman in her femininity, to the detriment of her participating quite simply in human life. By underlining the likeness, Genesis provides protection against the coarse *machismo* of the Mediterranean male, but also against the suspect cult of an Eternal Feminine, and against the Romantic speculations which make the masculine and the feminine, like yin and yang, the ultimate principles, the two poles of being.

This clear position deserves all the more attention in view of the Bible's parallel emphasis on the importance of sexuality. Its viewpoint, in both Genesis and other texts, could be summarized in Feuerbach's famous statement: it is 'a distinction which pervades the entire organism, which is everywhere present, which is infinite, and whose beginning and end are beyond discovery'[14] – infinite in the sense of extending to the whole personality. The 'tablets' of creation, like the consequences drawn elsewhere by the Bible, show that the neighbour, 'flesh of his flesh', whom God gives to the man *is* a woman; she does not merely add a few feminine attributes to a 'neutral' humanity.

[11] Matthew Henry, *Commentary on Holy Scripture* (1708–1710), *ad loc.* J. de Fraine, *op. cit.*, p.59, n.1, refers to a very similar, but less colourful, text from Aquinas.

[12] *De Gen. ad litt.*, 9, 17, 34, quoted by Renckens, p.227.

[13] Many modern authors adopt this position, *e.g.* Cassuto, p.134, who always shows great respect for the Torah. J. de Fraine, *op. cit.*, p.57, quotes Rémi de Saint-Germain of the 9th century.

[14] Quoted by Buytendijk, *La femme, ses modes d'être, de paraitre, d'exister* (Paris: Desclée de Brouwer, 1967), p.83.

As the hormones permeate the body, so femininity permeates the entire person, intelligence, feeling and will.

☐   The Bible does not relativize sexual differentation in the fundamentally rationalistic manner of Simone de Beauvoir; it does not confine the 'true' difference to a few bodily characteristics, in order to attribute all the rest to the choices of a sexless freedom.[15] But neither does it resort to the device of the two authors who have given the best answer to Sartre's companion, Buytendijk and Suzanne Lilar. They decide to call 'masculine' and 'feminine' those characteristics which blend in both man and woman, but in different proportions. Is this not somewhat arbitrary, since 'masculine' and 'feminine' could then be defined as the two different 'dosages' of common ingredients? Is there not a risk of reverting to the bi-polarization of being?[16] We would suggest that these thinkers lack the concept of creation as the image of God for measuring exactly the importance of sexuality. They consider humanity in its relation to itself and to the world. Faced with the great differentiation of man and woman, they either absolutize it or else they minimize it. They would need the primary truth of the link with God in order for sexuality to find its place as a dependent truth. What protects woman from being enclosed in an abstract femininity is that primarily and ultimately she is not 'out of' (*ek*) man, but 'out of' (*ek*) God (*cf.* the final phrase of 1 Cor. 11:12, where Paul's reminder *relativizes* what he has just said).   ☐

The first proposition of biblical anthropology does not only allow us to assert the difference and otherness in its true proportion, but to understand it in terms of correspondence and complementarity; the divine ordering which is its circumference and foundation prevents the duality from becoming an antithesis. The language of Genesis implies this positive correspon-

[15] We refer, of course, to her great two-volume work, *Le deuxième sexe* (Paris: Gallimard, 1949). We would point out that the dialectic of freedom and situation would imply that freedom, which is totally different from the situation (including sex), is also totally identical; but that dialectical moment does not appear in *Le deuxième sexe*.

[16] Suzanne Lilar, *Le Malentendu du deuxième sexe* (Paris: PUF, 1970), goes much further in this dualistic direction than Buytendijk. Influenced by Merleau-Ponty, Buytendijk seeks to establish a correlation between the masculine-feminine duality and the existential-ontological dialectic: one of *intentional awareness* and *deep-rooted feeling*, or of *work* and *concern*. The idea of bisexuality can be authorized by the mixture of the 'male' and 'female' hormones, in different proportions in man and in woman; at the anatomical level, the primary sexual characteristics are produced by a divergent development from an undifferentiated beginning, up to six weeks after conception; only with the chromosomes, XX and XY, is the division perfectly clear. The facts mentioned by S. Lilar, however, show that the division between male and female is not absolute but relative; they do not necessarily justify the theory of bisexuality, with its metaphysical extrapolations.

dence. God defines the woman whom he is going to make for the
man as 'a suitable companion to help him' (2:18, GNB). 'Help'
states plainly enough that the duality should not entail any
rivalry. 'Companion' requires more, for the Hebrew term means
literally 'as opposite him'; so the man and woman are not simply
side by side, far from it! They must be genuinely different, on the
basis of their common humanity. In the text, despite the
assonance the feminine *'iššâ* is different from *'îš*. In the first
chapter, the prologue with its 'male and female' speaks clearly;
the feminine word *n^eqēbâ* comes from *nāqab* 'to pierce', and
zākār, 'male', is not a euphemism.[17] It is as *others* that the man
and the woman are made for each other, and the man must
accept this otherness in order for the emptiness of his solitude to
be filled.

We would see the sign of his necessity in the strange sleep
that falls on the man and leaves him totally passive in the
mystery of the emergence of the woman. The rarity of the word,
which indicates an extraordinary sleep, perhaps even supernatural (LXX: *ekstasis*), should make us pause. The idea of an
anaesthetic that eases the surgeon's task is far removed from
the spirit of the account. The proposal that it contains a figure of
the passion of Christ, whose side was wounded in order that his
bride, the church, might be generated, is exaggerated allegori-
zation, as practised by some of the Fathers and by Karl Barth.[18]
But we must follow Barth when he writes: 'The widespread idea
that woman is the creature of man is implicitly rejected by this
part of the account.'[19] If she is his rib or his side, she is not a mere
extension of his body; the man must *suffer* this grace of God, the
gift of another being, as his partner. In this sense we can take up
Bonhoeffer's thought: the woman is the (creaturely) limit of the
man which has materialized – and God calls the man to love
her.[20]

We have seen that the being-with of the man and his neighbour

---

[17] Alphonse Maillot, 'Le sexe dans la Bible', *FV* 1975, 4, p.60, says that according to his
dictionary, 'Strictly speaking, this is the "virile member" and the first meaning of the verb
would have been "dig", "pierce".' Our dictionaries are more reserved and attribute this
precise meaning to the root only in Arabic. The link between this root *zkr* and the verb *zākar*,
'to remember', is disputed. There have been various hypotheses: males were suitable for
cultic commemoration; by reproduction the man leaves behind a memorial of himself (so
Maillot); commemorative monuments resembled phallic symbols. But the roots could simply
be homonyms with no semantic link.
[18] Barth, p.321. [19] *Ibid.*, p.325. [20] Bonhoeffer, p.60.

reflects (and should serve) the being-with of man and God. If the fundamental being-with is face-to-face partnership with the other sex in diversity, then our proposition is confirmed and sharpened. The face-to-face relationship with the LORD signifies for mankind respect for otherness in supreme and transcendent form and for the primary distinction – that between Creator and creature. Immediately we can understand why the apostle Paul makes a close association between idolatry and homosexuality (Rom. 1:22–27). This sexual perversion as a rejection of the other corresponds to idolatry in its relationship to God, the rejection of the Other; it is the divinization of the *same*, the creature. Other perversions of sexuality, because of the uniquely sensitive place it occupies in the centre of human life, could act in a similar manner as a tragic mirror of the corruptions of the spirit.

But Genesis is speaking so far only of harmony. A third theme completes that of likeness and difference, the theme of order. The God of the second tablet is no more a God of disorder than the God of the first tablet. The face-to-face partnership of man and woman is not a mere reciprocity, equally readable from right to left and from left to right. The apostle Paul drew from the narrative the lesson that the man is the head of the woman (1 Cor. 11:3), and the woman must not be entrusted with the authority of the teaching office in the churches where Timothy is working (1 Tim 2:12). We must not give in, through sheer pressure, to the temptation to conceal the fact: this is the teaching of Holy Scripture, whether or not our age likes it. But let us apply ourselves to actually *reading* the text, without emotional distortions! Certain people indeed are spreading a sexist caricature of Paul which is totally slanderous.[21] The order that the apostle upholds involves no inferiority. If he says that the man is the head of the woman, he adds in the same breath that 'the head of Christ is God' (1 Cor. 11:3). Now the order within the Trinity unfolds in the most perfect equality of essence and of glory. And further on, as we have noted, Paul turns his attention to relativizing the difference between the sexes (1 Cor. 11:11f.). The constitution of any real community requires that

---

[21] Gisèle Halimi, for example, in 'La femme enfermée', *La cause des femmes* (Paris: Grasset, 1973). Frequently Paul is confused with the Fathers, such as Chrysostom, on this point, and little notice is taken of such passages as Rom. 16 which testify to the apostle's high regard for women. In her quotation of patristic writings, even Simone de Beauvoir, scrupulous as she is otherwise, gives incorrect wording or attributions.

there be order; it cannot be done simply by joining together two people, but it must possess its own structure and its metaphorical 'head'. What traces of such an order was the apostle able to find in the text of Genesis? Emphasis has often been put on the element of *help*, as if it entailed subordination; but in the Old Testament, in fifteen cases out of twenty-one, it is God who is the help of man![22] The word would rather favour the priority of the woman. The making of the woman *after* the man would also point that way if it were considered in isolation; for in the first chapter (and *only* in the first chapter) it is the creature created *finally* that receives the lordship. If Paul, however, supports his argument about man as woman's head by the order of their creation (1 Tim. 2:13), it is because of its significance in the narrative: 'Neither was man created for woman, but woman for man' (1 Cor. 11:9). *That* argument is not a dubious one, and it gives meaning to the order of creation. Another clue is found in Genesis 2:24; the man has the role of initiating a new household.[23] Most particularly, the woman receives her name from the man: her generic name, *'iššâ* (2:23), and her personal name, Eve (3:20). By this factor the text reveals unambiguously that an order governs the relationship between the sexes.

If the apostle Paul adds: 'man is the image and glory of God; but woman is the glory of man' (1 Cor. 11:7), it is the fruit of his reflection on the order. He does not deprive the woman, as a human being, of the glory of being as the image of God, but he observes that *in the relationship of the sexes* the privilege of authority, which represents God, rests on the side of the male. If we may be permitted the comment, there is a kind of subtle balance. In all earthly relationships, the man represents God more obviously than does the woman: in active transcendency, in keeping an objective distance, in leadership and in work. But we realize at once that it is the woman who best represents humanity in its relationship *with God*: in the face-to-face relationship with the LORD, every human being, male or female, must accept a feminine position, existing from him and for him, receiving and bearing the seed of his word, receiving and bearing the name he gives. And the 'three things' that remain, faith, hope and love (1 Cor. 13:13), have they not all a feminine fragrance? Well did the Creator weigh the respective advantages

[22] Bonhoeffer, p.58.
[23] There are no grounds for seeing here the marks of a primitive matriarchy, see J. de Fraine, *op. cit.,* p.61, n.1, quoting Gn. 34:3.

of the male and the female. The scales are less unequal than is supposed. Each one of us, man and woman, finds it easier to live one dimension of the human portion, being as the image of God; one represents him, one corresponds to him.

The institution of marriage

In the Genesis narrative the man and the woman are simultaneously the first husband and the first wife. In order to determine in general the relationship of the sexes, we have used material which did not raise the question of the marriage bond. Now we must remove that restriction. The tablet of the *tôlᵉdôt* of the universe records not only the making of the woman but also the institution of marriage.[24]

The author's comment (and there is no need to suppose that it is a prediction made by Adam, suddenly changed into a prophet) is, 'For this reason a man will leave his father and mother and be united to his wife, and they will become one flesh' (Gn. 2:24, NIV). This is the inspired Magna Carta of the institution. Christ found in the Genesis verse the Word of God, a law about marriage which the Mosaic tolerance of easy divorce had not repealed (Mt. 19:1–9). In his instructions to husbands and wives, Paul refers to it naturally as the very formula of the conjugal state (Eph. 5:31). If in another letter he applies it in a more limited sense to copulation with a prostitute (1 Cor. 6:16), he does so because he wishes to bring out the inner contradiction of this sin 'against his own body' (v.18). This sin apes the marriage union and yet is a fleeting encounter and an abuse of the body which is no longer an expression of the person. Whereas the Genesis prologue does not touch on this matter – at the very most the institution of marriage is implicit in the command to be fruitful – the intention of 2:24 is not in doubt: to show the origin of this form of life that is known to all peoples, whether in a greater or lesser degree of conformity to God's design.

In biblical times the event the Bible calls marriage involved the whole society. The idea of a purely private marriage is simply a recent aberration, the result of individualism and of the disintegration of traditional communities. The marriage feast assured that the marriage was a public event. For Scripture the marriage bond is a part of those social realities supervised

---

[24] See Henri Blocher, 'Clartés sur le mariage', *Ichthus* 57 (Dec. 1975), pp.6–12.

by the civil authority; it is the law (Jewish or Roman, the commentators are uncertain) which binds a woman to her husband (Rom. 7:2; *cf.* Dt. 22). The commitment of the new couple consequently takes place under the eye of the magistrate, within his area of jurisdiction. The formula of Genesis 2:24 already suggests this, since 'leave father and mother' must precede the physical union. That is a fact of a social kind, an important development within the structures of society. Its mention here is all the more remarkable since the presence of just one couple, in the beginning, could have caused it to be omitted.

Kidner observes astutely, '"Leaving" before "cleaving"; marriage, nothing less, before intercourse'.[25] What in fact is the meaning of 'cleave' in order to become one flesh (the verb is used in Jb. 31:7 : 'if any spot has cleaved to my hands')? The phrase undoubtedly signifies firstly the consummation of marriage in the physical joining of the bodies. Without overstraining this prescriptive verse in Genesis, we can already detect in it the condemnation that will descend in the law on 'pre-marital' or extra-marital relations. In the language of the New Testament, they are *porneia,* the illicit use of sexuality. If sexual differentiation permeates the whole personality, and thus colours all relationships between men and women, it can lead to union only within marriage. That is the place, and the only place, that God has prepared for that purpose. But why this exclusiveness? No doubt we shall never fathom all the wisdom of this merciful and liberating provision of the LORD. We can nevertheless at least discern a reason suggested by the meaning of the word 'flesh', which is usually very wide in Scripture. The term 'flesh' can indicate simply the body, but more often it calls to mind the whole of human nature – as seen from without, usually in the bonds of creaturely solidarity, sensitive and vulnerable, but sometimes even without these characteristics being noticeable. 'All flesh' is a set expression for 'every human being'. 'To become one flesh' therefore in all probability goes beyond the first, limited meaning, to refer to a union which will embrace the various realms of human expression and form a new cell in the social, economic, juridical, political, cultural (*etc.*!) community. That is why the man must leave his father and mother. The requirement of marriage for the sake of, and before, the union of

[25] Kidner, p.66, n.1.

the bodies asks that sexuality be fulfilled throughout the whole range of human essentials: that it be integrated in the whole of personal life, assumed in responsibility and that it colour the whole range of human activity.

The Bible thus allows us to formulate a definition of the valid marriage: 'The covenant (*cf.* Pr. 2:17; Mal. 2:14) sanctioned by the authority in charge of social order, by which a man and a woman commit themselves unreservedly to each other to live a common life and to join in sexual union.' From the book of Genesis and from the objective of human completion in sexual fulfilment, the New Testament has drawn two commands of God for the well-being of marriage: 'What therefore God has joined together, let not man put asunder' (Mt. 19:6) and 'each man should have his own wife and each woman her own husband' (1 Cor. 7:2). Divorce and polygamy, which God can tolerate because of men's 'hardness of heart' (Mt. 19:8), do not answer to his original intention.

Despite the importance it attributes to the differentiation of the sexes, the Bible also relativizes it, as we have already observed. It follows that its fulfilment in marriage is not indispensable to the fulfilment of humanity. Beside the ordinary vocation and the gift of the conjugal state, God has in reserve for some an extraordinary vocation and another *charisma* (the word used in 1 Cor. 7:7), celibacy. The apostle Paul, who provided the example of this, as had Jeremiah six centuries earlier, insists on its practical advantages in the service of the Lord, especially in view of 'the present distress' (1 Cor. 7:26, 28, 32ff.). Jesus Christ himself lived in this state,[26] and the unmarried believer can rejoice in the thought that he walks in the footsteps of his Master.

Let us notice, however, that nowhere does Scripture extol the celibate in Jesus, even in 1 Corinthians 7; it is as if it wished to forestall the misunderstanding that attributes to the gift of celibacy an intrinsic value that is higher than that of marriage. In Scripture, Christ is called the bridegroom, and there is presented as the model for husbands.

In the marital fulfilment of sexuality, indeed, we find the

---

[26] Certain writers think that in Mt. 19:12 he is referring to John the Baptist and to himself. But this enigmatic *logion* remains difficult to interpret, as Jesus emphasizes (v.11). All commentators are agreed in rejecting the literal meaning (except the great allegorist, Origen). But is it about celibacy? The renunciation that Jesus speaks of could be the renunciation of a selfish use of sexuality, such as the disciples were suggesting (v.10).

relationship of the man and the woman mirroring the relationship of God and humanity. Already in the Old Testament, the covenant of the LORD with his people is daringly compared with marriage. With his symbolic marriage, Hosea says it with shattering force. Other prophets enrich the theme, *e.g.* Isaiah 62:4f.; Jeremiah 31:32; Ezekiel 16:8. When the prophecies begin to be fulfilled, John the Baptist hails Jesus Christ as the Bridegroom (Jn. 3:29). Jesus takes up this theme (Mk. 2:19), as later do Paul and the book of Revelation. Jesus Christ is the Lord who left the glory of the Father in order to join himself to his Church, his people, redeemed humanity, and become with it 'one spirit' (1 Cor. 6:17). Describing the order between man and woman which is the basis of harmony within marriage, the apostle proposes as the archetype of their relationship that of Christ and his Bride (Eph. 5:22–33). It is in the light of this model that we can best understand the horror of adultery, the tragedy of divorce and the bitterness of polygamy, for Christ remains eternally faithful to his one Church, for which first of all he gave up everything.

At what moment in the Genesis narrative is the institution of marriage located? The charter of marriage is summarized in Genesis 2:24, but marriage itself is not to be confused with the creation of the sexes. Could its origin be implicit? Calvin points out that the LORD took a specific step in order to bring the man his partner, and he comments: 'Moses now relates that marriage was divinely instituted'.[27] We subscribe to this perceptive judgment. Whether or not the author had it in mind, the narrative records clearly that God was not satisfied simply with forming the woman; by presenting her to the man, he was inviting them to a form of common life. And as the husband commits himself in front of the magistrate, he gives his positive answer to God; verse 23, which acclaims the woman, is addressed to God.

There remains one question. What weight should be given to the absence of any mention of descendants and of fruitfulness?[28] This gap is all the more surprising since the Old Testament celebrates the gift of children as an outstanding blessing. The text seemingly wishes to reserve for it the status of an added blessing (1:28), without linking with it the essence of marriage. Procreation is a purpose of marriage only indirectly, since sexual union will be the means of obeying the blessing-commandment

---

[27] Calvin, p.134.   [28] *Cf.* Barth, pp.312f.

of the first chapter. Procreation is not the purpose of marriage as such. For his institution the LORD gives only one reason: 'It is not good that the man should be alone'. The Song of Songs, which sings of the love of husband and wife as a flame of the LORD (Song 8:6), preserves a similar silence. This poem, 'a real return to the primal age, to the springtime of humanity', as J. J. von Allmen says,[29] presents the couple Solomon and the Shulammite as the counterpart of the couple *'îš-'iššâ*.

The love of Solomon and the Shulammite, however, 'is exposed to a thousand temptations, delays, hesitations, and breathless chases that the first couple did not know; sin has now taken a hand'.[30] The complexity of the Song contrasts strongly with the simplicity of Genesis: 'they were both naked, and were not ashamed' (2:25). We still have this final verse to interpret.

Here nakedness does not signify destitution or need, as it does frequently in other parts of the Bible. The atmosphere of the narrative excludes such connotations. On the contrary, it means 'not to be concealed from one another, but to be revealed and known without any cover'; the man and the woman had thus 'no need...to flee or to excuse themselves...They were thus free, and in the exercise of their freedom good'.[31] Indeed, basking in the sunshine of all their blessings, the man and woman in their nakedness enjoyed the glorious liberty of the children of God.

This conclusion to Genesis 2 could bring our study to an end, but no-one who grasps its meaning can fail to notice the correction it calls for to one of the most profound of all philosophical meditations on Genesis. The final touch to the picture of paradise forces us to reject the brilliant but wayward interpretation of Søren Kierkegaard. We must discuss it not only because it comes from Kierkegaard, but also because what is at issue is the vital connection in the biblical narrative, the relationship between Genesis 2 and Genesis 3.

The Danish philosopher's piercing insight duly discerned the importance of sexuality. He sees it as 'the extreme point of the synthesis' that constitutes mankind. But in his view this synthesis is one of *contradiction*, and as such is the source of anxiety even before there is any question of sin. It seems to us that this contradiction arises in his vision from an idealist concept of liberty, for he explains himself in these terms: 'The

---

[29] See the article 'Mariage' in his *Vocabulaire biblique* (Paris: Delachaux & Niestlé, ²1956), p.168.
[30] *Ibid.*   [31] Barth, p.329.

sexual is the expression for the prodigious *Widerspruch* [contradiction] that the immortal spirit is determined as *genus*'. Because of this contradiction, because of 'the spirit's feeling that it was a foreigner', it is in the ignorance of innocence that Kierkegaard places both anxiety (or 'dread') and modesty or shame (*Scham*).[32] Now, at this point Kierkegaard clashes with the text he is seeking to understand; the text is explicit: 'they were both naked, and were not ashamed'. Here something of a gap is apparent between the thought of Kierkegaard and that of the Bible. In God's creation liberty suffers *no* anxiety, for there is no vertiginous 'void' before. Liberty basks in the grace of God. The only option for created liberty is the response of love obeying sovereign love. There is no 'contradiction', for everything comes from God, the God of peace. When you take the creature as your starting-point and as your point of reference, then you bring in contradiction. The carefree nakedness of the first couple attests their liberty received from God – as long as they continued in obedience.

The final sentence of the second chapter says basically the same thing as the commendation in the prologue: 'God saw everything that he had made, and behold, it was very good' (1:31), and the same thing also as the paragraph on the seventh day, on the rest of God in which mankind should share. The work was very good, the man and the woman were without shame – before sin entered the world.

[32] Kierkegaard, pp.68f.

6
The covenant in Eden

In the second 'tablet' of Genesis, God is no longer called simply 'God', as in the first, but YHWH God. Why? The 'tetragrammaton' YHWH which derives from the verb 'to be' and was doubtless pronounced 'Yahweh' – replaced by 'the LORD' when read in the synagogue, in order to avoid the slightest risk of profanity – plays the role of God's personal name. This is the name God bears when he comes and visits his people and makes a covenant with them; this is his covenant name, his name for his 'marriage' with Israel.

It is YHWH, the God of the Covenant, who intervenes in Genesis 2. The agreement concluded between God and his people provides perhaps the most characteristic category in the Bible for the description of divine-human relations. It is not for nothing that it is used to designate the two divisions of Holy Scripture, the two *testaments*. *Testamentum* is the Latin translation of the Greek *diathēkē,* which the Greek translation of the Old Testament, followed by the New Testament, selected to render the Hebrew *bᵉrît*, covenant.[1] Classical Reformed theology which took the initiative in assigning a cardinal role to this notion found it also in the narrative of Genesis. God reveals himself there as YHWH. If the actual word 'covenant' is missing, the

[1] The choice of *diathēkē* instead of *synthēkē* merits a brief comment. The translators felt that the current word, *synthēkē* (a contract), suggested a kind of symmetry between God and man, which the texts exclude. Since in the covenants that he makes, the LORD makes his sovereign dispositions, they took the word which was used for testamentary dispositions, in which, of course, the testator lays down the terms.

reality of a first covenant appears in outline. This original covenant has been given various names: the covenant of nature, the covenant of life, the Edenic covenant, the covenant of works.[2] This view appears to us to be firmly grounded.[3] We find substantially in the second 'tablet' the arrangement found in covenant treaties between a vassal and his suzerain, which have become more familiar of late thanks to archaeological advances. The text suggests both the benefit granted to, and the fidelity required from, the vassal. It defines, as an agreement should, both the generosity of the LORD and the duties he imposes.

In order to give an account of the contents of Genesis 2, it seems helpful to treat it as an ellipse, revolving around the twin foci of the *place* and the *bond* of the Covenant. This duality does not correspond exactly to that of the advantage conceded by the suzerain and the demands he formulates in return, although the place is firstly a gift, and with regard to the bond we must stress the conditions fixed by God. But our method of procedure is best adapted to that of the narrator.

The place (and the four rivers)

The name says it all: *Eden*, 'delight'. It is not in fact the Assyrian geographical name (2 Ki. 19:12, *etc.*); the first vowel is not the same.[4] If there is any kind of reference, it is by way of a play on words. The connection that is frequently made[5] with the Sumerian *edin(na)*, 'steppe', giving the reading in Genesis 2:8 of 'a garden in the steppe' (*i.e.* an oasis), does not find universal acceptance either.[6] Cassuto in particular considers it impossible, and prefers recourse to a Ugaritic root in order to introduce the idea of irrigation: a garden generously watered.[7] This thought could fit certain other references (especially Gn. 13:10), but the lament of Ezekiel 28 situates Eden, the garden of God, on his holy mountain (vv.13f.), and conveys no suggestion of rivers. The

---

[2] L. Berkhof, *Systematic Theology* (London: Banner of Truth, 1959), pp.211ff. Augustine used the word for the bond between Adam and God, but the founders of covenant theology appear to be Bullinger (Zwingli's successor at Zurich) and Olievanus, who was one of the authors of the Heidelberg Catechism. Cocceius later elaborated and systematized it.

[3] In spite of the doubts of John Murray, 'The Adamic Administration' in *Collected Writings of John Murray* 2 (Edinburgh: Banner of Truth, 1977), pp.49, 55f. Murray is an exception in the theological tradition to which he belongs.

[4] Keil, p.80. Eden in Gn. 2 is written *'ēden;* the other *'ēḏen.*

[5] Speiser, p.16; Kidner (more cautiously), p.62. See also Arthur H. Lewis, 'The localization of the Garden of Eden', *BETS* 11 (1968), pp.170f.

[6] Lagrange, 'L'innocence et le péché', *RB* 6 (1897), p.343, voices his doubts.

[7] Cassuto, p.107. He also translates Ps. 36:9 as 'the river of Thy watering'.

name of Eden, therefore, did not necessarily call to mind plentiful water-supplies for the garden. Besides, whatever etymological connections there might be with other languages, the Israelite did not think in Sumerian or in Ugaritic. Eden must have suggested first of all to the person listening to the account the Hebrew term of the same form. 'Eden' is often used in the plural for 'delight', with other related terms and the corresponding verb, to mean a life of luxury and pleasure.[8] This must be the determinative connotation in Genesis 2. God had prepared for the man a place of pleasure, the very environment of happiness. The overtones that we associate with the word 'paradise' are in harmony with the purpose of the text. Those who translated Genesis into Greek borrowed it from Persian (as the Hebrew itself had done in Ne. 2:8; Ec. 2:5; Song 4:13 – for a royal forest, a park or a delightful orchard), and the book of Revelation uses it after them to refer to the garden of Eden (Rev. 2:7). The Lord immediately proves his generosity by installing his vassal in a paradise – that in summary is the first intimation of the narrative.

God's gift leaves nothing to be desired. There he makes fine trees grow which are of the most useful kind, more useful than those of the goddess Siduri in the Gilgamesh epic: 'these trees were pleasant to the sight, beautiful to behold', true enough, but their fruit was precious stones.[9] In Genesis, the man is able to feed on the fruits of paradise. The correspondence between the man and the tree, as we noted in our discussion of the prologue, is one of perfect harmony. Nor is that all. In the East there is no fertility except by water. How can this magnificent orchard prosper? A river – and it is no mere trickle – flows out of Eden (2:10).

Might this be the same water as the 'flood' which arose from the earth in Genesis 2:6? We must indeed follow the majority of recent commentators and translations and translate as 'flood' (NEB) or 'streams' (NIV) rather than 'mist'; the parallels and the verb 'watered' lean in this direction.[10] But verse 6 still belongs to

---

[8] *Cf.* 2 Sa. 1:24; Je. 51:34; in Gn. 18:12 it is used by Sarah of sexual pleasure; the verb *'āḏan* is used in Ne. 9:25. Keil, p.80, retained the meaning of 'delight'; von Rad, p.76, considers this a most important factor in the use of the word here.

[9] Cassuto, p.77.

[10] *E.g.* von Rad, p.74; Cassuto, pp.103f.; Young I, p.62; R. Laird Harris, 'The mist, the canopy, and the rivers of Eden', *BETS* 11 (1968), pp.177f.; and particularly D. Kidner, 'Genesis 2:5, 6: wet or dry?', *TB* 17 (1966), pp.109–114, which we shall follow. With Kidner and Speiser we can take as the closest word the Assyrian *édu* (= flood, deluge). In Jb. 36:27, the only other use of the word, this meaning is suitable too.

the description of the 'not yet' of verse 5, and suggests rather the wild waves of a kind of *tōhû-bōhû*.[11] The water 'rose', like an episodic, unpredictable flood, and soaked the ground in this unproductive manner (the same verb as in Ezk. 32:6). So we are not yet reading about the beneficial river, which flows *for the sake of the garden.*

We can imagine the vast volume of its water, for it 'became' four smaller rivers, of which at least two are well known and were among the most powerful rivers in the world that Israel knew. The number four very commonly symbolizes universality, both inside and outside the Bible.[12] And if the rare metal and precious stones of the lands crossed by the river receive special mention, it is doubtless in order that they should thus be connected with paradise, without, however, actually being within it as in Ezekiel 28. We are to understand that no riches of any sort are lacking in Eden. Kidner sees here a hint of the cultural development of mankind.[13] In every respect it is abundance.

With the list of the rivers and of the countries (Gn. 2:11–14), however, the text itself poses a problem which we admit is difficult to resolve: the problem of the location of Eden. Its difficulty was felt centuries ago by Calvin. He devoted several pages of his commentary to outlining a solution. Two trends emerge, depending on whether the geographical details given by Genesis are understood in a more literal sense or in a more figurative sense. According to the first approach, the courses of the Tigris and of the Euphrates are studied and an attempt is made to locate paradise near their mouth or else near their source; solutions in between are unusual. According to the second approach, the author is using the geographical concepts in a non-literal manner in order to communicate the idea of a primeval earth, or at any rate a choice place. In this debate minds are not divided along the usual lines of orthodoxy and modernism. What we saw concerning the literary genre of the second tablet leaves both possibilities open. Calvin himself, despite his literalist reading, speaks with unusual leniency of

[11] Kline, p.151, would like to see life-giving water here already, and seeks to translate: flooding waters 'began to rise', speaking of the 'inceptive' imperfect. But the grammarians (Gesenius-Kautzsch and Jouön) are not aware of such an imperfect, and we have searched in vain for a definite example. So we prefer to follow Kidner.

[12] Cassuto, p.114, reports that in antiquity Eastern peoples sometimes mentioned four primeval rivers.

[13] Kidner, p.61.

those who would wish to make Eden the image of the whole earth.[14]

☐　The young Bonhoeffer proposes that the language of imagery is inevitable for the primeval earth,[15] while Karl Barth pleads in more moderate but nonetheless powerful terms for a non-literal reading.[16] In the pages in question it would be difficult to accuse him of lacking in respect for the inspired Scripture. For Barth, paradise 'existed somewhere', but we have to accept 'also the fact that there can be no actual investigation of this "somewhere"'. The writer 'speaks of God's Garden as a genuine and original place on earth, just as the first witness spoke of God's week as a genuine and original period of time on earth'. By locating the garden towards the *East*, the writer, in Barth's view, points to the great desert and 'beyond it to the coming light of day' and therefore to 'the future already present with the creation of man'. The argument could be strengthened and amended – for its reference to the future is too Barthian – by noticing the author's word-play on *qedem* (2:8), which can be translated both 'orient' and also 'origin', as was understood by the majority of the ancient translations.[17] The garden is to be located 'towards the origin'. Barth detects a 'symbolic character' which is 'revealed by the fact...that a whole river bursts forth which Eden is not to keep to itself but to take its own share and then pass on to surrounding districts'.[18] Of the four branches (literally 'heads') he remarks that it is 'a process which can hardly be understood in terms of the familiar picture of the origin of a delta',[19] and admittedly a delta is scarcely what first springs to mind.

It is the second river in particular, the Gihon, that provides Renckens with the argument which eliminates the literal interpretation. It is a fact that the land of Cush which is watered by the Gihon is customarily taken as Ethiopia in the geography of the Old Testament. Is it to be understood thus here? 'The fact that some Greek sources do sometimes use the name Gichôn for the Nile would seem to suggest a confirmation'.[20] This is the case in

---

[14] Calvin, pp.113ff.

[15] Bonhoeffer, p.47: 'How should we speak of the young earth except in the language of fairy tales (*Märchen*)?... Who can speak of these things except in pictures?' Such an *a priori* judgment seems improper.

[16] Barth, pp.252ff.

[17] Aquila, Symmachus and Theodotion, who follow the Jerusalem Targum, and the Vulgate. Renckens, pp.210ff., shows interest in the double meaning, although he does not see it as the writer's.

[18] Barth, p.255.　　[19] *Ibid.*, p.251.

[20] Renckens, p.203. Josephus, *Ant.* I.i.3, makes the Pishon the Ganges.

the Greek version of Jeremiah 2:18. The Nile, like the Tigris and the Euphrates, is the source of life to a whole country. All you need is to identify the Pishon with the Indus, as does Renckens, in order to find in Genesis the four great rivers which supported life in the ancient world. The idea which then impresses itself on the mind, with regard to Eden, is that of Barth: 'There all the rivers of the earth have their common origin in a single river'.[21] The result is roughly the same if you make the Pishon and the Gihon the White Nile and the Blue Nile.[22] We agree that there is no question of accepting this geography in a literal manner; the author was well aware of the distance between the Nile and the Euphrates, and if he links them he does so by a deliberate transposition.

In support of the same thesis may be brought forward the freedom of Ezekiel's references. He does not hesitate to give the nations and rulers figurative designations such as 'the trees of Eden...that were in the garden of God' (Ezk. 31:9, 16, 18). He associates the garden of Eden with the mountain of God, an apparent borrowing from Canaanite and Syrian mythology, treated as a figure of speech.[23] In the New Testament, quite apart from the use of the word 'paradise' for the third heaven (2 Cor. 12:2f.; *cf.* Lk. 23:43), the reference in Revelation 2:7 does not favour a literal interpretation. Christ promises the one who conquers 'to eat of the tree of life, which is in the paradise of God'. This utterance supposes that the situation described at the end of Genesis 3 still survives; the present tense, 'which is', for example, excludes the destruction of paradise in the flood. But if that is the case, how may Genesis be understood literally? Do we think that a sufficiently determined explorer would finally discover the garden at x degrees longitude and y degrees latitude, and find himself face to face with the cherubim?[24] No-one imagines that today. Can the author be considered to have entertained such a thought? The vision of the cherubim (who are described only in the visionary pictures of Ezekiel) and the flaming sword which turned in every direction make this very unlikely. Never in the subsequent biblical text is there any question of Eden as a place

[21] Barth, p.253.

[22] Thus Y. Aharoni and M. Avi-Yonah in their *Bible Atlas* (New York: Macmillan, 1968): see A. H. Lewis, *art. cit.,* p.171; to Cassuto, p.116, it appears 'the most satisfactory explanation.'

[23] A. H. Lewis, *art. cit.,* p.173. In Ugarit, Mount Casius to the north was the mountain of Baal. Ps. 48:2, which has little regard for geography in situating Mount Zion 'in the far north', shows a comparable usage.

[24] Aquinas appears to have thought this, *Summa* 1, q.102, a.1 ad 3.

on earth which a traveller could reach.[25] Neither is there ever any
question of the garden being destroyed or removed. This fact
suggests that, in accordance with the writer's intention, we are
not to seek on any map the place where the four rivers became a
single one.

The case for a more or less parabolic interpretation of the
indication of the site very nearly persuades us. And yet the other
side of the scales is not empty by any means. It is not necessary to
interpret the cherubim and the sword literally in order to find a
plausible location in Genesis 2:11–14. This portion can have
literal value without other elements losing their figurative value.
The book of Revelation can speak of the spiritual reality which
the garden signified, the life of communion with God which is
beyond the sinner's reach, without prohibiting a literal accepta-
tion of the geographical details given in the Genesis paragraph.
The figurative interpretation runs a particular risk, that of
obscuring the difference, which is very clear in the text, between
the garden of Eden and the vast expanse of the earth, the ground
to which mankind will be sent after the fall. The specificness of
the place is of considerable importance; God chose it and prepared
it for the human race that he loves. The specificness comes out
much more clearly in the literal interpretation. It also has one
trump card: it is possible without forcing the text to envisage a
common region for the four rivers. The fact that the Tigris and the
Euphrates frequently flow close to each other, have their source
in the same mountains and join together before running into the
Persian Gulf suggests a literal meaning.

First we must resolve the difficulty of the Gihon. Cush, the
country that corresponds to it, does not *always* indicate Ethiopia.
Sometimes it has to do with Midian (Hab. 3:7), and several authors
follow Speiser in identifying the Kush of Genesis 2:13 with the
land of Kassu in Assyria.[26] The weak tradition identifying Gihon
with the Nile provides no attestation independent of the Ethio-
pian hypothesis, for it could have originated from the reading of
the verse in question; if one mistakenly read Kush to mean
Ethiopia, it was natural to conclude that the Gihon was the Nile.
Thus one of the strongest objects to the literal reading begins to
shift. As for the land of Havilah where flows the unknown Pishon

[25] Gn. 4:16 is a part of the same overall whole as Gn. 2 – 3, and if localization is taken
figuratively in these two chapters, it must be taken in the same way in 4:16.

[26] Speiser, p.20; A. H. Lewis, *art. cit.,* p.172; Harris, *art. cit.,* p.179. The Kassites are also
called *Kuššu* in the Nuzi texts.

and where there is gold, it can be located in plenty of places. The way is therefore wide open for all sorts of hypotheses concerning a literal reading, with the proximity of the Tigris and Euphrates remaining a fixed point.

The two most plausible locations are quite simply opposites; paradise must have been either at the source or at the mouth. Certainly the word 'headstreams' (NIV) used in Genesis 2:10 for the four rivers suggests a beginning and cannot signify the mouth of the river.[27] But the experts who locate Eden in Lower Chaldea either think that the four headstreams are the branches of a delta, seen where they start, or else think that the narrator's eyes look upstream, from Eden. The majority hold that four rivers joined their waters to make a single river in Eden, but that it has been expressed by the author in reverse.[28] Calvin was the first to propose that the garden was situated to the South-East of Babylon, providing the original solution of reducing the four rivers to two: Pishon and Gihon were other names of the Tigris and Euphrates, their names differing according to whether they were separating or joining: 'There are two rivers which flow together into one, and then separate in different directions'.[29] Many writers follow Calvin in the general region chosen, but not in the double name of the rivers. Some, including Friedrich Delitzsch (1881), locate Eden near Babylon and interpret Pishon and Gihon as semi-natural canals joining the Tigris and the Euphrates. Others, following Sayce (1894), identify the Persian Gulf with the single river of Genesis 2:10; the Babylonians, in fact, called it 'the bitter river' (*nar marratum*). Pishon and Gihon are then either rivers which flow into it or the two arms of the gulf.[30] Thus there is considerable diversity in the interpretation that locates the rivers near the mouth of the Euphrates. It would be rash to exclude any one of these proposals, but we must admit that none of them is in complete harmony with the impression conveyed by a literal reading of Genesis.

E. K. Victor Pearce has revived an old interpretation which situates paradise at the opposite extreme, in the rich valleys of

[27] Speiser, p.17, notes that the river mouth is called a boundary (Jos. 15:5; 18:19). Westermann *G*, p.252, assures us that the word 'heads' can indicate sections (Jdg. 7:16, 20; 1 Sa. 13:17f.) but his examples deal only with military sections, *i.e.* detachments. 'Head' can be used of the angle (or the top?) of a street: Ezk. 16:25; La. 2:19 (see Keil, p.81).

[28] So Kidner, p.64; T. C. Mitchell, 'Eden, Garden of', *IBD*, pp.408ff. Speiser, p.19, argues for Lower Chaldea.

[29] Calvin, p.122.

[30] Kidner, p.64. The arguments are summarized by Mitchell, *art. cit.*

Armenia, as also does an Armenian folk tradition.[31] The Tigris
and the Euphrates both rise in that area, an hour's walk from
each other. The Gihon could be the Araxes, whose source is
nearby, and which irrigates a region once inhabited by the
Kassites, before flowing into the Caspian Sea. Its Persian name
was *Djun* which bears some resemblance to Gihon. The Pishon
has often been interpreted as the *Phasis* of the Greek geographers
or historians, but Keil objects that the Phasis starts in the
Caucasus, further away. He proposes instead the Kur (Cyrus)
which also flows into the Caspian.[32] Pearce suggests the Halys,
which flows into the Black Sea. His new argument, however,
which takes up the old Armenian suggestion, springs from
discoveries about the beginnings of the neolithic civilization. It
seems likely that the revolution involving the cultivation of
cereals, the raising of cattle and the building of the first cities
centred on those fertile valleys. Such is the significance of the
discovery of Catal Huyuk on the Turkish Plateau by James
Mellaart, the city of 8,000 years ago.[33] From there the new human
race, our own, spread first of all on to 'the beautiful, wild land of
the Mediterranean shores' with its 'wonderful climate', as Germaine Tillion writes, that area whose outstanding quality 'was
maintained until the goats, the workmen and the Pharaohs, by
destroying the most beautiful forests of that earthly paradise,
wiped out a part of its resources'.[34] We quote an ethnologist who is
writing without the Bible in mind, because she uses the word
'paradise' quite naturally for that area of the first neolithic man,
whose origin is located so close to the sources of the Tigris and the
Euphrates. Chapter 2 – 4 of Genesis for their part present the
beginnings of cultivation, of cattle raising, of metal working and
of the building of cities – precisely the innovations of neolithic
man. It is easy to understand why Pearce makes the equation and
locates the biblical Eden at the birthplace of that civilization.
The traditional objection to this high location is that the single
river cannot be seen from there, but Pearce sweeps this aside. In
his view the narrative speaks of the waters which satiated the
region immediately after the end of the last Ice Age.[35] The idea
may not be so wild, but the exegesis is not literal; 'river' on this
reading becomes figurative. □

What conclusion are we to draw from this survey of the

[31] Pearce, pp.51ff.   [32] Keil, pp.82f.   [33] Pearce, pp.47ff.
[34] Germaine Tillion, *Le Harem et les cousins* (Paris: Seuil, 1966), pp.12, 56.
[35] Pearce, p.51, supposes anti-cyclonic winds that prevented rain (Gn. 2:5).

theories? Between the literal interpretation and the other, as between the Armenian and the Chaldean locations of paradise, the choice appears difficult. The path of wisdom is to suspend judgment, waiting for whatever it might be to turn up. Perhaps a tablet buried in the sands will throw light on the problem of the Pishon and the Gihon one day. Enough for us to know that in the beginning God did not cast mankind into the desert or into the jungle,[36] but showed kindness to him by taking care of him and by adding to the gift of being and life an abundance of good things for his happiness. Eden is the covenant gift, as will be Canaan in the covenant with Israel.[37]

When God, however, bestows gifts on those he wishes to love as his sons, he takes good care not to turn them into spoilt children. The concern represented by Eden wishes also to train mankind in responsibility. So paradise is 'no fairyland, no Utopia';[38] the man receives a charge to fulfil in that place. The LORD 'put him in the garden of Eden to till it and keep it' (Gn. 2:15). Engnell recognized in these two verbs the same royal and cultic overtones as in the terms of the prologue, on the sixth day.[39] Here we have certainly the rendering in another language of the mandate to subdue the earth that was given in the first chapter. We can immediately check how far the man's rule differs from that of a self-centred tyrant. In Hebrew 'to till' is literally 'to serve'. Even in his relationship with the soil, mankind must maintain his humility. The use of the verb paves the way for the condemnation of 'the destroyers of the earth' (Rev. 11:18), those guilty of ecological depredation. Not only will man rule over nature by obeying its laws (F. Bacon), but he will do so for the good of creation itself, so that it may fulfil its 'vocation', to glorify the Creator. The cultivated garden will be like a song of praise to the God of order and of life, the God of peace. The second chapter is also in agreement with the first with regard to imitating God in work; if the man devotes himself to horticulture, it is the LORD who planted the garden. In serving the soil, the man will do the works of God after him.

The man is also to *keep* it. Must he mount guard against a possible enemy? The term does not require the existence of a threat. 'Keep' does not necessarily mean 'keep *against*'. Since the narrative at this stage has not suggested the slightest hostile entity, it is dangerous to form any hypothesis to that effect. As

[36] *Cf.* Heidegger's *Geworfenheit*. [37] Barth, pp.267f.
[38] Westermann *C*, p.81. [39] Payne, p.28, n.5.

the keeper of paradise, the man is responsible for it. He is there not only as a servant but with the authority delegated to him by the Sovereign. If we must look for the foundation of the right of property in Scripture, that relationship between freedom and material objects, it is to be found in this creational right to 'keep' the garden. This original relationship of mankind to the earth is an analogy, and no more than that, of the relation of God to his property, and by that very token it is also limited by that divine relation. By the charge and the right to keep the garden, the man is placed entirely in *his own* place.

The bond (and the two trees)

The man's responsibility receives an initial definition in the mission which he receives. The LORD wishes to make it more explicit, more formal. It is in the double clause of the formula which follows (Gn. 2:16f.) that he pronounces the chief provisions of the covenant agreement. There the bond receives, as it were, a juridical expression.

What rigorous symmetry! Twice the same grammatical procedure is used, which in Hebrew allows the greatest force: the infinitive absolute. To the phrase 'EATING you shall eat' responds the phrase 'DYING you shall die'. In the first case the tone must be that of the fullness of the permission: you shall eat *freely*, eat your fill without lacking any of the good things that I have created. All the trees of the garden represent all the riches of the earth, placed at mankind's disposal. God reveals himself in this first provision as the God of superabundant grace, the opposite of the castrating father of our pitiful fantasies, the bestowing Father who rejoices in the happiness of mankind. God *commands* this permission, says the text. It is an order for the man to benefit from the life God gives him, to explore the magnificent park and taste its fruits. By refusing to be content with a stunted existence, the man will show his gratitude and glorify his LORD.

In the same vein the apostle Paul exclaims triumphantly, 'all things are yours' (1 Cor. 3:22). 'And you are Christ's', he adds (1 Cor. 3:23), for that is the condition of the royal liberty of the children of God. Likewise, it is stipulated in the creational agreement: 'you shall not eat'; otherwise 'DYING you shall die'. That is the condition that is the basis and the safeguard of the happiness of the human race.

As Bonhoeffer could state with considerable force, the prohibition does not imply any temptation.[40] In order for it to have stirred up any covetousness, it would have required a sin that was already latent in the man and which would then have been awakened, revealing the virulence of sin (Rom. 7:8–13). In Eden mankind is pure and has nothing to rebel against. The prohibition shows him his *limit*, and Bonhoeffer emphasizes, 'the limit is a gift of grace, for it is the basis of creaturely existence and of freedom'.[41] Mankind cannot, without destroying himself, be anything other than what he is by God's decree. That is what the second clause tells him, for his own good. It does so in a manner suitable to the creature made as the image of God, who will make decisions and act in the image of his Creator. Exalted above the passive docility of the animals, the man will be responsible in his choices and his actions for a permanent ratification of the dependence that is the basis of his existence. It will be his privilege to say Yes and Amen to the divine provision to continue to live. In that there is no temptation. The warning, 'DYING you shall die' hammers home the absolute certainty: on the monstrous, unthinkable hypothesis of a different form of conduct, *surely* you will die; the consequence is inescapable. The formula is found in texts of condemnation, both human and divine.[42] The use of this language brings out the importance of the man's responsibility and the juridical aspect of the covenant. On the one hand, then, is enjoyment of the Lord's munificence; on the other is the condition, that the free creature shall freely approve of his creaturely status in order to continue in his state of happiness.

The symmetry is admirable. Two trees in the garden correspond to the two clauses in the contract.[43] Let us start with the tree of life, which represents the gift that is central to all the gifts made by God to the man, as central as the tree itself in the midst of the trees of the garden (Gn. 2:9). God gives life. Life from him, constantly renewed, is necessary in order to enjoy all the other gifts. That, we believe, is the meaning of the text.

In order to understand the biblical narrative, it is indeed important to make a simple affirmation: the tree of life is one of

---

[40] Bonhoeffer, p.52.   [41] *Ibid.*

[42] Gn. 20:7; Je. 26:8, for example. In legal declarations a similar formula is found, but the verb, after the infinitive, is in the hophal, which perhaps suggests better the putting to death, the execution. However, the verb is also found in the qal, without the absolute infinitive.

[43] Westermann *G*, p.290, brings out the masterliness of the composition.

'all the trees of the garden' allowed and given to the man. He was to feed on it and enjoy it more than any other. Strangely enough, many commentators assert that he had not eaten from it.[44] But the clause in 2:16 logically implies the contrary. And the decision of the LORD in 3:22 to prevent the disobedient man, after taking the forbidden fruit, from taking also of the tree of life in no way signifies that he had never eaten from it. In order to draw that consequence from the text, it is necessary to suppose that to eat of it once was sufficient in order to have eternal life that could never be forfeited. But that is not stated by the text. It can be equally well understood as representing the ceaseless communication of the life given by God, and that after the fall the man could no longer have the benefit of it. Since he was given freedom to eat of it, he *had to* eat of the central tree, unless the fall followed immediately on the man's settling in Eden. It is true that a sermon attributed to Augustine says that the state of innocence in Eden lasted only six hours,[45] but the procession of the animals, the formation of the woman and the carefree picture, 'they were both naked', suggest a considerably longer time-span.

Other religions have often given a place to the theme of the plant or the tree of life, frequently a vine.[46] Since ordinary fruit sustain everyday life, mortal man dreamed of an extraordinary fruit which would ensure life for ever, obviously conceived in some magical manner. Does the second tablet of Genesis put forward such an idea? How are we to interpret it? A strictly literal reading can scarcely avoid the idea of the magic fruit. In 3:22 God appears to be worried that the eating of the fruit, in spite of himself and in spite of the sin of the man, should by itself produce an effect of immortality. And that is quite simply magic. But the author of Genesis has given us adequate proof of his mastery of naïve language for mature theological ends to prevent us falling into that trap. Magic supposes a view of the world and of the divine that are diametrically opposed to that of Genesis; magic harnesses blind forces in which the divine and the human are not clearly distinct, where Genesis reveals the absolute LORD, the holy God, the God of order and of grace. The entire

[44] Barth, p.256; Murray, *art. cit.,* p.48; A. H. Lewis supposes it was hidden, *art. cit.,* p.172.
[45] Calvin, p.156.
[46] *Cf.* Mircea Eliade, *Traité d'histoire des religions* (Paris: Payot, 1964), pp.244ff. In most cases, gaining access to the tree is a task of great difficulty for the man. If in the Bible this access is easy, then in this we should see a preliminary preaching of grace. Eliade, preoccupied with extra-biblical analogies, has unfortunately not understood this contrast.

Bible, whose inspiration is equally shared by the Genesis 'tablets', excludes the idea of any supernatural effect attached to any kind of food. It does not permit us to understand in literal terms what we read about the tree of life.

☐   An important tradition that Kidner, without insisting on it, considers still possible to follow,[47] takes the existence of the tree as literal but assigns to it a sacramental function. God had chosen a tree and made it the sign of the grace that was offered. If the man had fulfilled the spiritual conditions, he would have received life at the same time as the sign. There is no denying the attraction of this hypothesis. No objection of principle can be raised against the idea that God did this. But where does the text give the slightest hint of this meaning? Genesis 3:22 goes against the 'sacramental' principle when it appears to link eternal life to the eating of the fruit, regardless of the man's frame of mind.[48] True enough, without faith and obedience the sacramental sign 'is of no value'. But if we see that in this instance the literal sense misleads us, what right have we to maintain the literal existence of the tree?   ☐

With regard to the tree of life the exegete may be thankful because the rest of Scripture comes to his aid. There are, in fact, several references made to the tree at the centre of paradise. For the book of Proverbs with its passage in praise of wisdom, 'She [wisdom] is a tree of life to those who lay hold of her' (3:18; *cf.* 11:30; 13:12). The reference to Genesis is as clear as daylight.[49] It does not incline towards literalism, even in part. The tree acts as a symbol for that life-giving communication given by revealed wisdom. The book of Revelation promises to 'him who conquers' that he will share in the tree of life (Rev. 2:7) and places it at the centre of its final vision, with other elements (Rev. 22:1–5). Study of this passage uncovers many riches. The seer of Patmos combines the description in Genesis with that in Ezekiel 47, with its monthly harvests and healing leaves. He found it quite natural to link the two passages, for in both he found the river

[47] Kidner, p.62. This traditional exegesis of orthodox Protestantism (*cf.* Keil, p.85; Young III, p.155) is already to be found in Calvin, pp.116f.

[48] This causes obvious embarrassment to John Murray, who faces the difficulty with characteristic courage. He is forced to accord a *double* meaning to the fruit – in the case of the sinner the tree has a sealing significance in the opposite direction, as 'confirmation in the life of sin and death', *op. cit.,* p.55.

[49] The article is not used before 'life', but that difference is scarcely significant because the construct state implies that the absolute is definite, and in any case the article is often dropped in poetry.

with the tree, the river springing suddenly from the garden or the sanctuary, a mighty river which cannot be explained in terms of natural hydrology. Although the name 'tree of life' is not present in Ezekiel, the thought cannot have been far away from the prophet who dealt allegorically with the trees in Eden (Ezk. 31) and who depicted very freely the fall in the garden of God (Ezk. 28). In any case, John works out his synthesis in a very open manner. The features taken from the two passages overlap to such an extent that it is not at all clear whether we are intended to imagine several trees of life on both sides of the river (as in Ezk. 47), a single tree of life straddling the river like an arch, or else the tree of life 'in the middle of the main square of the city with the river flowing on both sides'.[50] Obviously we are not meant to picture the vision so much as to understand it; John is combining the *ideas* represented by the symbols. The river of living water undoubtedly means for him the Holy Spirit which proceeds from the Father and from the Lamb (*cf.* Jn. 7:37–39). Similarly, in Revelation 2 and 22 the tree of life is obviously a symbol. So, the following question confronts us: when reading Genesis, would John have thought of a literal tree with a sacramental function, and would he then have transformed it into a symbol for the new Jerusalem? There is nothing to indicate that he followed such a course. He appears rather to take the tree of life as he finds it, 'in the paradise of God', and to attribute to it in all respects, including its existence, a spiritual meaning. In the same way as the book of Proverbs, therefore, John authorizes a non-literal reading of this element of the narrative. In addition, he helps us to clarify the meaning of the symbolism: the tree of life represents communion with God, the inexhaustible source of life. The communion is made possible by Wisdom, who is the Father's delight and who delights in 'the sons of men' (Pr. 8:30f.), who acts as the link between the LORD and his covenant partner, his quasi-son, his living image on earth.

If the tree of life is figurative, the same must be said for its counterpart, the tree of the knowledge of good and evil.[51] This is the tree which is dealt with in the second clause of the covenant

[50] JB has the first solution; RSV and NIV the second; the third is suggested by the reading in AV and in RSV mg. The quotation above is from Jean Cambier, *L'apocalypse de saint Jean lue aux chrétiens* (Paris: Cerf. 1955) and comes closest to the Greek text.

[51] We translate it thus because *ṭôb wāra'* functions grammatically like a single noun; *hadda'aṯ* possesses both the properties of the noun (the article) and the verb (accusative), *cf.* Gesenius-Kautzsch, para. 115 d.

agreement: 'you shall not eat'. It illustrates it and makes it specific. It appears too, in its turn, 'in the midst of the garden' (Gn. 3:3). Two trees in the one middle? There is no contradiction between 2:9 and 3:3, as some have claimed, but rather we are able to see in the apparent conflict the indication of symbolic usage. In the harmony of the primeval peace, it is the tree of life that is at the centre. At the hour of crisis, the hour of temptation, it is the second clause which plays the decisive part.[52]

No parallel for the second tree has been found outside the Bible.[53] The idea that it was an apple tree rests solely on a Latin word-play, *malus/malum* (evil/apple).[54] The mythologies know plenty of trees of knowledge or of wisdom (and thereby trees of life), but they have no tree of the knowledge *of good and evil* which is forbidden when the first is permitted. The biblical text alone therefore can show us its meaning. We have already interpreted the fact of the prohibition as the reminder to the man of his limits and of his creaturely dependence. We must go further and understand the name of the tree. What is this knowledge of good and evil? The question has given rise to most extensive debate.

☐ The terms of the formula are more than somewhat elastic. 'Know' in Hebrew covers a whole range of meanings: to know with the mind, to experience, to discern, to choose, to determine. The words 'good' and 'evil' can mean the helpful and the harmful, happiness and misfortune, but these meanings are not primary and do not fit the highly ethical context of obedience and disobedience. The best translation is 'good and evil'. And why should God have refused mankind the knowledge of what was helpful and harmful, the translation suggested by Wellhausen?[55] But when the moral force of the two terms is maintained, how are we to understand their association, the 'and' between them? Is the sense *conjunctive*? According to several writers, the pair constitute a figure of speech known as *merismus,* a way of expressing totality by means of two opposite extremes. 'To speak neither bad nor good' (Gn. 24:50)

[52] Young III, pp.29, 154, protests against those who have alleged a contradiction here that the language does not have mathematical precision and that the trees could both be in the middle. He is right, but our solution has this advantage over his, that it explains why the text assigns centrality to the first only in 2:9, and to the second only in 3:3.

[53] It was quite wrong to take as a parallel the cylinder-seal which presents two characters – gods, in fact – with a tree and a snake. As for Langdon's alleged discovery in 1915, no scholar after him has found it in the text he 'translated'.

[54] Michaëli, p.52; Young III, p.45 (apple and evil are homonyms in Latin). Song 8:5 definitely does not refer to this tree.

[55] Wellhausen's translation is thoroughly criticized by Cassuto, p.111, and Barth, p.285.

means to say nothing, and 'they can do neither evil nor good' (Je. 10:5) means they can do nothing.[56] Or is the sense *disjunctive*? If that were so, it would not be a case of totality, but of the separation between good and evil. The two words often occur with the thought of antithesis, of mutual exclusion. When God sets good and evil in front of his people, it is in order that they may choose between them (Dt. 30:15). Amos exhorts the people to seek good and not evil, to hate evil and love good (Am. 5:14f.).[57] Or is the sense *additive*? Is it a question of knowing good and, in addition, knowing evil? The knowledge in question might be cumulative.[58] This way of reading it cannot be excluded automatically, for it is quite a natural way to take it, in spite of the absence of other examples in the Old Testament. The choices are by no means straightforward.

The task of focusing the meaning of the words is merely the start of the interpretative enterprise; we must also understand how they are put together, within their context. By what light shall we be able to decide between the proposals? The material in the narrative is our starting-point, especially Genesis 3:5, 2. The five passages in which the antithetical pair, good and evil, and the verb 'to know' recur, will provide confirmation or otherwise (Dt. 1:39; 2 Sa. 14:17; 19:35; 1 Ki. 3:9; Is. 7:15f.); the meaning of the formula is not likely to be radically different. With these points of reference, let us examine the hypotheses.

From the vast array of interpretations we must once again isolate a few principal types. First we shall discard the suggestions that appear to us to be least well supported. Keil ingeniously considered that the tree was to give the man moral discernment by his *abstention* from it. The man would have known good and evil by refraining from eating, trained by that discipline. But Keil is forced to conclude that, by eating, it was a quite different knowledge that the man acquired.[59] This is at odds with the natural suggestions of the narrative in 3:22, according to which the tree gave the forbidden knowledge as the tree of life gave life,

---

[56] This interpretation has been quite popular since the article by Honeyman, quoted by Robert Gordis, *art. cit., JBL* 76 (1957), p.131. Other examples of the *merismus* good-evil are found in Gn. 31:24, 29; 2 Sa. 13:22; Is. 41:23; Zp. 1:12.

[57] J. Coppens, *La connaissance du bien et du mal et le péché du Paradis* (Paris: Desclée de Brouwer, 1948), p.83, objects that there is no necessity to see a *merismus* here. Other examples of the disjunctive sense can be found in Lv. 27:33; Jos. 24:20; Pr. 31:12; Mi. 3:2; 6:8.

[58] This is Coppens' thesis, *ibid.*, pp.17f.

[59] Keil, p.86. A similar opinion held by Franz Delitzsch is criticized by Barth, p.285.

by the eating of its fruit. Likewise the idea that the prohibition was to be in force only for a time, that it was provisional and that God's intention was to make the man eat later from the second tree also, falls to pieces on the silence of the text. This argument also answers those who, without having recourse to Keil's subtle reading, take knowledge to be mere moral discernment. Why would God have waited before granting it?[60] Does not the actual command suppose this, since it invites the man to limit himself to the good, to the will of the LORD?[61]

The objection against the hypothesis of a merely temporary prohibition is also valid against a simple and moderate form of the sexual explanation. Certain thinkers have suggested that the fruit had aphrodisiac qualities and was forbidden in order to prevent a *premature* sexual union. But the sexual interpretation, which can boast the support of Origen, Ibn Ezra, Thomas Hobbes, Gunkel, Coppens and recently Gordis (not to mention the psychoanalysts), assumes a variety of forms and requires separate consideration. If we concentrate our attention on the knowledge of good and evil, postponing until later our study of the nature of the fall in Genesis 3, which is a related but distinct topic, we find we are left with only two possible indications of a sexual meaning: the verb 'to know' is sometimes used in that sense, and the phrase might be understood that way in 2 Samuel 19:35. The material is scarcely substantial.

'Know' is sometimes used as a euphemism for sexual relations (Gn. 4:1), but it is also used regularly in Hebrew without that reference. With 'good' or 'evil' as its object it never has a sexual meaning. It goes against all the laws of semantics to imagine that every use of the verb is coloured by the occasional euphemistic use.[62] As for Barzillai, if he declines David's invitation and argues that at the age of eighty he can no longer 'discern between the good and evil' (AV) and no longer appreciate the attraction of the court (2 Sa. 19:35), he may after all be thinking of something other than the pleasures of the courtesans! There is nothing to require the sexual interpretation given by Gordis.[63] The alleged parallel of Enkidu in the Gilgamesh epic, appealed to by Gordis,

---

[60] Cassuto, p.111, criticizing Dillmann.

[61] Gordis, *art. cit.*, p.124. Bonhoeffer, pp.53ff., carried away by his hostility towards moralism, joins discernment indissolubly to perdition. This thesis, which is important for the whole of Bonhoeffer's theology, is not supported by the overall message of Scripture.

[62] Our criticism at this point is directed in particular against Coppens.

[63] Gordis, *art. cit.*, p.136. He also refers to Dt. 1:39 and Is. 7:15, taking them to refer to puberty, but nothing in these verses, taken in context, suggests sexual relations.

scarcely merits quotation. Enkidu, the wild man who lived with the animals and who was finally civilized by spending six days and seven nights with a prostitute, sees the animals flee from him, and the woman congratulates him: 'You are wise, Enkidu, you have become as a god'.[64] Can anyone really claim that this story throws light on Genesis, with regard to the 'knowledge of good and evil'?

In favour of the sexual interpretation there is only one argument that can be drawn from the Genesis narrative, and that does not come directly from the passages about the tree. It is that the awakening of shame (3:7) and the punishment of the woman (3:16) refer directly to the area of sexuality.[65] We shall return to that later. Let us point out for the moment that the disturbance of this central point of human existence, our sexuality, can simply confirm the centrality of our sexuality, without the fall itself having occurred there.[66] This settles nothing concerning the meaning of the forbidden knowledge. And if the argument in favour of this interpretation is unsubstantial, the case against is massive, presenting powerful objections. Genesis 2 simply does not depict the man and the woman as two children before the age of puberty, and casts no shadow across the marriage union; on the contrary, the text provides the charter of this gift from the Creator. If the objection is made that the 'evil' mentioned is an illicit sexual practice, the narrative gives no grounds for any such suppositions.[67] Furthermore, in the text the knowledge of good and evil is the divine prerogative (3:5, 22). The implications of extending this view to the Creator God of Genesis are obviously grotesque, not to say blasphemous.[68]

Coppens, who advocates the sexual exegesis, shows what difficulties these verses put him in. He has no trouble with 3:5, since it is the snake speaking, but he contorts 3:22 into the following: 'Behold, Adam, like anyone who shall be born of him, will have to experience good and evil'.[69] This translation defies the norms of grammar and deserves a special place in the museum of exegetical

[64] *Ibid.*, pp.134f.
[65] Coppens, *op.cit.*, pp.21, 91.
[66] Barth, p.286.
[67] Gordis, *art. cit.*, p.133, argues that 'to do evil' signifies homosexuality in Gn. 19:7 and Jdg. 19:23. But this is a strange way of doing semantics. If homosexuality is the evil in these two passages, it does not follow that evil always means homosexuality. See below, ch.7, pp.136–146, on the transgression of Gn. 3.
[68] Cassuto, p.111, Gordis, however, *art. cit.*, p.134, tries to forget the biblical vision of God.
[69] Coppens, *op. cit.*, pp.118–122.

freaks.[70] It almost constitutes a proof by *reductio ad absurdum* of
the impossibility of giving a sexual interpretation to the name of
the second tree. We firmly reject it.

Several more cautious writers bring out the dimension of
experience in the Hebrew concept of knowledge. They propose a
very simple explanation: God forbade his creature to taste evil in
the concrete manner that he was already tasting good.[71] What
God wanted was to protect man from knowing evil as well as good.
By eating the fruit he underwent a double experience and
discovered that he knew, in the words of Milton, 'Both good and
evil, good lost, and evil got'.[72] The interpretation has the ever-
valuable advantage of economy. Unfortunately it also founders
on attributing to God the knowledge in question. God does not
'know' evil in the sense suggested; he remains radically outside it
(*cf.* Jas. 1:13). Furthermore, this meaning does not fit any of the
five passages which we must compare with Genesis for the use of
the formula.

Two theories remain in contention. They are rivals to each
other, but a slender bridge could be constructed between them.
According to the first, it is *total knowledge* that is represented by
the forbidden fruit, the supreme knowledge which gives total
power and which God reserves for himself. According to the other
it is *autonomy,* particularly *moral autonomy,* the ability to decide
oneself about good and evil: 'It is a higher knowledge which
towers above good and evil, and which decides about good and
evil'.[73] The first theory prefers to take good and evil in a conjunctive
manner; the other can accommodate both conjunctive and
disjunctive. Neither appears to run into difficulties with the
wording of Genesis.

The first gets caught for a moment on 3:22, since there the LORD
asserts that the man has become 'like' a god, knowing good and
evil, and it is perfectly clear that the man has not acquired total
knowledge. But this interpretation can survive on the supposition
that the remark is ironic. This could be admitted at a pinch,

[70] R. de Vaux has quite clearly demonstrated its impossibility, *RB* 56 (1949), p.303; *RB* 58
(1951) p.157. True enough, taken on its own *'ehād* can take on an indefinite meaning and
mimmennû can be 'of him' as well as 'of us'; but Coppens does not mention any parallel for
the construction that he proposes, with *hāyâ* translated as a future and 'will be born'
arbitarily understood. Goldstain, unfortunately, has allowed himself to be caught out the
same way, p.172.
[71] Lagrange, *art. cit.,* p.344; Young III, pp.40f.
[72] *Paradise Lost*, Bk. 9, l. 1072.   [73] R. de Vaux, *RB* 56 (1949), p.303.

although the beginning of verse 22 gives in a serious tone the reason for the measures taken by God.[74] With the latter there is no problem. If the knowledge of good and evil is the pretended sovereign choice in the matter of good and evil, 3:22 makes good sense. The verse expresses the paradox of life under sin: it is a kind of autonomy by which mankind apes the independence of God, though this autonomy is illusory and is actually alienation.[75]

With both propositions, particularly the second, the meaning of the forbidden knowledge connects with and extends that of the prohibition as such, which is to remind mankind that he is not God and that his dependence is his very life. Thus either theory would be acceptable.

In order to decide between the two, we must refer to the more or less 'parallel' passages. As we review each one, we shall give the literal translation of the formula that interests us in order to help our appraisal of it. The texts seem to divide easily into two groups: two concerning the king, two concerning the child, with Barzillai's reply to David forming a separate case.

1. The formula of this last text, 2 Samuel 19:35, 'know between good and bad' can mean 'to discern' between wines and between meats; but it can also be understood as to play the part of the king's counsellor (for which duty Barzillai now considers himself too old). If it is taken in this sense, the passage simply belongs with the next group.

2. The two royal texts are the compliment paid by the clever woman of Tekoa to David: 'My lord the king is like the angel of

---

[74] J. de Fraine, *Mélanges Robert*, pp.51f., sees irony here. Strangely enough, von Rad, who first of all adopts the interpretation 'omniscience' (pp. 79, 86f.), rejects any suggestion of irony in 3:22 and moves to the concept of autonomy (p.94). Charles Resplandis, *Le fruit défendu de Genèse 2 – 3* (Paris: Le Centurion, 1977), pp.69f., strongly resists the proposal of irony.

[75] Resplandis has not noticed this paradox. He argues that the knowledge of good and evil, resulting from eating the fruit, cannot be autonomy, since man did not become metaphysically autonomous. But our interpretation of 3:22 dissolves the objection. He argues also that man already has the autonomy of moral choice, since he proved his free will by sinning (p.28); but we do not accept this idea of free will, which diminishes the scandal of evil, and in any case is not the same thing as autonomy in the sense that we take it. As Resplandis has properly discerned in sin the wish to escape the eye of God and the desire of independence, he distinguishes the *objective* of sin (divine autonomy) from its *object* (the power within the fruit). The *object*, the knowledge of good and evil, would be an *increase* in knowledge, a larger dose of intelligence, which the couple desired in order to raise themselves up to the same level as God (pp.31f., 51, 80f., *etc.*). Apart from the difficulty of separating the object and the objective, this ingenious solution runs into a number of problems. Why would God have forbidden an advance in intelligence? If this progress occurred, as Resplandis asserts, can it be said that mankind has attained a *god-like* understanding, as Gn. 3:22 would imply? That is quite impossible. And the idea that the fruit simply makes one *more* intelligent seems to us quite out of keeping with the tenor of the narrative.

God to discern good and evil' (2 Sa. 14:17), and the prayer of Solomon on the occasion of his dream at Gibeon, when he asked the LORD for 'an understanding mind to govern thy people, that I may discern between good and evil' (1 Ki. 3:9). In the first case it is generally considered that the woman is trying to flatter the king by attributing total knowledge to him, as she does expressly a little later (2 Sa. 14:20). This is not, however, certain, for the verb 'understand' can also be rendered 'hear' (AV mg.), which suggests the judicial role of the king: he 'hears' the cases presented to him and decides with supreme wisdom what must be done. Solomon clearly distinguishes good from evil, or rather asks for the ability to do so since, as judge, he will be the representative of YHWH, the King of Israel.

3. The prophecy of Immanuel announces that this child will live in close communion with God ('Butter and honey shall he eat', AV) in the years of his minority, 'until he knows how to reject evil and choose good' (Is. 7:15). Before that time comes, Assyria shall lay waste Syria and Ephraim (v.16), which in fact occurred after an interval of approximately thirteen years. Here the phrase definitely refers to the age of responsibility, thirteen years being the age of the bar mitzvah. Lastly, Moses speaks of young children by describing them as those 'who this day have no knowledge of good or evil' (Dt. 1:39). This text, which is closest in form to Genesis 2 – 3, certainly concerns the total dependence which makes children unsuitable to answer for their actions or to control their own conduct. We may also compare the phrase in Jonah 4:11 about the 'hundred and twenty thousand persons who do not know their right hand from their left'. In comparison with the condition of the children, what constitutes the privilege of the adults? They seem independent and can decide on their conduct themselves, they can themselves decide good and evil. ☐

The study of this information allows us to draw definite conclusions. Only once is the theme of total knowledge suggested, without compelling our recognition completely. Elsewhere the knowledge of good and evil corresponds to the ability to decide. It is the prerogative of the king who judges his subjects and of the father who brings up his son. What analysis could be more suitable for Genesis? It shows the man as the vassal of the LORD by virtue of his covenant of grace. It makes him as it were a son of the Creator God. The LORD reserves for himself the royal prerogative to decide, the Creator God alone knows good and evil, he alone is autonomous. Relative to God, mankind must, in order to be happy, constantly approve his dependence as a vassal and renounce all conspiracy against his suzerain; relative to God, mankind must rejoice in his filial dependence and reject the mirage of a truant autonomy like that of the prodigal son. Thus the final interpretation of the knowledge of good and evil is the one which is confirmed. In our view it is certain. Those who have subscribed to it include such varied thinkers as the neo-orthodox theologian Karl Barth,[76] the Catholic biblical scholar and archaeologist Roland de Vaux,[77] and the liberal Protestant philosopher Paul Ricoeur.[78] Before them it was upheld by the orthodox Protestant scholar G. C. Aalders[79] and by Calvin himself. Why did Calvin say the tree was forbidden to the man? 'Not because God would have him to stray like a sheep, without judgment and without choice; but that he might not seek to be wiser than became him, nor by trusting to his own understanding, cast off the yoke of God, and constitute himself an arbiter and judge of good and evil.'[80]

The tree of the knowledge of good and evil represents ingratitude and rebellion against God's provision, the absurd pretension to abolish dependence and the disastrous misuse of the privilege of being freely accountable to God. It represents our deviation into death and the absurd. If with the book of Proverbs we should say of Wisdom, 'She is a tree of life', then the tree of the knowledge of good and evil is nothing other than the tree of folly.

Should we follow a notable tradition and add that, by placing the man under the terms of the covenant, in front of the two trees, God was putting him to the test?[81] Should we think that God was merely establishing a temporary system, in order to raise mankind later if he passed his examination? Such speculation is manifestly a long way from the text, and we share G. C. Berkouwer's reticence in this matter: 'there is reason to question whether the term "probationary command" is actually a correct expression of that which Scripture means to tell us in the Genesis account'.[82]

As Berkouwer felt, the hypothesis formed is, as it were, an

---

[76] Barth, pp.286ff. He adds Nu. 24:13 to the proof texts.
[77] R. de Vaux, *art. cit.*   [78] Ricoeur, p.250.
[79] Quoted by Coppens, *op. cit.,* p.77, n.1. Coppens does not refute him.
[80] Calvin, p.118.
[81] Keil, p.85; Murray, *art. cit.,* p.49; Young III, p.155.
[82] G. C. Berkouwer, *Man: the image of God* (Grand Rapids: Eerdmans, 1962), p.345.

attempt to explain sin by what preceded it. Since sin arose, the theory goes that it was 'possible', and so there was a test with an uncertain outcome. This attenuates the scandalous originality of the fall, which is radically *other* than the good creation of God. Scripture never encourages that kind of logic. Between the work of God and evil there is no continuity.

Before considering the narrative of the unthinkable disobedience, let us for a moment recall with delight the peace and harmony of the creational covenant, with its foundational permission and its protecting condition. There was no covetousness! There was no anxiety! Before those two trees, 'the man and his wife were both naked, and were not ashamed'.

7
The breaking of the covenant

Traditionally the churches, commentators and theologians entitle the third chapter of Genesis 'The Fall'. There is nothing in the text, however, to suggest that metaphor. It could put the reader's thoughts on the wrong track altogether by implying that the event was a sudden, dramatic change of level downwards, of a metaphysical order: a fall from the heavenly to the earthly, from a higher, spiritual stage of being into the lower material realm. The Bible would condemn such contamination from Greek and Gnostic themes. True, when the prophet Ezekiel, in his satirical lament against the prince of Tyre, recalls the sin of the first prince of this world, in Eden, he shows him 'cast to the ground' (Ezk. 28:17). But he is not dealing with the offence, which was rather one of exaltation, rather he is dealing with the punishment, a return to the earth, the ultimate, total humiliation of death which was already proclaimed in Genesis (Gn. 3:19; *cf.* Ezk. 28:8f.). Elsewhere in Scripture sin is a fall only in the sense of a stumbling (*skandalon*), tripping as one walked or making a false step. The image of a fall does not occur in the tablet of the first *tôlᵉdôt*.

What title would be more accurate? Paul Ricoeur suggests 'the myth of "deviation," or "going astray"' rather than 'the myth of the fall'.[1] We shall investigate later the question whether Genesis deserves to be classified as a myth. For the moment let us appreciate and accept the metaphor of deviation as an improvement on the usual title. The word 'transgression',

---

[1] Ricoeur, p.233.

however, would agree even more closely with the text. Mankind did not so much deviate from the prescribed path as cross a forbidden frontier. He overstepped the limit, symbolized by the forbidden tree. But other phrases are legitimate too. The apostle Paul speaks of disobedience at the same time as transgression (Rom. 5:14f., 17f., 19).[2] He sums it up like this: 'Sin came into the world' (Rom. 5:12). And for the event of Genesis 3 Western theology coined the term *peccatum originale originans*. But since we have detected in the first part of the narrative the terms of a covenant between the Creator and his vassal-image, why should we not adopt the title, *the breaking of the covenant*? The prophet Hosea, more than seven centuries before Christ, gave the term his support, since he censured his contemporaries in these words: 'But they, like Adam, have transgressed (the) covenant' (Ho. 6:7).[3] By this comparison Hosea confirms the existence of an original covenant and understands the disobedience of Genesis 3 as its violation by the first patriarch.

Of the narrative of the first transgression or 'breaking of the covenant' in Eden we shall make three successive readings, drilling down, as it were, to three successive levels. First we shall attempt to follow the story as it is told. Then we shall listen more closely in an effort to grasp what it implies. Finally we shall grapple with the crucial question of the historicity of the offence, with which is bound up not only the meaning of the whole of the beginning of Genesis but also the biblical doctrine of evil.

The narration of the events

We shall not waste time extolling the literary merits of the chapter, the subtlety of its psychology and the skill of its dramatic

[2] *Parabasis* (Rom. 5:14) is the precise Greek word for 'transgression'; *paraptōma* (Rom. 5:15–18) is rather 'a false step', but it is not certain that the etymological image was still remembered in current usage. *Parakoē* (Rom. 5:19) is 'disobedience'.

[3] Our translation of Ho. 6:7 is strictly literal, word for word. Translators have often distanced themselves from it, whether because they have not discerned the existence of a covenant in Eden, or because they have considered the references to original sin foreign to the thought of the prophet. But their confusion is in this instance most significant. JB amends the text: 'But they have violated the covenant *at* Adam', *cf.* RSV, GNB. NIV gives the accurate rendering, which RSV offers in a footnote. NIV offers as alternatives 'as at Adam' and 'like men'. The latter is clearly the closer of the two, but comparing his contemporaries with mankind in general would scarcely fulfil Hosea's purpose of summoning them to be what they ought to be! The undoctored rendering of NIV, which we defend, is supported by J. Barton Payne, *The Theology of the Older Testament* (Grand Rapids: Zondervan, 1962), pp.92, 215.

construction. The question we want to put to the author at once is this: what happened? Two sentences could act as a summary of the development. The author tells us of the act of revolt: the man and the woman ate of the forbidden fruit. He tells us of the deadly enticement: the man and the woman yielded to the snake. We shall direct our attention to the first and second statements, interspersing an observation on the motives which, according to the text, we can attribute to the woman.

Revolt against the LORD. This is, in categorical terms, the manner in which the text requires us to characterize the conduct of the man. By eating the fruit, the first couple violated the prohibition and flouted the authority of the Sovereign. When the LORD begins his judicial enquiry, he emphasizes this categorical aspect: 'Have you eaten of the tree of which I commanded you not to eat?' (Gn. 3:11). If we consider not the prohibition itself but the 'knowledge of good and evil' which mankind wished to seize under the symbol of the fruit, then we get a similar view; as we have seen, what is at stake is independence from the Sovereign Father. To seek to have it meant revolt for mankind. The form of words used by the tempter adds a further confirmation: 'You will be like God [or, like gods]' (v.5).[4] The vassal was being pushed towards rebellion; let him reject the status defined by the agreement. We are reminded of the equation John makes between sin and *anomia*, the violation and rejection of the law (1 Jn. 3:4).

In Eden there is no explanation for this revolt. Its occurrence is without excuse. The freedom of the creature-as-image can on no account provide an explanation. Created completely good, the creature had no reason to bring forth evil. God's quasi-son on earth ought to have persevered in the freedom of goodness, as does God's eternal Son who is free and cannot sin, and as shall the children of grace, liberated and recreated in him and who shall be without sin for ever and ever.

☐ Kierkegaard, possessed as he was by a passion for freedom, a freedom which he wrongly calls 'infinite', rightly denounced the 'foolishness' of those who explain sin by free will: 'To maintain

---

[4] Young III, p.37, argues for the translation 'You will be like God', on the following basis: the snake insinuates that God forbade the fruit out of jealousy; what is at stake, therefore, is equality with God. The first Adam, we should add, considered it 'a prize to be seized' (Phil. 2:6). C. Resplandis, *op. cit.*, p.65, argues on the contrary that if the singular had been intended, the text would have read 'like him', a relevant argument.

that freedom begins as *liberum arbitrium* (which is found nowhere, cf. Leibniz) that can choose good just as well as evil inevitably makes every explanation impossible'.[5] But to link sin, as does Kierkegaard, with the secret anxiety of innocence – even underlining the 'qualitative leap' when sin is posited – is equally unsatisfactory. For there is no anxiety! In Eden, freedom knows of not vertiginous void, but the fullness of communion with the Father, Freedom is not 'infinite' and does not arise out of nothing. It is the gift of God, constantly renewed.[6] The attempts to find an opening for sin in liberty or in the anxiety that is inseparable from liberty fall into the same trap. They import into Eden *before* Adam's sin what is true about freedom (more or less true, about more or less freedom) *after* Adam's sin. Once the illusory autonomy has been won (Gn. 3:22), the rebellious freedom that is sundered and uprooted can experience anxiety over the void it has created around it; within itself it bears evil as its potential (and even as its slavery). But it was not so in the beginning. The logic which weaves a continuity back from the *afterwards*, after Adam's sin, to the *beforehand* of creation seeks to mitigate the scandalous oddity of sin, the monstrous nature of its emergence. Such logic is well on the way to pleading extenuating circumstances or even just making excuses. Such is the deceitfulness of the sinful heart. This logic must be rejected. In Eden there is nothing to explain, and so nothing to excuse, the rebellion. Even the concept of human *fallibility* is unsafe; if it suggests a crack preceding the split, a sort of tendency in one direction or fragility before the fall, it must be categorically denied. One can speak properly of fallibility only after Adam's sin. Before that we may say in the strictest sense of the words that there was no cause to suspect it. ☐

Doubt and desire. The narrative permits us at least to imagine these two motives for the foolish and wicked revolt of humanity. It has frequently been pointed out that the tempter's first words insinuate doubt into the woman's mind (v.1). Current versions translate: 'Did God really say...?' (NIV, *cf.* GNB), which conveys the idea that the snake invited her to doubt the *word* of God. But this rendering does not appear to be the most accurate; for *'ap̄ kî*, the expression which introduces the tempter's first sentence, is not an interrogative but rather a strong affirmation. Derek

---

[5] Kierkegaard, p.112.
[6] 'Freedom is infinite and arises out of nothing', *ibid.*

Kidner suggests: 'So God has actually said...?'[7] It is not a plain, straightforward question! Luther wrote: 'I cannot translate the Hebrew either in German or in Latin; the serpent uses the word *aph-ki* as though to turn up its nose and jeer and scoff.'[8] Speiser comments: 'The serpent is not asking a question; he is deliberately distorting a fact'.[9] The tempter makes a massive affirmation, adopting a tone of surprise and indignation or else of feigned compassion, because he wishes to make the fact seem *outrageous*. Playing craftily on the denial, 'You shall not eat of any tree of the garden', he presents the ban as a monstrous deprivation. It is not so much God's word on which he casts doubt as his *goodness*. Of the God who is generosity itself he sketches a portrait of miserliness. He projects the false perspective of a rivalry between God and man; he suggests that man will be the less free as God will be the more sovereign, and vice versa. How many generations since that very first one have swallowed the same bait!

The snake's attack on the truth of God's word is launched in an indirect manner, by imputing hidden motives that God's revelation passes over in silence, by subjecting the terms of the covenant to 'the hermeneutic of suspicion'. Even when he is so bold as to contradict the terms of God's words, 'DYING you shall not die' (v.4), there is still ambiguity. The unusual placing of the negative leaves open the possibility of understanding it as: 'It is not proper death that you will undergo'; in other words, dare to experience the trivial death-like change that will bring you the experience of full humanity![10] The emphasis remains on the criticism of the character of God, depicted by implication as selfish, jealous, oppressive and repressive. Since the narrative

---

[7] Kidner, p.67. Keil, p.94, and Cassuto, p.144, maintain an interrogative sense, but without giving an example that proves their case. Keil quotes 1 Sa. 23:3 and 2 Sa. 4:11, but one usually translates *'a fortiori'*. Cassuto quotes Is. 54:6, but there it is *ki* on its own. The dictionaries give no example apart from Gn. 3:1. J. Coppens, *La connaissance du bien et du mal et le péché du Paradis* (Paris: Desclée de Brouwer, 1948), p.62 and Robert L. Reymond, *PCSR* 1 (1975), pp.51–56, emphasize that the meaning is in the affirmative.

[8] Quoted by von Rad, p.83 n.   [9] Speiser, p.23.

[10] The negation of a form with the absolute infinitive is regularly placed after the infinitive and before the form (Gesenius-Kautzsch, para. 113 v). Now here, instead of *môṯ lô' tāmûṯû*, we have *lô' môṯ tᵉmuṯûn* ('not DYING you shall die'). There are only two other examples of this unusual order: Ps. 49:8 and Am. 9:8. In Am. 9:8, this order being followed, the negation bears on the intensification itself: 'not DESTROYING I shall destroy' = 'I shall *not utterly* destroy'. Ps. 49:8 is less clear, but it can be understood: 'not REDEEMING he shall redeem', *i.e.* a man cannot redeem totally, *Cf.* v.9, 'he *will lack* always' something. Thus in Gn. 3:4 it is permitted to understand: 'You shall not die utterly (really, *etc.*)'. J. de Fraine, *Mélanges Robert*, p.55, suggests 'You shall not die *immediately*'.

aims at being more than just a tale, it certainly intends us to discern within sin itself, as contained in this particular sin, doubt concerning God – doubt about his motives, doubt about his goodness, and, above all, doubt about his love. It is not possible to sin as long as one remains in the knowledge of the love of God.

'The woman saw that the tree was good for food, and that it was a delight to the eyes, and that the tree was to be desired to make one wise' (v.6). The temptation played upon the whole range of human desire. Just as in ourselves 'desire gives birth to sin' (Jas. 1:15), in Eden we find it linked with disobedience. It would be difficult to miss the theme here, even if the correspondence with the threefold temptation of Jesus and the threefold lust of 1 John 2:16, expounded by so many preachers, remains somewhat tenuous.[11] But what is the meaning of the attractive appearance of the tree, if we agree on its symbolic nature? Is the knowledge of good and evil 'good for food'? A simple observation points the way to the solution of the difficulty. In the narrative, the forbidden knowledge, which is not a created entity, is representated by a fruit, an element of the created order. What is the full implication of this 'detail'? It is immense. It recalls this point: it is always in his use of the created order that mankind exercises the autonomy that he pretends to have seized. When mankind decides to be like God, 'knowing good and evil', he fails lamentably to create anything at all. He cannot withdraw from God's world, neither can he bring about any innovation except by *misusing* the wealth that God has given him. Thus, it is always with regard to one of the fruits of God's garden, a fruit that is genuinely beautiful, pleasant and useful, that mankind is tempted. Evil is not in the good that God has created, but in the rejection of the order that God has instituted for the enjoyment of the world. Temptation plays with facets of things that are good, and highlights the attractions of the beauties in creation. Sin then perverts the excitement which these objects quite rightly cause within us. Thus, to revert to John's words, 'the lust of the flesh' perverts and corrupts the excitement which

---

[11] It is in the third clause, 'to be desired to make one wise' that the sense must be forced in order to find a parallelism with the third temptation of Jesus, to hurl himself from the pinnacle of the temple (following Luke's order), and with 'the pride of life' (1 Jn. 2:16c). C. Resplandis, *op. cit.*, p.78, emphasizes the third clause: it would show that the knowledge of good and evil would be a growth in intelligence. But the equivalence is not explicit: the autonomy represented for us by the forbidden 'knowledge' certainly includes intellectual supremacy.

drives us towards what is good and beneficial. The 'lust of the eyes' likewise corrupts the drive towards what is beautiful and true. The 'pride of life' perverts the rightful effort to be, and to be valued. Thus, in the temptation of Jesus, the devil offered him things which by right belonged to the Son of God; but he invited Jesus to invert the order established by the Father. Thus, in Genesis 3, the fruit of the tree planted by God was intended to be beautiful and good – the opportunity for sin was an innocent creature – but the human race perverted the order of the Creator.

It was by doubting God and by desiring in a wrong way something good in creation that the first couple sinned. Might doubt and desire, then, make us understand why evil arose? One might be tempted so to think. But in fact, nothing has been explained. If doubt exists, then ungodly sin has already entered on the scene. Similarly, throughout the Bible 'lust' in the sense of covetousness is not only the mother of sin, it is a form of sin. How did doubt and covetousness arise? The woman in Eden had no reason to doubt God, and every reason to trust him. The woman in Eden had no grounds for dissatisfaction, nothing within her should have disordered or misdirected her desire.

At this point the interpreter must pray for a share in the narrator's own care and precision! Certain writers have concluded from the presence of the sins of doubt and of covetousness that the conversion to evil had preceded the eating of the fruit – that this sin was in a sense a second sin.[12] But that is to throw the narrative off centre; its whole construction bears out the fact that the decisive moment occurs in Genesis 3:6. Besides, the text, with its rigorous care, does not say that the woman welcomed the blasphemous insinuations of the snake. It does not say that she coveted; it limits itself to recording that she *saw* (v.6a). We have definite knowledge of her doubt and greed only by the conclusion: 'she took…and ate'. The two motives suggested, then, do not constitute an antecedent act; they form part of the first sin. In no way at all do they explain its occurrence; they belong to its emergence.

What, in the last analysis, is the reason for the role that doubt and covetousness appear to play in the narrative? It shows that the first sin was a human act. A human act is never completely simple, and sin, being a corrupt act, is less simple than any other. As soon as it enters, sin is just as we know it – complex,

---

[12] Young III, p.48, leans in this direction.

involved, multivalent, like an octopus with its spreading tentacles or like a cancer with its manifold metastases.

The seduction by the snake. When we get into the story, it is impossible to overlook that another party brings in the doubt, arouses desire and incites to disobedience. What significance for the description of the fall has the fact that humanity committed this sin at the snake's instigation, and was thus led into evil?

The second summary of the dramatic events in the garden of Eden – the first couple *yielded* – allows us to observe three features of sin from the very beginning. The tempter's role reveals *weakness* beneath the false strength of self-affirmation. The sinners of Genesis 3, like so many after them, imagined themselves greater in the arrogance of their gesture. Were they not making a superhuman challenge against heaven? Rebellion seeks to masquerade as heroism. But it is a laughable disguise, for at the very moment that the sinner is intoxicated with the sense of his own power, he is being manipulated by *another* mind. In actual fact, sin is defeat. At the same time, it is from another perspective an *inversion* of the true order of things. The fact that the other party takes the form of an animal (the text underlines that the snake belonged to that category, Gn. 3:1) is not an insignificant detail. Reptiles were a part of the animal kingdom over which the man and the woman were to have dominion. If, as they sin, they obey the snake, there is the evidence that orders established at creation are being twisted and smashed with the violation of the divine covenant, either directly in the commission of the offence, or else in its repercussions (as the continuation of the narrative will show). Sin is accompanied by an alteration in the original hierarchies and harmonies; one has only to think of the puzzling problem everyone has in living with his own body (*cf.* Jas. 3:2ff.). Finally, the tempter's presence brings out clearly the truth that sin is foreign to mankind's being. It comes, in some sense, 'from outside'. Here we may borrow the language of Paul Ricoeur: man 'is not *the* Evil One, the Wicked One, substantively, so to speak, but evil, wicked, adjectivally'.[13] Suggested by the *other*, sin is clearly

[13] Ricoeur, p.259. We think, however, that we must say of the Evil One himself that he is not wicked by essence, and that he became so by disobedience, by a 'fall'. Otherwise one could not assert his reality without falling into Manicheism. But it is less obvious in his case than in the case of man, since the Evil One comes on to the scene, in the biblical narrative, already wicked.

alienation for mankind; it is captivity under an inhuman principle, a parasitic infection.

It seems that only the woman had anything to do with the snake. This element in the narrative also calls for reflection. Is the author some kind of misogynist, and is he laying all the blame on the woman? The idea is nonsense, of course. The construction of the chapter proves that it is not the case. The eyes of both of them opened uneasily when the *husband* ate (v.7). And when God pronounces sentence, it is to the man that he addresses in verse 19 the fulfilment of the threat, 'you shall die' (2:17). The apostle Paul gives a faithful reading of the passage: 'sin came into the world through *one man* and death through sin...the transgression of Adam' (Rom. 5:12,14). The woman's role in the temptation does not allow us to blame her solely or principally; it allows the narrative to make the guilt rest on both the man and the woman, without either being able to give an excuse. If the man had taken the initiative in the transgression, the woman would have appeared to be a victim. If the woman's offence had been the fatal point of rift, the man would have appeared almost innocent.[14] But the woman opened the way and the man took the determining decision, within the responsibility conferred on him by the covenant. Each in turn seems more guilty than the other! If they put the blame on one another, they only make their situation worse. They both sinned, and they even did so in agreement with each other. They were accomplices in the same way as Ananias and Sapphira and other criminal couples. We can simply notice again, within the context of their complicity, the reversal of the creation order. The woman takes the initiative, contrary to the indications of Genesis 2. The apostle Paul, in a passage defining the order that God requires between man and woman, underlines the inversion: in creation it is the man first and then the woman, in sin it is the opposite (1 Tim. 2:13f.).[15] But the man shares the responsibility for this reversal, since he consented to it.

But why did the snake launch his offensive against the

[14] This would be implied by the romantic idea that Adam followed his wife only out of chivalry. Something of the kind was suggested by the nineteenth-century American theologian, W. G. T. Shedd, referring to 1 Tim. 2:14, quoted by John Murray, 'The fall of man' in *Collected Writings of John Murray* 2, p.70. This is a long way from the Bible.

[15] In our opinion 1 Tim. 2:15 should be taken as a third allusion to Gn. 3 (v.15). In the promise of redemption, the woman appears as the one who gives birth; when God restores the order that has been overturned by sin, he gives back to the woman her 'differential' role of woman.

woman? That too deserves comment. Here, it seems, we find 'the mediation of weakness'. Ricoeur writes: 'Here the woman represents the point of least resistance of finite freedom to the appeal of the *Pseudo*, of the evil infinite'.[16] And he recalls Shakespeare's line, 'Frailty, thy name is woman!'. Since Scripture admits the notion of 'the weaker sex' (1 Pet. 3:7), the quotation is apposite.[17] But what constitutes the weakness of the woman?

☐   Kierkegaard takes his analysis much further: 'Eve is a derived creature' and this fact 'may seem like a hint of the sinfulness that is posited by propagation', for 'it is the fact of being derived that predisposes the particular individual' to sin.[18] He explains himself by positing that woman has more anxiety (which, he says, is not an imperfection), because she is more sensuous, and that thus the 'cleft' between the two parts of the human synthesis 'becomes deeper' ('the dissimilarity'). He proves that woman is more sensuous *aesthetically* – she is represented by artists as more beautiful when she is sleeping – then he proves it *ethically*, because 'woman culminates in procreation'.[19] We have rejected the idea of anxiety before the offence, and we refuse to define mankind as originally the synthesis of contradictory elements; therefore we shall not follow the great Danish philosopher in seeking to locate the inclination to sin in sensuality. And furthermore, Genesis gives no clear indication that the woman is really more sensuous than the man. On this point too we shall hesitate to follow Kierkegaard.   ☐

In the narrative it is indeed the woman's role to be 'derived' from the man and dependent on him. Might the snake have chosen her as his target for that reason? A single detail could well confirm that. When the woman repeats the divine command not to eat the fruit, she does not quote it exactly (3:3); she adds that they must not even *touch* the fruit, and she says, '*lest* you die'. Her paraphrase definitely takes liberties! But Ceuppens pushes imagination too far when he explains that Adam had transmitted the precept and added a little to it, just to be on the safe side![20] Young is severe in his judgment on the modifications the woman brings to God's words. He argues that they show that Eve's trust in her Creator had already begun to waver.[21] Calvin,

---

[16] Ricoeur, p.255.

[17] Young III, p.19, also thinks of weakness as mentioned in 1 Pet. 3:7.

[18] Kierkegaard, p.47.   [19] *Ibid.,* pp.64–66.

[20] J. Ceuppens, *Genèse I – III* (Paris: Desclée de Brouwer, 1946), p.142.

[21] Young III, pp.31f.

however, approves of the addition of the word 'touch'. Eve 'expressed her pious disposition by anxiously observing the precept of God', but he blames her for adding the 'lest', which might imply doubt about the certainty of the punishment.[22] In our view, the change of wording could suggest incipient legalism, or else a magical conception of the fruit. But none of this is definite. It is wiser to stick to the simple assertion: there is a change, and that change recalls the distance between the woman and the conclusion of the covenant (2:16f.), and hence her status as a 'derived' being and her dependence. It does not seem too arbitrary to associate the idea of weakness with that situation. The woman, taken from the man and created for him, receiving from him her name and waiting for him to leave father and mother in order to join himself to her, naturally found herself in a receptive attitude. She thus provided an easier prey for the cunning stranger, whom she ought not to have welcomed. And as the narrative presents us with a 'model' situation, we may draw from it this more general lesson: temptation seeks to induce in mankind (both male and female) a 'feminine' attitude towards it; it asks that sin receive a welcome, an opening, sympathy and consent to this determined approach from outside. It must be resisted in a 'manly' way, by gathering all one's energies, by fighting it head-on, and by deliberately holding fast to the objectivity of the commandments.[23]

The snake's influence on the woman and then the woman's influence on the man *qualify* the first sin – from this we may derive instruction. But it explains nothing about its sudden emergence. As John Murray writes forcefully, the temptation was the occasion of the fall; it was not its *cause*.[24] 'Weak' as the woman was, she had no reason to let herself be persuaded. There was no tendency in her nature that drove her on to the fatal slope. Neither did anything direct the man to his foolish acquiescence. There was no fault in his will – before sin entered.

---

[22] Calvin, p.149.

[23] Two texts come to mind. First, a literal translation of La. 3:39: 'Of what shall living man (*'ādām*) complain? Man strong (*geber*) against his sins!' The meaning seems to be that instead of complaining man should assume his responsibilities and fight sin; *geber* is a word for man in his virile strength (*cf.* Je. 31:22). Further, Paul exhorts all Christians to acquit themselves *like men* (1 Cor. 16:13). Perhaps to these could be added the mysterious word to Cain: 'sin is couching at the door; its desire is for you, but you must master it' (Gn. 4:7). The end of that verse takes up the language of Gn. 3:16 exactly, where God described the wretched fate of woman after the fall, under the tyrannical authority of her husband. God seems to invite Cain to treat sin as a hard, dominating man treats his wife.

[24] Murray, *art. cit.*, p.68.

145

Why did they yield? The enigma remains total, and the evil rebellion inexcusable.

Suggestions from the form of the text

No-one who has appreciated the subtlety of the second tablet of Genesis (chs. 2 – 3) and the skilful use of popular imagery will be content simply to follow the thread of the story. The first reading that we did, of a meditative nature, will not satisfy him. Since it is certain that the author distances himself from the language he uses, the reader must ask questions about his hidden motives or his designs. The reader cannot hold back two questions, which are linked together: those concerning sex and concerning the snake. Must we think in terms of a sexual offence, if we wish to define what exactly the sin was? And, in the narrative, what exactly is the meaning of the snake? We have commented on the intervention of a tempter and have sought to determine its full significance, but we still have to understand the fact that 'the snake' plays that role.

Our study of the 'knowledge-of-good-and-evil' showed that that formula bore no sexual connotation. Other elements in the text, however, could suggest that the act of arrogance by which the man and the woman claimed to win their autonomy and free themselves from filial dependence was a forbidden use of their sexuality. This interpretation, that has generally been suspect in orthodox circles, retains remarkable resilience. This is not just a question of the last traces of the old anti-sexual asceticism of the West, with its Gnostic overtones. Paul Fueter reports the reactions of the Nyakusa and the Safwa of Tanzania. A group of African students told him: 'We know perfectly well that you Europeans are hiding the truth from us, or else you are extremely simple-minded! God did not mean, "You shall not eat", but "You shall not go to bed with her"...The snake...taught Eve the sex act and she committed it with Adam'.[25] When asked where they got that idea from, they replied: 'We know it ourselves; no missionary has told us that'. Such confidence in young readers who had apparently come to the text with fresh minds suggests that we should listen more closely; might we pick up some hidden message?

Others have already saved us the trouble of looking for 'clues'.

---

[25] Paul D. Fueter, 'L'historicité des récits de la Genèse', *Chantiers* 65 (1970/71), p.8.

Some of the arguments are so light-weight that they disappear as soon as you look at them; all they prove is the weakness of the arguments proposed. For example, since the apostle Paul says that the woman was 'seduced' (1 Tim. 2:14), it has been claimed that he was adopting the rabbinic interpretation of a *sexual* seduction of Eve by the snake. But the Greek verb used by Paul does not normally bear a sexual connotation, and the Hebrew verb of Genesis 3:13 never has that meaning in the Old Testament.[26] It means to lead astray, to deceive, and we must not ourselves be deceived if some choose to translate it 'to seduce'. Some have appealed to the name of Eden and to the presence of the tree of life as references to sexual pleasure and reproduction. But pleasure and life are themes that are too vast to be restricted to the idea of sex. Besides, Eden and the tree of life nowhere have any connection with or bearing on the offence in Genesis.[27]

Three considerations carry more weight and deserve closer attention. The man was led on by the woman to disobey; can one not assume that the temptation was connected in fact to feminine attraction? Pierre Grelot, who is too careful a scholar to resort to poor reasons, argues his case with skill. Sin, he argues, which is the rejection of the creaturely condition, 'must be partly connected with the awakening of self-awareness'. Now, 'is it possible in the case of two partners who are man and wife to separate the awakening of the awareness of the *self* and the experience of *the other*? If the problem of the original sin is approached from this perspective, it will be impossible to rule out every sexual element'.[28] The figure of the snake, the representation of the divinities of the ground, is associated throughout the ancient Near East with fertility cults. It acts as a phallic symbol.[29] It must also have made the first recipients of the narrative think of the area of sexuality. Lastly, if the first reaction of the man and the woman, once the offence has been committed, is to cover their nakedness (3:7), are they not indicating the point of their

---

[26] Goldstain, p.166, employs the argument, seeking support from M. Dibelius' commentary on the Pastoral Epistles (1913); but neither gives any proof of the sexual use of *exapataō*. According to Coppens, *op. cit.,* pp.22f., who remains most careful, the sexual use is 'possible, particularly since Polybus', but it is certainly not usual. Bauer-Arndt-Gingrich makes absolutely no mention of it for *exapataō*, but gives three references with *apataō*. 2 Cor. 11:3, insisting on the cunning of the snake and on the mind, does not imply this meaning. As for *nāšā* in Gn. 3, no-one disputes its simple meaning 'to lead astray'. In Ex. 22:16 another verb, *pātâ*, is used for the seduction of a virgin.

[27] Goldstain, p.166, n.5, seems to take on board the argument that we reject.

[28] Pierre Grelot, *Le couple humain dans l'Ecriture* (Paris: Cerf, 1962), p.44.

[29] Coppens provides ample documentation, *op. cit.,* pp.21f., 91–117.

new experience, of the 'knowledge' they have just acquired?[30] It
is not possible to see in their sudden shame of nakedness simply
the sense of their destitution;[31] it is definitely a sense of shame
concerning their *genitalia*. Some would add as the fourth indication the nature of the woman's punishment, her pain in childbirth and the desire which submits her to the domination of the
male, the punishment fitting the crime.[32] But this principle
should operate also in the case of her husband, who fell into the
same sin, but there is nothing in the sentence pronounced on
him that refers in any way to sexual life. This fourth supposition
must be rejected.

There remain, then, three features which one could take as
suggestions made by the text. As soon as we move in this
direction, however, a formidable difficulty bars the way. If it
was a sexual offence, what offence could it have been? Philo,
whom Gunkel was still following, thought it was the act of
conjugal love. But in the opinion of our text, that act is
thoroughly good (Gn. 2), as it is throughout the Old Testament.
It could not have been forbidden as premature in Genesis 2 – 3,
for there the man is adult, the one who is responsible for the
garden and who rules in wisdom over the animal world. Gregory
of Nyssa and other church fathers imagined that some kind of
illicit pleasure had slipped into the carnal union.[33] But what
was this illicit pleasure? This hypothesis obviously bears a
neo-Platonist flavour, one of metaphysical hostility towards the
body and its pleasures. But the Bible leaves the married couple
free to enjoy the gift they have received.

☐　　The 'demography' of the garden of Eden made homosexuality,
incest and adultery impossible. Out of the complete list of sexual
offences, the only one that can possibly be envisaged is bestiality,
as certain Rabbis dared suggest. But Coppens himself recognizes
that Adam's presence at his wife's side in 3:6 rules that out as far
as she is concerned,[34] and the man sinned without having anything
to do with the snake. Coppens tries to get out of this difficulty by
supposing that the first couple sought fertility *from the pagan*

---

[30] Coppens, *op. cit.,* p.91; Goldstain, p.164.

[31] As attempted by Romano Guardini, *La Puissance. Essai sur le règne de l'homme* (Paris:
Seuil, 1954), p.32; C. Resplandis, *op. cit.,* pp.84ff., 101–122. If it is true that nakedness more
often suggests dishonour in the Old Testament than the arousal of sexual desire, nakedness
is also a euphemism for the sexual organs, and the modesty which covered them was not
unknown (Ex. 20:26; *cf.* Gn. 9:21f.; Hab. 2:15).

[32] Coppens, *op. cit.,* p.21; Goldstain, p.165.

[33] References in Goldstain, p.166, n.4.

[34] Coppens, *op. cit.,* p.24. *Ibid.,* pp.22f. for the Jewish folklore.

gods.[35] R. de Vaux points out that in that case it is no longer a sexual sin that we are discussing but a religious sin.[36] The first occurrence of shame is explained equally well by any other concrete sin. And nothing in the text suggests that the man and the woman had been motivitated by the desire for descendants.[37]   □

These difficulties more than outweigh the three points which favour the sexual interpretation of the offence, and which we deem far from being conclusive. The narrative does not say that the woman tempted the man by means of her femininity, and Grelot is perhaps a little too quick to accept the link between the transgression and 'the awakening of self-awareness'; for did the man not sing of his awareness of the other and of himself back in 2:23, when he awoke from his enchanted dream? According to the text, the offence is not found *between* the man and the woman; they both sinned, in turn.[38] The symbolism of the snake could certainly suggest the licentious cults of Canaan and elsewhere, but this fecund symbolism could suggest many other things: the snake was also the beast of wisdom, of the occult, of divination and of magic.[39] As for the shame, it can signify the effect of the first sin without indicating its nature; if the relationship of the man and the woman, shown by their sexuality, reflects the relationship between God and man, as we have said, the breaking of the covenant cannot fail to have repercussions in their sexual relationships. At any rate, the consequence of rebellion against God must be embarrassment and shame of both the man and the woman in front of one another. So we must conclude with the majority of commentators that the sexual interpretation of the offence lacks serious foundations.

Why is the theory constantly emerging again from its ashes? We suspect that its strange attraction, if it flouts careful exegesis, arises from the very disturbance spoken of in Genesis 3:7. By imagining that this is a sexual offence, people are confessing *their* difficulty in being in full control of themselves at that point where they are supremely 'flesh', and their difficulty in living with integrity the pattern relationship with the other. At the same time they obscure the problem, since they take the effect

---

[35] *Ibid.*, pp.25ff.; Goldstain, p.167.   [36] R. de Vaux, *art. cit., RB* 56 (1949), p.306.

[37] Coppens, *op. cit.*, pp.27f.; Goldstain, p.165, take up the idea of A. van Hoonacker: as at Babel mankind sought to transgress the commandment to fill the earth, in Eden their disobedience must have referred to the only precept given them at that point, 'be fruitful and multiply'. But this precept is not given in the second tablet, and disobedience would have meant the *refusal* to procreate.

[38] De Vaux, *art. cit.*   [39] *Ibid.*, p.307; Renckens, pp.279f.

for the sin itself; their obsession with the disturbed area conceals the true cause, the breaking of the covenant and the claim to autonomy. It is a diversionary tactic. Karl Barth comments: 'It is the genius of the sin which entered the world to declare the relationship between man or woman, or sexuality, the *pudendum* of humanity, and thus to make it its real *pudendum*'.[40]

The snake plays too large a part in the drama of Genesis 3 to allow us to be satisfied with the remarks that have already been made about him. Von Rad appears to us rather short of inspiration when he minimizes the snake's importance: 'The mention of the snake here is almost secondary'.[41] The curse that is specifically pronounced upon him, and the announcement of his future destruction by the woman's seed prove, on the contrary, that he is one of the principal protagonists in the story. It is impossible to refrain from asking oneself the question: Who is the snake?

Everything concerning the serpent can be read in a 'naïve' manner. The story as a whole retains its coherence. He is an animal that is more cunning than the others, and that uses his animal cunning to deceive the woman. He speaks completely naturally.[42] He will be punished by being made to crawl, whether he previously had legs of which he will be deprived, or whether the judgment confirms an original humiliation. Between the human race and the snake, enmity will be unwavering. Women do not like snakes, men crush their heads, but snakes give as good as they get.

Such a reading, which is simply 'literal', is possible, but it carries us into the world of legends and popular fables. In the style of folk stories, it is *the* snake with which we are concerned, just as in Jotham's fable *the* fig tree and *the* vine speak (Jdg. 9:8ff.).[43] Does the writer share the naïvety of this language, or does he adopt it for figurative purposes? What we have seen of the writer's approach and his treatment of the two trees make it almost certain that he does not speak literally. He makes several word-plays about the snake. We have already mentioned '*ārôm*-'*ārûm*-'*ārûr*. To this we can add *nāḥās* (snake) and *nāsâ* (deceive), and undoubtedly *nāḥās* is intended to suggest the other use of

[40] Barth, p.311.   [41] Von Rad, p.85.

[42] Young III, pp.12, 17, asserts that the fact that the snake speaks is abnormal, 'out of order', but nothing in the text of Gn. 3 suggests this. Young makes this assertion on *a priori* grounds.

[43] Young III, p.16, wants to take the article in 3:1 as generic: snakes as a group were the most cunning of the animals. But he forgets that every subsequent time that he is mentioned, the article is kept for the *individual* snake that converses with Eve.

the same root (*nāḥas*) for magic and divination.[44] The language of 3:15 also appears ambivalent. It attributes to the snake a length of life that is foreign to the animal kingdom, when it announces its final defeat – the snake's own personal defeat, not that of its descendants – after many generations of the human race. The writer unquestionably has in mind another figure, behind that of the snake.

The book of Revelation, which once again corresponds to Genesis, gives us the key. On two occasions it explains, 'the dragon, that ancient serpent, who is the Devil and Satan' (Rev. 20:2; *cf.* 12:9). The apostle Paul had earlier made the same identification when he feared that the thoughts of the Corinthians might be corrupted by the snake (note yet again the definite article). The continuation of his exhortation shows that he is apprehensive of the wiles of Satan (2 Cor. 11:3,14; *cf.* 2:11). Jesus himself had pictured the defeat of Satan as treading upon snakes (Lk. 10:18f.). This is probably an echo of Genesis, as is the reference to the devil as a murderer from the beginning and a liar (Jn. 8:44). The Hellenistic book, the Wisdom of Solomon, prepares the way with its own interpretation: 'through the devil's envy death entered the world' (Wisdom 2:24). In any case, Scripture itself leaves us in no doubt; the snake is the devil.

☐ Orthodox Christianity has never sought to cast doubt on the point. But in most cases, from Augustine to E. J. Young, it has defended a further proposition. According to this addition, the devil took possession of the body of a literal snake and used it in order to deceive the woman. In that case there are two creatures to distinguish in the account, the evil one and a snake that he used as his cover.[45] Such a manifestation of Satanic possession would by no means be inconceivable to us. We must simply ask, does Scripture support the idea? In fact neither in Genesis nor anywhere else do we find the least suggestion in this direction. Nowhere is the role of the snake presented as that of a disguise or of an instrument; nowhere does the Bible indicate that the tempter was twofold.

The silence of the texts is not the only difficulty in the theory. What they quite clearly state fits the theory badly. If the animal is only the devil's tool, why does the narrative insist on the animal cunning that it displays (3:1)? Why is the snake alone punished?

---

[44] Goldstain, pp.147f.   [45] Calvin, p.140; Keil, pp.92f.; Young III, p.23.

Young himself recognizes: 'the punishment which fell upon the serpent was really a symbol of the deeper punishment to strike the evil one'.[46] Augustine had also detected a figure of speech, and Lagrange rightly responds: 'But why not be consistent and recognize in the snake not the instrument, but a creature representing the devil?'[47] He points out at the same time that it would be more in line with the book of Revelation, which does *not* say, 'the ancient serpent, the *instrument* of the Devil'. ☐

By linking the dragon with 'the ancient serpent', Revelation gives any confirmation that may be needed that it is showing how to interpret symbolic language. The dragon, that is to say Leviathan of Isaiah 27:1, the monstrous sea serpent, fleeing and twisting, better known to us today thanks to Ugaritic literature, was already in use as a symbol amongst the prophets.[48] It represents the power of paganism rising up against the LORD and against his people. No-one imagines that the devil took possession of the body of a sea monster in order to deceive the nations! Revelation interprets the snake of Genesis 3 and the dragon from other passages in exactly the same way; thus it respects the laws of language which require a clear choice of the figurative meaning if it is necessary to depart from the literal. Learning from the approach of Revelation, we shall understand the information about the snake as a whole as extended symbolism; since the snake is the devil, we must transpose all that is said about the snake in terms that are suitable for the devil.

☐ Before we do this, however, we must meet certain objections. Several writers think they are in a position to challenge the New Testament's interpretation and believe it is a mistake to see Satan in Genesis. Some minimize the role of the snake, like G. von Rad. Westermann rules out the possibility of its being the evil one, since it is a good creature that God has made, and here he finds the 'paradox' of the emergence of evil without a cause.[49] Bonhoeffer finds it typical that here there is no *diabolus ex machina*.[50] But these commentators overlook the importance of the snake in the structure of the narrative and the enormous symbolic weight of such a figure in the ancient world of biblical times. Paul Ricoeur proposes an alternative reading that is much better worked out: in the 'myth' of Adam the snake is the

---

[46] Young III, p.96.   [47] M. J. Lagrange, 'L'innocence et le péché', RB 6 (1897), p.365.
[48] *Cf.* Heidel, pp.103ff.; C. Pfeiffer, 'Lotan and Leviathan', *EQ* 32 (1960), pp.207–211.
[49] Westermann *C*, p.92. He is wrong if he believes that the presence of Satan eliminates this 'paradox'; we have shown the contrary.   [50] Bonhoeffer, p.64.

effective, invincible trace of the tragic myth.[51] The biblical narrative attributes the origin of evil to mankind's use of liberty. The tragic myth, on the other hand, locates darkness in God and evil within being itself. It is the myth of the 'cruel' God and of blind, malevolent fate. Now the snake in Genesis 3 'represents the aspect of evil that could not be absorbed into the responsible freedom of man', the 'already there', the 'cosmic structure of evil' which is the invitation to betray. Although Ricoeur also takes later demonology to be a sequel to the concession made by the book of Genesis to the tragic view of life, thus bringing Satan and the snake closer to one another, he departs from the New Testament doctrine of the devil. For the New Testament, the devil is precisely not an element of the essential structure of the cosmos, and we must reaffirm that in God there is no darkness at all (1 Jn. 1:5). Was there any risk that the Israelites, who were the first readers for whom the book of Genesis was intended, would hear in it an echo of the tragic myth? To us it seems that the answer is no.[52] In the account, the snake is a particular creature, carefully distinguished from the others. The LORD judges, condemns and punishes it separately. That does not suggest some obscure part of reality, but a particular agent. The symbolism of the snake could not suggest the tragic; in the mythologies it is rather the ally of mankind, giving life, health, power and secret knowledge. Its deception of humanity and cause of human death could not therefore be taken as a reflection on the evil inherent in being (an idea that is simply a device of the snake to excuse sin),[53] but as a polemical thrust against the rejected mythologies. □

Just as Leviathan represents the arrogant, tortuous power that stirs up the sea of the nations, the snake of the Garden of Eden stands for the attraction of pagan religion and its magic spells. It was the emblem of fertility rites and of cults involving prostitution. It was the animal of divination. We have already pointed out that the word *nāḥaš*, which has an almost identical pronounciation, is used for divination procedures (Nu. 23:23; 24:1). It was 'the magical animal *par excellence*',[54] as is still recalled by the symbol of the medical profession today! By its

---

[51] Ricoeur, pp.256f.

[52] Dubarle, p.62n., quotes Eichrodt as an Old Testament scholar who asserts the merits of the assimilation of the snake and Satan.

[53] François Laplantine, *Le philosophe et la violence* (Paris: PUF, 1976), p.65n., sees that this subterfuge dates back to the very beginnings of tragedy: man seeks to remove his own guilt by projecting evil on to God.

[54] Barth, p.288, quoting T. C. Vriezen.

chthonic origin it represented the attraction of occult mysteries and of the experiences of darkness (*cf.* Pr. 9:17). Through its cunning and suppleness it provided the image of the way that religious influences work. Erwin Reisner has even imagined that the resemblance *'ārôm/'ārûm* (2:25/3:1) signified 'that the snake by its *intelligence* was closer to mankind in his nakedness than were the other animals, and that, consequently, *intelligent* and *naked* meant the same thing in their deepest sense'.[55] Whether or not the nakedness of mankind (which distinguishes him from the other mammals) is the sign of his possession of spirit, the suppleness of the snake easily represents cunning, which is an attribute of the mind. There is nothing arbitrary about seeing in the snake, in Genesis, the representation of the lying spirit which empowers paganism. This we believe to have been the thought of the writer.

We need take only one more step in order to align ourselves with the book of Revelation in its elucidation of Genesis. In the light of later revelation, what name are we to give to that spirit which constantly opposed the LORD and sought to turn Israel away from him, unless it is the devil and Satan? All the items in the text can be rendered without difficulty. Just as the stealthy snake appears more cunning than any other animal, so was the Adversary the most intelligent of all the creatures of his order. He was the first to rebel and he became the tempter of mankind, particularly through the pernicious methods suggested by the symbolism of the snake. He is as certainly cursed as the serpent eats the dust.

The historicity of the material

The mediator of revelation who rewrote the first *tôl^edôt* in order that they might provide instruction (*tôrâ*) for Israel – Moses, if we must put a name to him – slipped a *doctrine* into his colourful, dramatic account of man's first disobedience. In view of our study to date, we no longer have any doubt on the question. By definite suggestion, he tells us that at the heart of sin lies the claim to autonomy, that sin is rooted deep in our hearts by doubt and covetousness, that it overthrows the created order, that it is both weakness and arrogance, and that it brings alienation to the human race, to the advantage of that spirit of false wisdom

[55] E. Reisner, *Der Daemon und sein Bild.*

which corrupts the religion of men. For those who have seen these lessons, there yet remains the weightiest question. What is the ultimate object of our clear-sighted author? While he tells his story so well, playing with words and images, to what reality is he referring? Is he pointing to a specific event which occurred once only, or is he trying to present the timeless features of human experience in all ages and in all places? Is this story basically history, or is it to be classed as a myth, a condensed summary of a theory of existence, presenting in dramatized form creatures that symbolically portray aspects of the human condition?[56] Did the change from innocence to guilt take place in the space-time continuum, or is it rather a picture of the enigma of guilt as one of the many phenomena of human existence?

The traditional view has held firmly to the historicity of the narrative. The majority of critical scholars today, however, treat the second tablet as a mythical story, revised merely in order to fit the monotheism of the Old Testament. They willingly emphasize that the era of rationalistic scorn for the value of myth has long since passed, and that they confer value on Genesis by reading from it a deeper and more universal truth than that of isolated facts. Faced with this choice, it would be pointless to equivocate. While retaining our flexibility and objectivity, we must also avoid any ambiguity in our response.[57] The stakes, as we shall show, are considerable.

Let us recall first what we settled when we were considering how to approach Genesis.[58] The presence of symbolic elements in the text in no way contradicts the historicity of its central meaning. To argue that the use of figurative devices reveals the

---

[56] The seventh (1982) edition of *The Concise Oxford Dictionary* reads: '**myth** *n.* traditional narrative usu. involving supernatural or fancied persons etc. and embodying popular ideas on natural or social phenomena etc.'. *Le Petit Robert* reads: 'A fabulous narrative, often of popular origin, which presents beings which, in a symbolical form of the forces of nature, personify aspects of the human condition'.

[57] Ambiguity persists in Renckens' treatment, p.164: he finds in the text and metaphysical thesis 'transposed into a chronological and material dimension', but later (pp.256ff. esp. p.261) he gives good arguments in favour of historicity. Dubarle, who has provided several of our arguments, is clearer in his chapter on *Genesis*, published with the first edition in 1957, than in the concluding chapter added in the 1967 edition. In the latter he seeks for 'an intermediary position', admitting that the narrative depicts 'not a rigorously individual event, but a universal condition transmitted in the human heritage' (p.194). It would certainly be possible to conceive of an intermediary position that was totally clear of any ambiguity: the fall could have been the act of a numerous human race, at the beginning of our history, which was at first innocent and later sinful; in this way historicity would be kept, but the individual couple could be jettisoned. This solution, however, would have few advantages and would run up against several of the considerations that we shall show.

[58] *Cf.* above, ch.1, pp. 15ff.

nature of the narrative, showing that it is a literary fiction used to make a synthetic representation of sin in all men and women, would be an inexcusably strong-armed approach. The Bible gives us too many examples of most varied styles of presenting historical facts by means of images, symbols and allegories, to prevent us from confusing the two distinct categories: language and the actual subject.

☐   Our study of the characteristics of the narrative and the light shed on it by the New Testament have clearly revealed as figurative the two trees in the middle of the garden, the 'character' of the snake, perhaps the four rivers and also the removal and shaping of the rib. But it would be arbitrary to deduce from there that Genesis 2 – 3 is the mythical expression of a general truth. Likewise, to reject the symbolic use of language as does E. J. Young in order to defend the essential historicity of the content implies an unwarranted uniformity of form and content.[59] In our opinion that great evangelical scholar is making an unfortunate transposition from the art of warfare to the art of reading. The interpretation of the various details seems in his view to be a bulwark in the strategic question of the central historical reference. To allow one single symbol would seem to him a concession of ground to the opponent who would then advance closer to the heart of the battle-ground. But exegesis is not called to establish a series of fortresses, like the 'hedge' of supplementary commandments that the Pharisees built around the Law. Its vocation is the quest for truth – the meaning of the Word, nothing more and nothing less. Derek Kidner, an equally orthodox exegete, comments more cautiously: 'it may still be an open question whether the account transcribes the facts or translates them: *i.e.*, whether it is a narrative comparable to such a passage as 2 Samuel 11 (which is the straight story of David's sin) or to 2 Samuel 12:1–6 (which presents the same event translated into quite other terms that interpret it)'.[60]

Even in the case of a 'translation' that is full of imagery, it is legitimate to retain the notion of historicity, since it is a question of the communication of facts which occurred, of a 'true knowledge of the past', however far we may be from the methods of investigation and composition of history in the scientific sense.[61] Of course, the symbolism of the language would be equally suitable if we had to give up the historicity of the text, if it were completely

---

[59] Young III, pp.48ff.   [60] Kidner, p.66.   [61] Dubarle, p.53, *cf.* p.49 n.1.

symbol. Thus, once the two issues of form and content are properly distinguished, the real problem is not to know if we have a historical account of the fall, but the account of a historical fall. James Orr, a stout defender of biblical truth, had already perceived this at the end of the nineteenth century: he considered 'very probably' that the third chapter of Genesis was 'an old tradition clothed with an oriental allegory', but said: 'The truth incorporated in the narrative, the fall of man from an original state of purity, I consider vital for the Christian vision'.[62] Is this 'truth' so vital? Is it indeed the meaning of the passage? There lies the question. □

What arguments are employed by those who class Genesis 2 – 3 as myth? They appeal to the collective meaning of the name *'āḏām*, which means mankind; the name, it is said, reveals the intention of recording universal experience.[63] Then, the similarities with mythological material provide general corroboration. As there is a striking lack of substantial parallels, however, emphasis is laid on similarity in the method of composition. It is evident that the writer had no eyewitness accounts at his disposal when he was writing about the garden of Eden, and it is supremely unlikely that an exact account could have been handed down the centuries without being changed, so that the story in Genesis must be taken as the product of an imaginative projection into the past, starting from the conditions of the writer's present existence. And that is equivalent to myth. In order to understand properly, continues the argument, one must sympathize with the author's understanding of the enigma of existence which he expresses through imagery, instead of clinging stubbornly (like orthodox exegesis) to the fictitious historical information that he appears to provide.[64] Lastly, the decisive conviction which lends substantial strength to the preceding arguments is stated bluntly by Paul Ricoeur: 'Every effort to save the letter of the story as a true history is vain and hopeless. What we know, as men of science, about the beginnings of mankind leaves no place for such a primordial event'.[65] Ricoeur, who is the most penetrating thinker in his camp, relies essentially on his scientific certainties in order to reject 'the passage from myth to mythology', a fatal transition which takes as a causal explanation what is in fact an archetype of human

[62] James Orr, *The Christian View of God and the World* (Grand Rapids: Eerdmans, 1960 reprint), p.185.

[63] *E.g.*, C. Tresmontant, quoted by Dubarle, p.197, n.2.

[64] Westermann *C*, pp.119f., strongly opposes the notion of historical information.

[65] Ricoeur, p.235.

157

experience.[66] From this modern position he draws the assurance to make the following denunciation: 'The harm that has been done to souls, during the centuries of Christianity, first by literal interpretation of the story of Adam, and then by the confusion of this myth, treated as history, with later speculations, principally Augustinian, about original sin, will never adequately be told'.[67] In taking this step, Ricoeur seems to us quite typical. Doubt about the historicity of the 'original sin' has come about with the reconstruction of the past by Science. Such doubt is merely the other side of faith in a rival 'history' – or that is at least understood as a rival.

Our diagnosis of the strongest motivation behind the 'mythical' interpretation already suggests the position we shall adopt. More substantial arguments would be necessary to sweep away our conviction, at least in so far as our exegesis is intended to remain free of all outside factors. The last argument, which is also the major one, is out of court, if we wish to avoid a scientific authority being imposed on the text. Does Genesis itself indicate that it is outlining an archetype of universal validity rather than the historical origin of evil and death? Or indeed, does the larger biblical context of the narrative imply this? If that is not the case, it is better to recognize the fact, in order to gauge the distance that separates this conception of origins from that of the natural sciences. It is also better to recognize it in order to make a choice if necessary, than to attempt a salvage operation on the old story by separating 'myth' and 'mythology'.[68]

☐   As for making oneself the spokesman of Science in order to exclude irrevocably the occurrence of the first act of disobedience, he is a bold man who ventures so far. Ricoeur surely shows such boldness in expressing himself as he does. 'What we know about the beginning of mankind' surely leaves a lot of space. The lines that have been drawn are no more than dotted lines. The data are fragmentary and the gaps are enormous. Supposing one neverthe-less accepts the current evolutionary sketch, nothing is easier than

---

[66] The phrases come from his *Conflit des interprétations* (Paris: Seuil, 1969), pp.279f.

[67] Ricoeur, p.239. It is significant that a thinker with such a scientific approach should have no other real recourse for a thesis that is so important in his view. In his long footnote criticizing Lagrange and Dubarle (pp.235f.), he has only one more consideration to advance: 'It is hard to see how the story as a whole could have a bearing on real history when all the circumstances, taken one by one, are interpreted symbolically'. Such fallacious reasoning we have already refuted, *i.e.* the confusion between form and content that is contradicted by such texts as Ezk. 16 and Rev. 12.

[68] The ambiguous concessions made by Dubarle in 1967 are clearly consent made under the pressure of evolutionist thought (pp.187, 198ff.).

slipping in a 'miraculous parenthesis', to use Labourdette's phrase.[69] If we admit that there are revealed reasons for so doing, nothing in the observable phenomena today rules it out absolutely. And 'What we know'! What do we *know*? The bold assurance relies on a certain naïvety. Have we forgotten the fragility of the reconstructions of the distant past, all the hypotheses – and they are no more than that – that have been verified by nothing more than hope? In the most likely of theories operates a coefficient of conjecture, because of the conditions of study, not to mention the clandestine metaphysics that may enter via the diplomatic bag.

The rest of the evidence is rather thin. The original features of the narrative of Genesis 2 – 3 far outshine the outward resemblances with the documents it is compared with. Not only is the heart of the story unique, but also its tone and atmosphere, its style and 'spirit'. 'In this respect,' writes von Rad, 'the reticence, indeed soberness and calm of the biblical story, is especially noticeable in contrast to the arrogant and harsh colours in the myths of other peoples.'[70]   □

If we recognize that the first event of history is reached by means of mental reconstruction,[71] intuitive and imaginative at first and then taken up by the theologian, we by no means admit thereby that its historicity is unimportant for the writer. It is precisely because the historical cause is so important to him that he reconstructs what occurred. Indeed, he starts from contemporary human experience, but not merely to express his opinion on the matter. Like Pascal, he is seeking to throw light on the incomprehensible monstrosity of man the sinner by disclosing how, through historical actions, man became what he is. The myths around him were already seeking to explain reality by telling how (and therefore why) it came into existence.[72] Genesis aims to supply the true reconstruction, guided and guaranteed by divine inspiration, over against the fantasies and errors reconstructed by others. There is nothing in that which allows us to take the event as a symbol. Lastly, the first argument that we mentioned, which directs attention to the

---

[69] Quoted by Dubarle, p.199, who recognizes that such a reconciliation 'is not absurd, considered in itself' (p.200).

[70] Von Rad, p.97. *Cf.* p.85, where he contrasts the transparency and lucidity of the narrative with myth.

[71] Dubarle, p.190n., quotes Renckens, K. Rahner and L. Alonso-Schökel as sharing this opinion. We admit that it is probable, without excluding a more immediate form of revelation.

[72] Mircea Eliade, *Le Sacré et le profane* (Paris: Gallimard, 1965), p.94.

collective sense of *'āḏām*, either breaks down a door that is already open, or else falls into the trap of inaccuracy. If the argument means that the Man in Genesis does not act as any mere individual, but represents humanity, concentrating it in his person and carrying its destiny, then the orthodox interpretation which holds to a historical account has never said anything different. The disobedience in the garden of Eden is of interest to the author and to us because that man is the Head of mankind, with whom God concluded the creational covenant and *in whom* everyone has his definition and standing before God. But if the argument seeks to deny that *'āḏām* is also the actual name of the first man, then we have a head-on collision with the text, starting from Genesis 5:3ff.[73] None of the reasons, therefore, that have been put forward to identify Genesis 2 – 3 with myths will stand up to close scrutiny.

It is not sufficient, however, in order to assert the text's historicity, simply to refute contrary arguments. On what positive data is the orthodox view founded?

The contrast between our narrative and the myths deserves that we consider it *in its central thrust*. No-one has put this better than Ricoeur: 'The etiological myth of Adam is the most extreme attempt to separate the origin of evil from the origin of the good; its intention is to set up a *radical* origin of evil distinct from the more *primordial* origin of the goodness of things'.[74] For theogonic myths, such as the Babylonian ones, evil is incorporated into the cosmos as one of the primary ingredients of reality. Heidel reminds us that in Babylon man is held to have been *created* evil.[75] For tragic myths, an obscure malignancy is hidden in God himself, a cruelty is concealed in fate, so that evil is still situated 'in the basic principle'. For the myth of the exiled soul, whose misfortune arises from being mingled with the body, and for allied themes of antecedent, prehuman, ahistorical sin, which U. Bianchi contrasts with the Christian

---

[73] On *'āḏām* as a proper noun, without the article, *cf.* Gesenius-Kautzsch, paras. 125f and 126e. The Septuagint kept *Adam*, in Greek, treated as a proper noun, from Gn. 2 and for the rest of our narrative. In 4:25 it could be the proper noun in Hebrew; at the end of 2:20 the word is used without an article, but the exact implication is not clear. Other usages for the first man as an individual (apart from Ho. 6:7): Goldstain, p.90 n., instances Jb. 15:7 ('Are you Adam, born the first?'); 31:33 ('Have I like Adam hidden my rebellion?'); Ps. 73:5 ('Like Adam they are not stricken'); R. Gordis, *art. cit., JBL* 76 (1957), p.127, n.16, interprets Ps. 82:7 in the same way ('Like Adam you shall die').

[74] Ricoeur, p.233.   [75] Heidel, p.126.

doctrine,[76] evil is inextricably linked with the metaphysical composition of mankind. In the various myths, then, it remains something prior. Now, if evil belongs to being, how can we protest against it? How can we repent of it? Ricoeur understood the point clearly: 'Evil becomes scandalous at the same time as it becomes historical'.[77] It is the exclusive characteristic of the Genesis narrative to bring this out. Consequently the firm etiological purpose that it manifests – to take account of the presence in creation (made by a God who is perfectly good) of shame, fear, tyranny, suffering for the woman in childbirth, toil and weariness for the labouring man, and death[78] – is far weightier than the corresponding half-hearted efforts of the myths. It requires us to take as essential the historicity of the fall.

☐   Myths, it is true, claim to give an explanation of the origin by telling the story of it. But because they want to integrate evil with ultimate reality, they tend to function as timeless models, a balancing of formulas and an ordering of relations. On this point the structuralist studies of Lévi-Strauss link up with Mircea Eliade's propositions from the standpoint of the phenomenological approach to religions. While looking like history, myth is profoundly allergic to it – it seeks to destroy it by the repetition of the archetypal pattern which keeps evil firmly fixed within it. That is the view that Eliade continually illustrates. Myth seeks to stabilize the dialectic between nature and culture, acts as a tool of logic to reconcile contrary elements and mediates between the rival forces. That is the analysis of Lévi-Strauss and of those whom he has influenced. These two quite different methods converge in a remarkable manner. The etiology offered by the myths is not really intended to be historical; rather, it is ontological — Eliade spoke of an 'ontological obsession'[79] – or systematic. That is why they are not completely distorted if they are treated as pure archetypes. But with Genesis the case is completely the reverse. It stands in clear opposition to the myths by giving evil a historical

[76] Quoted by Goldstain, p.141n.
[77] Ricoeur, p.203.
[78] J. de Fraine, *La Bible et l'origine de l'homme* (Paris: Desclée de Brouwer, 1961), p.51, n.3, has seen clearly that the 'mentality' of the author is 'etiological and therefore "historical", i.e. anxious to base his narrative on facts'. Payne, p.19, recalls also that etiological does not mean non-historical: 'the best explanation of present circumstances is presumably the true facts about how they arose'.
[79] M. Eliade, *op. cit.,* p.81.

161

beginning and by refusing to integrate it into a cosmic order.[80] It is impossible to respect its intention without affirming its historicity. ☐

Renckens recognized this point: 'It is most certainly the sacred author's intention – for this touches the heart of his message – to *explain* our present situation. This Adam of whom he speaks is not only a reflection, an image, but also the *real cause* of our predicament'. And he adds: 'This causality is only clearly evident, if Adam was indeed the real ancestor of all'.[81] We would not be as categorical as Renckens when he uses the word 'only'; it is possible to imagine a causality which is not dependent on blood relationship! The role of head of the human race that implicitly devolved on the first man in the conclusion of the covenant counts for more than does his mere paternity. Nevertheless Renckens puts his finger clearly on a second proof of the historical intention of the text. It is as the father and mother of the human generations, of 'all living', that Adam and Eve figure in the narrative. The mention of their posterity makes this clear to anyone who might not have grasped it.[82] The genealogies that follow will give further confirmation. Adam is considered, therefore, as a character who lived in the past. The events in the garden of Eden must affect all human beings in the same way as the deeds of the patriarchs influence the destiny of their descendants, from the faith of Abraham to the pre-eminence of Joseph, with the sole difference that the role of the head of the human race is unique and more decisive. Now this idea supposes that he is situated in time at the very head of the race.

The plan of Genesis brings out very clearly the link, within the same linear history, of the offence of the first couple and of the events of the second millennium BC. The tablet of the Eden narrative is only the first of the *tôlᵉḏôṯ* sections which form the body of the work, after the prologue. In spite of the great breach caused by the flood, and in spite of the different form that history must take when no trace of the ages in question survives, the author has only one series of *tôlᵉḏôṯ* and invites us to place Genesis 2 – 3 at the beginning of a sequence of events that are

[80] Edmund Leach, *Genesis as Myth and Other Essays* (London: Cape, 1969), pp.7–23, has attempted a structural analysis of Genesis, but it is brief and carries little conviction. Manipulation is obvious. For example, it requires that the sin of Adam and Eve was incest, Eve being his sister, and that the sin of Cain also included homosexual incest (p.15)! We do not deny *a priori* the possibility of a structural study of our text, nor its interest; we think that in it sin should appear neither as one of the poles of a binary opposition of reality, nor as the mediator of a position (for there is no logical mediation between life and death).

[81] Renckens, p.261.   [82] Dubarle, p.58.

in principle localizable and datable. Dubarle points out that Genesis 'creates an imperceptible continuity between the memoirs that are properly speaking historical and the traditional narratives that deal with origins', and he makes the careful observation: 'Amongst the other peoples of the ancient world the myths did not undergo a similar treatment'.[83]

The broader context of divine revelation as a whole confirms that no other interpretation is possible. The analogy of faith and the light mutually shed on one another by the various parts of Scripture give a clear verdict. The brief allusions that can be gathered suggest already that the inspired writers understood the transgression of Genesis 3 as a specific event (Jb. 31:33; Ho. 6:7; 2 Cor. 11:3; 1 Tim. 2:14).

The reference in Ezekiel 28 points in the same direction (in particular v.15). The Johannine texts which refer to the snake of the garden of Eden associate him with the beginning (*archē, archaios*), which would be pointless if Genesis simply set forth universal human experience (Jn. 8:41–44; Rev. 12:9; 20:2). Two passages especially go further: they develop a line of thought which presupposes the historicity of the fall.

The first requires only a brief commentary. Jesus explains that Moses, in spite of the Creator's intention for marriage, permitted an easy divorce because of the need to accommodate mankind's hardness of heart (Mt. 19:3–8). As Dubarle has shown clearly, nothing is further from Jesus' mind than to criticize Moses for conniving with evil. As always, he unreservedly approves of his law as the expression of the will of God (*cf.* vv.18f. in the same chapter!).[84] Jesus does not see tolerance as having only a human origin. It is not inferior for being later, for Jesus does not habitually follow the rule that an ancient law prevails over a more recent one. Dubarle's summing up is excellent:

'The word, "From the beginning it was not so" brings into direct opposition not a law, strictly speaking, but a primitive state of things which conformed with the divine ideal for marriage and a later law which made concessions to the hardness of the human heart. The blame, if blame there is, falls not on the fact of the concession but on the attitudes of human beings that have made it necessary.'[85]

In order to reason in this manner, Jesus must posit the succes-

---

[83] *Ibid.*, p.53.   [84] *Ibid.*, p.106.   [85] *Ibid.*, p.107.

sion of two orders, that of the upright heart and that of the slavery to evil, *and hence the historicity of the rupture between the two,* of the evil rebellion that broke the original harmony and brought about the new situation of hardening (*cf.* Ec. 7:29 for an earlier statement concerning this succession). Will a believing Christian look for a more authoritative exegete than his Lord?

The apostle Paul's commentary on the effects of Adam's sin in his famous antithesis between Adam and Christ (Rom. 5:12ff.) remains faithful to Jesus' interpretation and is the final weapon in the hands of those who uphold the historical interpretation.[86] It could not possibly be any clearer. Paul underlines the sequence of the events: 'sin came into the world through one man and death through sin, and so death spread to all men' (Rom. 5:12). He underlines the definite individuality of the transgressor and continually contrasts the *one* with the *many* (or 'all') – from one man springs the cause, upon many fall the effects (vv. 15, 18f.). He specifies concerning a whole category of men affected by Adam's deed that they did *not* sin in the way that Adam did (v.14), which is completely contrary to what is postulated by the mythical or symbolical interpretaton. Paul underlines the connections between the divisions of the historical sequence; after the introduction of sin he distinguishes a stage 'from Adam to Moses', and then another from the introduction of the law to the coming of Christ (vv.13f., 20).

☐   The Epistle to the Romans dots all the i's so thoroughly that those who deny Adam's historicity are forced to use pretty poor bolt-holes. Thus Franz Leenhardt gives us the grand assurance that, for the apostle, Adam 'is humanity', and that in Genesis 'he could read the statement of a fundamental structure of human existence'. The reasons he gives are the freedom and pertinence with which the apostle applied the pages of Genesis in Romans 7, and 'the mythical mode that he uses here to speak of sin and death'.[87] The phrase 'mythical mode' is the totally subjective assessment of the modernist theologian without the first vestige of proof. As for the description of the awakening of covetousness (Rom. 7:7–11), we do not decline to detect in it a reference to the temptation in Eden, but it is by no means a proven fact. At any

---

[86] *E.g.* Young III, p.61.

[87] F. J. Leenhardt, *L'Epître de saint Paul aux Romains* (Paris: Delachaux & Niestlé, 1957), p.83. For a different perspective, see John Murray, *The Epistle to the Romans* (Grand Rapids: Eerdmans, 1960).

rate, there is no explicit reference, nor is there any interpretation of Genesis in that passage that is contrary to the historical interpretation of Genesis 3. Leenhardt carefully avoids commenting on the contrast which Paul so often underlines between the uniqueness of Adam and the great number of people who suffer because of his sin. He suggests that Jewish speculation had extended the character of Adam 'to the dimensions of a collective, cosmic being'.[88] But he gives no evidence of any sympathy on Paul's part for such speculations. Nor does he establish that this extension has dissolved the distinction between the individuality of the ancestor and mankind collectively, a distinction which contemporary Judaism expressed forcefully at the same time as human solidarity in the famous passage from the Apocrypha:

> O Adam, what have you done?
> For though it was you who sinned,
> the fall was not yours alone,
> but ours also who are your descendants   (2 Esdras 7:48).[89]

Paul Ricoeur, who is more concerned to limit himself to the probable, does not challenge the apostolic testimony head-on. First he seeks to minimize the references to the Adam narrative in the Bible: 'In every way the addition is belated and, in certain respects, non-essential...the Prophets ignore him...[and] Jesus himself never refers to the Adamic story'.[90] We have cited sufficient texts which invalidate these hasty conclusions. Then he attacks the Pauline passages. His tactics, calculated to deflect the force of Paul's recourse to Genesis, are most adept. It was on the model of Christ, 'as the inverse of that Christ', that the figure of Adam was set up and personified. Therefore it plays only a subsidiary and accidental part, and the construction of original sin 'is only a flying buttress'.[91] We consider that we should challenge both the premise and the deduction of this argument. Undoubtedly the apostle Paul has developed the 'Adamic' doctrine – he had received the gift of a theologian! – but by no stretch of the

[88] *Ibid.,* p.82. Note that Leenhardt, because he takes liberties with the text, also uses expressions that contradict his main thesis, *e.g.* 'Adam is the initiator of a humanity that is given over to sin and death' (p.82), and 'heirs of Adam' (p.84).

[89] The passage is found in the Jewish part of this apocalypse (chs. 4–14), which dates from the last part of the first century. It is perhaps more moving than the present Jewish tradition, but it is no less distinct. According to Dubarle, it was 'classical' to attribute death and the sufferings of this life to Adam's sin, and to attribute eternal damnation to one's own individual faults. As for the unrestrained speculations about Adam – that his head touched the sun, but that after the fall his height was reduced to fifty yards, *etc.,* – one ought not to overestimate them as representative, nor conclude that they cancelled his individuality.

[90] Ricoeur, pp.237f.   [91] *Ibid.,* p.239.

imagination did he invent the theme. Before him the importance of the first man had been already brought out, and emphasis had been placed on the transgression of Genesis 3 as the cause of the misery of Adam's descendants. To the material mentioned above we should add the forceful statements in the great intertestamental books of Ecclesiasticus (25:24) and especially The Wisdom of Solomon (1:13f.; 2:23f.). When he writes 'as in Adam all die' (1 Cor. 15:22) and that through him sin and death entered the world (Rom. 5:12), Paul is not surprising his readers with a homiletical device that he has just invented for the sake of symmetry; he is taking his stand on a very strong opinion that he shared with them. Even had the apostle's argument been a complete innovation, Ricoeur's logic would still have been strange, for he argues from the parallel with Christ in order to diminish the scope of the apostle's words. Paul linked Adam to Christ, therefore we may unlink him! If Romans 5 were merely rhetorical, it could be argued that Paul exaggerates Adam's role for rhetorical purposes; but the passage presents itself as an argued proof. It is an argument *a fortiori*, the key formula of the chapter (vv.9, 10, 15, 17). Paul wishes to prove that our present justification, by the grace of Christ, assures us of final salvation and of reigning in life (vv.9f.). His arguments follow one another without difficulty, in spite of the enthusiasm of his discourse: the transgression of the first Head of the human race had, for all those who are 'in him', the effect that we all know; the work of the second Man, the Head of the new humanity that is 'in him', must be infinitely more effective, since it restores against all expectation a situation that was bereft of hope (v.16); 'much more' are we assured in him of reigning in life more abundant.[92] The proposition concerning Adam is very far from being a 'flying buttress'; it serves here as the very foundation. To cast doubt on it is to oppose the thought of the apostle Paul and the authority of his inspiration. No device can manage to obscure the evidence: in Romans 5 and elsewhere, Holy Scripture teaches that an individual Adam existed, created upright, and that he subsequently became the initiator of sin in human history.

Precision in our reading and acceptance of the inspired Word are not optional. They take priority, and that is why we began by examining the text. They are attended, however, by blessing, a

[92] We limit ourselves to what is of interest to our discussion of Genesis. How, according to Rom. 5, the offence of Adam affects the many is another problem. The usual solutions are not entirely satisfying; perhaps we shall publish some suggestions one day.

blessing on the understanding of faith, a blessing which proclaims that the gamble of faith will be justified. As we meditate on these truths, we understand and discern what is at stake. To the arguments of exegesis we shall now add those of theology.   □

The Genesis narrative stands in contrast to the myths by reason of the historicity that it attributes to evil. The whole biblical conception of evil, we dare suggest, is inextricably linked with this unique feature. Nowhere else is evil denounced with such a tireless zeal, intransigence, horror and indignation. It is the disorder that finds no justification, the enemy and the work of the enemy. Nowhere else is the problem of guilt placed in such a central position. Nowhere else do you find such a clear insistence on the conversion of the human heart, that heart from which evil emerges and which must turn away from it. This 'nowhere else', which is plain for all to see, has an explanation, which we shall now disclose. Since elsewhere evil is inherent in the original being of reality and is part of the very definition of humanity, then elsewhere it must be excusable because it belongs to fate, and as such it must be invincible. There can therefore be no voice raised in protest against it. The myths and the philosophies that spring from them inevitably stifle the innate sense of the intolerable nature of evil, whether it is the evil one commits or the evil one suffers. But the Bible can stand as accuser and can awaken this sense, because it knows that evil was not there in the beginning, but arises from a subsequent, historical use of human freedom.

And at the same time the Bible is free to state a doctrine of God which is totally beyond the capacity of the myths. It can affirm the complete goodness of God – 'God is light and in him is no darkness at all' (1 Jn. 1:5). It can also affirm that all that is comes from him – 'For from him and through him and to him are all things' (Rom. 11:36). The myths are forced to locate evil in God or else to opt for a dualism in which evil is equal with God, in an implicit or explicit polytheism. So it is crystal clear that in the affirmation of the historical fall all the main themes of divine revelation come together.

□   What is amazing is that Ricoeur sees clearly the link between the historicity of the fall and ethical monotheism, as well as the indictments and appeals of the prophets: 'By thus dividing the Origin into an origin of the goodness of the created and an origin of the wickedness in history, the myth tends to satisfy the twofold confession of the Jewish believer, who acknowledges, on the one

167

hand, the absolute perfection of God and, on the other hand, the radical wickedness of man. This twofold confession is the very essence of his repentance'. Ricoeur sees clearly the need to distinguish finitude, which is metaphysical, from guilt. But he makes the tragic mistake of supposing that he can keep the biblical sense of sin *without* its historical beginning. Instead of a temporal sequence, he speaks of the states of innocence and sin as superimposed 'in the Instant'.[93] That is the content of the meaning that he extracts from the myth-symbol. But his procedure is illegitimate. The purpose of the Genesis narrative is to point us back to a real event, contrary to all the mythical systems. To seek to preserve the historical significance by suppressing it is like trying to swim in an empty pool.[94] Responsible thinking does not evade the choice: either evil belongs to the very being of humanity and one must be resigned to couple evil with finitude (or some other dialectical category), or else one must recognize in it what is unjustifiable (of which one must repent) and what is *inhuman*, and an origin must be assigned to it. Furthermore, since the spread of evil is universal, this origin must be supposed as unique for the whole immense body of the human race – in fact, as it is presented in Genesis.[95] In point of fact, Ricoeur does not escape from the grip of this either/or; and if anyone could, he could! This exemplary thinker demonstrates in fact that you cannot have it both ways, for the meaning changes. Having so well understood the intention of Genesis, Ricoeur goes into reverse and crosses it with the message of the pagan tragic myth. This latter, he assures us, is 'invincible', and makes us go beyond ethical monotheism

[93] Ricoeur, pp.243, 251.

[94] Ricoeur is the ablest of a large number of writers for whom the narrative expresses the following intuition: the sin in which we are born is something *other* than the component parts of our nature; it is a use of liberty and of responsible conduct. According to Dubarle, p.48, n.2, this interpretation goes back to Kant, as does that which sees in the fall an advancement of human awareness. Emil Brunner, *The Christian Doctrine of Creation and Redemption (Dogmatics* 2) (London: Lutterworth, 1952), shows the same illogical clarity as Ricoeur: 'We cannot believe, in Christian and Biblical terms, without holding firmly to the distinction between Creation and Sin, and therefore to the idea of a Fall' (p.51); and yet for him it is impossible after Copernicus to believe in a historical Adam!

[95] In *The Concept of Anxiety*, Kierkegaard seems to have carefully retained the sequence of innocence and sin: 'If he was not innocent before becoming guilty, he never became guilty' (p.35). But he refuses to give Adam a special role. He attacks orthodox dogmatics and makes the individual, just as much as Adam, 'both himself and the human race'; each one of us loses an innocence analagous to Adam's in the same way as he lost his. Then how is the universality of sin to be explained? After Adam, the first man, Kierkegaard admits a quantitative increase in anxiety and sinfulness (pp.57ff.), but this mere 'quantitative approximation' (p.57) does not explain any more than in Adam's case the qualitative leap by which the individual posits sin (pp.57, 61ff.). Since the universality of sin does not amaze

(the God who desires the Good and only the Good); there are 'aspects of the Ineluctable', of fateful ruin.[96] This slide on Ricoeur's part, which also affects his interpretation of the snake, brings a solemn warning: one only remains firm in one's grasp of biblical truth by abiding resolutely by the historical interpretation of Genesis 3. □

The second issue is no less weighty than the first. And, once again, Ricoeur was fully aware of it. While myth seeks to annul time and invites us to repeat the archetypal motions which restore evil 'to its place', the narrative that makes evil begin *afterwards* permits a totally different concept of the remedy: 'Neither can Salvation any longer be identified with the foundation of the world; it can no longer be an aspect of the drama of creation re-enacted in the cult; it becomes itself an original historical dimension like evil'.[97] To which we can only respond, Amen! If only the illogical Ricoeur had remembered these words of the lucid Ricoeur when he was expounding Romans 5! Paul's argument, making the link between the two Adams, between the Head according to the original covenant and the Head according to the new covenant, specified this precise logic: to a historical sin corresponded a historical redemption. If evil were an ingredient of humanity as such, the only way of deliverance would be by stripping off one's humanity or creaturely condition, and such dreams of divinization are alien to the Bible. And in this whole process the cross of Christ is reduced to a mere symbol.[98]

Kierkegaard so much, presumably sin, despite the 'leap', is linked with the metaphysical contradiction in the synthesis that constitutes man, and which implies anxiety in innocence; and, since 'In innocence, man is not qualified as spirit' (p.41), sin seems inevitable in the development of man. Here Kierkegaard moves away from the intention of Genesis and of Scripture as a whole. If he refuses to recognize that Adam has a role as the Head of humanity, and if he has no place for the Pauline category, 'in Adam', this is because of the same absolutization of individual liberty which makes him speak of a contradiction in the constitution of man. With a creaturely liberty, grounded in God, measured by him and held in his hand, an organism of liberties that are united (but not 'one') and distinct (but not isolated) is possible.

[96] Ricoeur, pp.306ff., 314ff., 317ff. This concession has connections with other parts of Ricoeur's work, in particular in the 'disproportion' of the finite and the infinite, which constitute man, as *fallibility*. The other writers likewise, when they reject the historical fall, end up linking sin with man's metaphysical situation. For Kant, evil does not lie in the tangible world and remains an inscrutable enigma; but its presence is related to the antinomy of Reason (liberty) and the world of the senses (nature). E. Brunner, *op. cit.*, pp.100f., gives up the attempt to provide a coherent account.

[97] Ricoeur, p.203.

[98] For the consequence of this in Ricoeur's thought, see our study, 'L'herméneutique selon Paul Ricoeur', *Hokhma* 3 (1976), pp.37–40.

The liquidation of sin 'once for all' in the datable, localizable event of Golgotha, on the contrary, presupposes the teaching of Genesis. Twice the same structure, instituted by God, has come into play: the organic solidarity which united the members of one humanity under its Head, and gives him power to be its representative.[99] On both occasions it had to be a real act, otherwise the second Adam would not have been able to put right the work of the first. The obedience of the unique Man on that Good Friday has set free a great multitude because the evil which held us enslaved had its origin in history, and we all contracted it through the offence of the first man, on that first evil day. For a historical sin there is a historical redemption.

The cry from the cross, 'It is finished', is nothing short of the gospel. Along with ethical monotheism and the doctrine of sin, we see that in the debate on the 'historicity of the content' of Genesis 3 nothing less than the gospel is at stake. But let no-one be deceived by our words, 'at stake'. The person who has received the gospel knows very well that in staking his faith he has won. The harmony of the inspired testimonies and the very beauty of the text of Genesis had already told him as much.

---

[99] The structure that has been called 'corporate personality' (though we prefer to speak of the 'Head of humanity', by reason of the covenant) does not operate in the same way in the two cases. Rom. 5:15f. emphasizes that there is a difference. Adam acts as a representative, but not as a substitute; he constitutes as guilty those sinners who will be born of him. Christ bears the sins of his people in their place: he constitutes sinners as righteous. We enter the humanity of Adam by natural birth, we enter into the new humanity in Christ by the new birth, by the work of the Spirit and the decision of faith.

8
The wages of sin

'The wages of sin is death' (Rom. 6:23). When the apostle Paul formulated this axial truth of biblical teaching, he was no doubt thinking of the protective clause in the first covenant: 'in the day that you shall eat of it, DYING you shall die' (Gn. 2:17). After the account of the mindless rebellion by which mankind broke the covenant, what else is there to tell except the coming of death?

In the Bible, death is the reverse of life – it is not the reverse of existence. To die does not mean to cease to be, but in biblical terms it means 'cut off from the land of the living', henceforth unable to act, and to enter another condition. Even in the Old Testament, when the revelation of the life beyond is shrouded in mist, and despite the affinity between death and destruction, since death disintegrates the power to live, this condition is not confused with the extinction of being. It is a diminished existence, but nevertheless an existence. Proof of this is found in the representation of the departed as meeting in 'the house appointed for all living' (Jb. 30:23), who are 'joined to their fathers' and who greet and speak to one another (Is. 14; Ezk. 32). The whole question of literary freedom affects only the details here; the passages presuppose the idea of death that we have described.[1]

[1] Note too that the dead can receive the name of *yidd$^{e^r}$ōnîm* (from *yāda'*, to know), Lv. 19:31. R. H. Gundry, *Soma in Biblical Theology with Emphasis on Pauline Anthropology* (CUP, 1976), pp.128ff., underlines that the reunion of the dead with his fathers does not piling up the bones in the same tomb, for the phrase is often used – in fact, most of the time – when there is no common burial place. The texts that are brought against our position are

This is important for Genesis. Such an idea of death can indeed broaden and diversify. If dying were ceasing to be, nothing more could be said about it beyond that simple statement; but since dying is still existing, other changes in existence will, by extension, be able to bear the name of 'death'. In all the experiences of pain, discomfort, discord and separation, we can recognize a kind of funeral procession. (How forcefully Calvin put it, when recalling the thousand diseases our body carries: 'A man cannot go about unburdened by many forms of his own destruction, and without drawing out a life enveloped, as it were, with death'.)[2] This is the precise viewpoint of Genesis 3. The narrative shows us that the threat 'You shall die' is fulfilled in a multiplicity of ways, by a whole succession of disastrous changes. In order to take full account of the doctrine of the text 'the wages of sin', we must follow the progress of the gangrene that it describes and announces.

The picture of 'wages' in the apostolic statement corresponds to the great biblical theme of retribution: 'For the LORD is a God of retribution; he will *repay* in full' (Je. 51:56, NIV; literally, 'PAYING, he will repay').[3] In this regard we must point out, however, that the Bible shows the connection between sin and its penalty in two different lights. Sometimes death follows evil as its inevitable consequence, by virtue of an internal necessity: 'He who sows to his own flesh will from the flesh reap corruption' (Gal. 6:8) – a kind of biblical equivalent of *karma*! Sometimes death on an individual scale appears to be specially inflicted according to the decree of the divine Judge, and the sanction is applied in the natural course of events. The two presentations are by no means mutually exclusive. They complement each other and protect each other mutually against any misunderstanding on the part of the reader. The first reminds us that there is nothing arbitrary in the judgment of the Judge: the rebellion against the Giver of being and life can lead only to

---

either parts of a debate (Ec. 3:19, but see Ec. 12:7), or else moving passages where death is viewed negatively in contrast to this life (*e.g.* Is. 38:18f.). The New Testament, of course, in agreement with Judaism, also refutes the idea of death as annihilation (Lk. 16:23ff.; 2 Pet. 2:9, *etc.*).

[2] Calvin, *Institutes* I. xvii. 10. 1 Cor. 15:43, 53 justifies the association of weakness with mortality.

[3] For this reason we may be sure that it is God who pays the wages of Rom. 6:23, just as he makes the gift (*charisma*) of eternal life to those who are in Jesus Christ. The word could be used of the gratuity that a Roman soldier would sometimes receive as a supplement to his pay.

death. The second emphasizes that the law of destructive corruption is not a mere physical fact: it operates in the spiritual order, as divine justice. In the first we see God reacting to evil as the immanent God, and in the second as Transcendent One. This duality is to be found also in Genesis. Some of the elements of the funeral procession have the appearance of 'spontaneous' effects of the fall, and others, defined by the sentence passed by the LORD, look like additional punishments. We shall classify them in this double manner, therefore, for the sake of our study, before exposing ourselves to the rays of light which manage, in the final part of our chapter, to pierce the ever-increasing darkness of death. But let us remember that even the 'spontaneous' effect is an effect of justice, willed by God. Even the Judge's decree is the fruit of a rigid logic: it could not have been otherwise, for God to remain God.

The effect

The sentence is executed without delay. As soon as the disobedience is committed, the beauty and harmony of existence is shattered, and in their place come shame, fear and pathetic excuses.

The narrative does not take up the word 'shame', but the deliberate contrast between 3:7 and 2:25 suggests it immediately, and it is confirmed by the couple's behaviour. For what is shame, other than a feeling of embarrassment which makes us hide? The carefree nakedness signified a perfectly transparent character, a harmony in all their relationships; and now these gifts of the Creator are lost. Can we understand, however, how shame followed the eating of the fruit? What is the reason for this consequence? It seems to us that it can be discerned in two complementary ways: in terms of vulnerability and in terms of the division within the self.

As soon as they claim to be like God (or gods) in their autonomy, these human beings, the earthlings, undertake the defence of their claim. This is an obligation, since they wish to be supreme. It is impossible for them not to discover at once the gulf between their intent and their resources. How vulnerable are they in their finitude, how tender and defenceless is their flesh. Their first reflex is to protect themselves by concealment. The threat springs in particular *between* the man and the woman. By posing each as absolute, they absolutize their

173

difference. Being face to face now means that they are opponents. By rejecting the divine reference that united them, each claims for himself and herself the position of ultimate reference. Each wishes to make the other his or her creature, an object to dominate. Each finds in the other a rival god and an independence that threatens their own. In order to get out of this war, they will dream haphazardly of total fusion, for they also absolutize their common humanity, but they will not be able to forget for a long time the danger that each holds for the other. In order to evade the aggressive or seductive look, which seeks to captivate and to capture, they attempt to cover their nakedness which is so vulnerable – and thereby they admit to it, according to the paradox of shame.[4]

At a still deeper level, the claim to know good and evil divides the human being within himself. The demands of the ego which sets itself up artificially sharpen one's conscience and self-awareness, and project us into an unhealthy hyperconscience. The bond of unity which subsists in the duality of the created conscience (knowing with oneself, and knowing oneself) is stretched to breaking-point. As a matter of plain fact, mankind cannot avoid the knowledge that the composition of his being is a fact that is not of his own making. If in his foolishness he proclaims himself to be self-created, he cannot eliminate what he has in fact been given, which he arrogantly credits to his own initiative in his pretended self-creation. As long as he recognized his whole self, including his liberty, as *given* by the Creator, he remained at peace. Now that he rejects it, he would like to hide the *givenness* of his being. The self setting itself up as autonomous resents as something alien the self as something given. So there is inner division. There is shame. There is shame about the marks of dependence which belie the assertion of self-sufficiency. There is shame over the body, which most eludes the absolute mastery we have conferred on ourselves. There is the shameful effort to regain a grip on what has eluded our mastery, by making a code of *behaviour*.[5] It is in terms of this role in our code of behaviour, an expression of the intention of

[4] Bonhoeffer has caught the paradox well: the attempt to hide is also a way of emphasizing, pp.82f. In his *Ethics* (London: Fontana, 1964), pp.20f., he returned to the subject of shame, an important theme in his thought.

[5] In the French there is a remarkable play on two distinct meanings of *la tenue*, 'discipline' and 'clothing'. In the former sense it is used of good behaviour, including the notion of restraint; in the latter sense it has the idea of uniform, or of clothes appropriate to an occasion: *e.g. tenue de soirée* is evening dress, *tenue de ville* is a lounge suit. There seems no

mankind, that clothing (by another paradox) acquires a revelatory value. The covering reveals by showing the will to cover and thereby, in the symbolism that different clothing customs have in different cultures, the image that the individual or collective will chooses to ascribe to it.

☐   If that is indeed the way that shame follows sin, we can certainly see with E. J. Young that the silly attempt by the man and the woman to cover their nakedness is 'an effort at saving themselves'. They fall to this level, 'so perverted is their reason, so dark their light, so ignorant their knowledge'.[6] But that does not justify modern-day nudism, or naturism (*cf.* the contrary teaching implied in 1 Tim. 2:9, for example). Far from it: its religious significance appears profound. Nudism is another example of pseudo-salvation. It is a desperate attempt to recover the lost Eden, with its complete openness, and to overlook the fact of sin and the upheavals it has brought. In it can be detected a tendency to extol animal life as the true life of mankind, hence the term 'naturism', and to exonerate mankind of his responsibility and privilege that raise him above the other creatures that were made on the Sixth Day. To deny the disordered state of human relationships and to repress shame is merely an illusory solution. In a world where sin has entered, clothing has become indispensable. Only in the state of marriage, by the power of common grace, does God provide for man and woman to know some reflection of the freedom of Eden without shame.   ☐

Two further questions which are connected with each other require an answer. Why in Genesis 3:7 does shame affect sexuality, as the making of 'aprons' or coverings indicates clearly enough? And how are we to distinguish between two types of shame: the shame that belongs to evil and the shame that we call modesty? If man and woman cover themselves because they feel themselves vulnerable beneath the eye of each other, it is not so surprising that they hide what differentiates them. Since sexuality gives their impoverished relationship its specific form, each can be apprehensive of being no more than a sexual object for the other. Without forming the thought precisely, they no doubt experienced the feeling intuitively in the form of a sense

---

neat way of conveying the dual meaning in English. It should be pointed out, however, that this is not just a semantic trick: the author is clearly exploring a profound point. The two senses were once current in English, too, though the former survives chiefly in a military context and in the expression, 'a dressing down' (translator's note).

   [6] Young III, p.69.

of unease that they had not known before. But above all sexuality engraves in the flesh of man and woman their purpose in God's design, their being-each-for-the-other. Sexuality preaches the message, 'It is not good that the man should be alone', and seeks to open up existence. The message is directly contrary to the fundamental desire of sin: autonomy, self-sufficiency. The man who wishes to be like God is ashamed of this visible reminder in his body that he is not self-sufficient. He makes himself a loin-cloth to bridle the formidable power of sexuality, over which his mastery is all the more diminished because sin has overthrown the hierarchies in nature. He needs the discipline of dress to permit the will to regain some control over the situation.[7] This analysis allows us to discern how the shame of evil and modesty are similar and different. In the first, mankind wishes to hide something which is attached to him – a fault, a stain, a habit – of which he disapproves out of sympathy with the negative judgment of others, and which he cannot master; the fault remains, the stain is not washed away, the habit enslaves him. In the second case, mankind wishes to hide the power of sexuality, which opposes his project of godlike autonomy and which he cannot master. In the first, mankind is ashamed of sin because the function of judgment has not been abolished. In the second, he is ashamed because of sin, since sexuality flouts his pretentions to be a miniature god. In both cases he is ashamed because he does not manage to master what is within him.[8]

[7] Our interpretation accords with what Claude Lévi-Strauss reports in *Tristes tropiques* (Paris: UGE, 1966), p.252. Certain rare peoples live in complete nakedness, but they 'are not unaware of what we call shame'. What they hide is the erection. Since their threshold of excitability is not very high, they run no risk in ordinary social relationships and thus can live naked. Lévi-Strauss thinks that in general the loincloth's function is 'to reveal the peaceful intentions of the wearer'; we suggest that its purpose is to give the wearer a certain control over sexuality. The two explanations support each other, since the social demand under discussion in *Tristes tropiques* is basically the same as the control of which we are speaking.

[8] As sin also brings disorder into sexuality, the two types of shame of which we are speaking can form complex combinations. A closer analysis would be necessary for the shame over good (*i.e.* over a good action). One of its components is often sympathy with the negative judgment of the other person. I am ashamed of the good (of Christ!), because he is 'not well thought of' and the judgment of the other person penetrates my soul, in spite of myself. It is also the protection of the very vulnerable point of personal intimacy where the motive for good has been at work: I dare not expose it, for fear it be wounded, even with the best intentions in the world. Once again it is a question of protecting ourselves. Or, if the good I have done were to come to light, I would not resist the temptation to vanity. Shame of the good can also resemble sexual shame in this way: the good deed attests my destination according to God, so I hide it lest by it I become *too* committed to the path of obedience! So tortuous is our heart! Discretion, of course, is close to shame, but the two must not be confused.

Between shame and the *fear* which the man admits in Genesis 3:10 there is a closer connection than just kinship. Shame is already the fear of the alien look. Under the dominion of fear, exposed in their nakedness, the man and the woman do their best to hide – behind the trees of the garden, as well as behind the leaves they have sewn together. The new factor in the development of the narrative is that their relationship with God is directly involved. Fear paralyses the rebels as the LORD approaches. Are we to conclude from this that the radical sense of insecurity which fills every conscience is always fear of the LORD? We would dare to suggest that the deep fear of death, whether conscious or unconscious, is not fear of the unknown, but rather fear of the Unrecognized, of the One whose approach calls us radically into question. We would dare to suggest that existential fear, *Angst*, is not really fear of nothing; for the void which rebellious liberty creates around itself is in fact fallacious. At the very moment that it denies God, our liberty stands before him. Existential fear is also fear before God.

Fear makes us flee. The flight of the first couple prefigures all the flights of sinners. Firstly, it is pointless. Adam is a lamentable figure as he thinks he can escape his judge. 'Everything is uncovered and laid bare before the eyes of him to whom we must give account' (Heb. 4:13, NIV). Of those who are guilty, the LORD says:

Though they dig into Sheol,
    from there shall my hand take them;
though they climb up to heaven,
    from there I will bring them down.
Though they hide themselves on the top of Carmel,
    from there I will search out and take them;
and though they hide from my sight at the bottom of the sea,
    there I will command the serpent, and it shall bite them.
                                                        (Am. 9:2f.).

The narrative brings out the pointlessness of the attempt of the first sinners by an apparent illogicality: God has only to call, for the man to answer him immediately (Gn. 3:9f.). The effort to hide is worthless. But – a second point of universal application – in the effort they resort to the trees of the garden. God's excellent gifts are used as a screen or as a shield against him! And thus there emerges not only man's powerlessness but also his ingratitude. But what else could he have taken to hide behind? Nothing, of course. Man's ingratitude is becoming more

177

and more blatantly obvious. What else do we take? Always the gifts of the Creator, which we use as a refuge when in our terror we attempt to escape from him. But the wealth of the world is a pitiful protection: it offers comprehensive life assurance which fails to comprehend the only important risk, and which gives no assurance of eternal life.

With the failure of the first flight, the sinners try another: an *excuse*. The third effect of the fall is revealed in the answers the couple give when questioned. The man and the woman avoid their responsibility by putting the blame on another party. The man accuses his wife, showing that the wine of their love has turned sour. At the same time he seems to insinuate that God himself is not above reproach: 'The woman you put here with me...' (Gn. 3:12 – *this* is where you hear the echo of the tragic myth). The woman accuses the snake, as if she had not of her own free will taken the decision to yield. But the very excuse points the finger back at her, and our narrative thus shows the device that sinners have recourse to: accuse another to excuse oneself. The words of self-justification, fed by grievances against neighbour or spouse, is distinct progress in the cancer of evil. That is what has to be broken by conviction of sin, in order that healing may begin: 'Woe is me! For I am lost; for I am a man of unclean lips, and I dwell in the midst of a people of unclean lips...' (Is. 6:5).

There are few more clear symptoms of persistence in sin than the accusing quest for excuses. The effect of sin is the sin of denying sin, and it grows worse, both with regard to God and with regard to our neighbour.

The reply thus given was made to the Judge. Westermann has clearly seen the judicial character of God's inquiry and the importance of this feature. The man and woman are given leave to speak. The minute they seek to evade their responsibilities, God treats them as responsible.[9] By highlighting this, the text is in agreement with the biblical predilection for forensic categories, and makes the transition from the 'spontaneous' effects of the fall to the punishments that were specially inflicted. The continuation of the narrative then indeed relays the Judge's sentence. Here the order mirrors that of the examination, for after the questioning of man, woman and snake in that order, the sentences fall on the snake, the woman and the man.[10]

---

[9] Westermann *C*, p.97.   [10] Young III, p.122 has pointed this out.

The sentence

The condemnations fall, but not like the blade of a guillotine. They retain a very personal tone and are shaped to fit the particular situation of each of the three guilty parties.

The *snake* will be cursed. Are we to understand: 'cursed are you *above* all animals' or '*by* them all' (3:14)? Speiser argues strongly that it means 'to hold off, ban'.[11] At any rate, it is some kind of adverse destiny that sets it apart. By submitting the tempter to the curse, the LORD demonstrates both that he severely reproves its manoeuvres and that he remains master of that creature – two methods of excluding the 'tragic' myth. He makes it eat dust for its effrontery in rising up against him (3:14b).

□   A naïve, literal reading might, for a moment, seem possible. One might imagine that snakes formerly possessed legs and then lost them in Genesis 3. But even as strong a literalist as E. J. Young discounts the idea of such a biological mutation.[12] In their references to this, the prophets show that in the snake eating the dust they saw the humiliation of pagan power and the overthrow of the forces of evil (Is. 65:25; Mi. 7:17). Genesis in point of fact is making use of the snake symbolism; its crawling, which classifies it amongst abominable beasts (Lv. 11:42), acts as a symbol for the humiliation of that spirit of opposition to God represented by the snake.   □

The second verse of the judicial sentence (3:15) strikes the snake as the Adversary. His grand plan to carry humanity with him in his war against God shall not succeed. His plan will be thwarted. A permanent hostility will prevent him from making humanity his obedient plaything (v.15a). The text no doubt contains an allusion to the moral struggles that humanity continues to experience; in spite of its fall into sin, humanity still retains a certain horror of evil, of the evil it commits, even though it commits it. Thus divided against itself (*cf.* Rom. 2:14–16; 7:14–24), humanity nevertheless resists the snake to the same degree. And, above all, God prophesies to the Evil One the final and utter failure of all his schemes; the seed of the woman will crush, or will bruise, its head (3:15b).[13] Since this defeat is

[11] Speiser, p.24.
[12] Young III, p.98, following Calvin (p.80) and Aquinas (who is quoted by Renckens, p.286).
[13] Some commentators and translators move away from the meaning 'crush' or 'bruise' for

located at the conclusion of a long warfare between the descendants of both snake and woman,[14] and yet affects the snake itself, the snake here must of necessity represent *another* figure which lives on while generations come and go; here we have a further indication of the snake's symbolic character. In the inspired writer's subtle composition, the repugnance that human beings, and women in particular, feel towards reptiles acts as a symbol of the horror of evil, the moral horror which sin will not succeed in suppressing; and the way in which men kill snakes acts as a symbol of the fate which ultimately awaits the Power of falsehood. Note that the snake will be struck *in the head*. The detail fits the imagery, but it has also a symbolic implication, for *rō'š* ('head') also means 'principle', 'essence', 'sum' and 'summit'. The Adversary will be *totally* vanquished. The apostle Paul recalls the condemnation in Genesis 3:15 when he reminds his readers: 'The God of peace will soon crush Satan under your feet' (Rom. 16:20).

Next the *woman* hears herself designated by the sentence that falls on her in her own particular condition. Since she shares the man's humanity, she too will experience the penalties suffered by mankind in general. But the text describes 'the wages of sin' in the two characteristic relationships of womankind: as a mother and as a wife.

'MULTIPLYING I shall multiply your pain in childbearing; in pain you shall bring forth children' (Gn. 3:16a). We agree with Speiser that the Hebrew terms, 'thy sorrow and thy conception' (AV, RV), are a typical example of the Bible's love of hendiadys, as the renderings of RSV and NIV concur. It is talking about the sufferings of pregnancy and of childbirth.[15] By announcing that he will 'multiply' them, or 'make them numerous', God does not mean that there were already sufferings in the former dispensation.[16] He is simply saying that henceforth

---

the verb *šûp* in Gn. 3:15. They follow the Septuagint and the Old Latin, and render it 'aim at', 'seek to strike' (*tēreō, observare*). In point of fact, no other passage of the Old Testament can be shown, where the verb *šûp* must take this latter meaning; recourse is made to a related verb, which is *not* the same word, *šā'ap*, meaning either 'crush', or 'lie in wait for'. But the method is faulty; why should we look for a meaning that is not attested, when the ordinary meaning is perfectly suitable? We do better to follow Jerome (*conterere*), as do the vast majority of scholars; *cf.* Keil, p.100; Renckens, p.296. See further notes 61, 62, below, p.193.

[14] The descendants of the snake suggest the proliferation of adverse powers. When the symbolism is deciphered, it can be understood of the other evil spirits, the disciples or spiritual sons of the devil. Thus Young III, p.116.   [15] Speiser, p.LXX.

[16] The verb has not always the narrowly mathematical meaning of 'multiply'. In Nu. 26:54 it means 'give a plentiful share' (no share having yet been distributed); in Jb. 9:17 it means

they will be abundant. On the other hand, the sentence seems to presuppose the woman's vocation to bring forth children, as included under the creation mandate of the sixth day (Gn. 1:28a). Mankind retains the blessing and the power to procreate. But with it there is mingled bitterness, so that the blessing becomes a burden. The great disorder of sin so affects the good that God had brought forth, that everything remains and yet everything is changed. Here the gift of generation becomes, so to speak, a caricature of itself.

'Yet your desire shall be for your husband, and he shall rule over you' (Gn. 3:16b). The second part of the sentence unquestionably concerns the relationship of the woman to the man – from (*ek*) whom and for whom she was created, as Paul states (1 Cor. 11:8f.). This relationship too continues, but it suffers disruption. It will operate, but with difficulty.

☐ What, more precisely, is the calamitous change which follows the entrance of sin, on which the text now focuses? Opinions vary. Susan Foh has put forward an original interpretation, and her forceful argument deserves our attention.[17] She discards the idea that the 'desire' of the woman is sexual desire or the psychological need of dependence on man. The Hebrew word, *t^e šûqâ*, conveys the thought of a desire to possess or control, and since it is used shortly afterwards for sin couching at Cain's door (Gn. 4:7), she concludes that the reference is to the desire to dominate. Woman, rejecting the creation order, will want to dominate her husband, but he will have to dominate her (the jussive, not the future), *i.e.* restore the relationship intended by God. The basis of this argument, however, seems fragile to us. There is nothing in the word *t^e šûqâ* to give the precise connotation of the desire to dominate. Even sin's impetus towards Cain can be conceived without that idea, as a desire of union in some sense.[18] In the Song of Songs, the lover is carried by his desire towards the Shulammite (Song 7:10), where it is unlikely that the idea is of domination.[19] This reference

---

'make numerous' wounds (Job was suffering from no kind of wound or injury before his trial).

[17] Susan T. Foh, 'What is the woman's desire?', *WTJ* 37 (1974–1975), pp.376–383.

[18] The word 'couching' (*rōḇēs*) conjures up the picture of a savage beast, and therefore of being devoured rather than dominated!

[19] Susan Foh mentions Song 7:11 only in a brief note (p.379, n.19). Rather diffidently she suggests the idea of domination could fit this passage, since it speaks of possession: 'I am my beloved's'. But the parallel in Song 2:16 requires that to 'Towards you is my desire' should correspond the clause 'My beloved is mine'. It concerns the desire that drives the man and the woman to join together, and not to the authority structure within the couple.

favours the sexual interpretation, taken in its broad sense, in Genesis 3:16. Besides, 'dominate' can appear stronger than anything suggested by the narrative concerning the man's authority in the created order before the fall. And what happens to the idea of punishment in this verse, on the basis of Susan Foh's interpretation? According to her, the Judge foretells the woman's sinful behaviour and exhorts the man to overcome it. Does that match up to the pronouncement of a verdict? Obviously not! We rather settle for this understanding: the LORD declares at this point the permanence of the attraction that he has implanted between the sexes, for it is not good for man to be alone, and he also declares what will be the wages of sin. ☐

The destiny of woman as help-meet and companion will not cease to make itself felt. But, because of sin, this blessing too will turn into a caricature of itself. The man will abuse his status, take advantage of his position and exploit the desire that drives the woman towards him, turning it into the chains of slavery. He will dominate the woman who seeks his love. How can we contradict the precision of this description, if we consider the relationship between man and woman, both on a global scale and throughout history?

The sentence pronounced defines the logical 'harvest' of the offence, and it must not be confused with a *precept*. Male tyranny and the corruption of the harmony that existed between the sexes at creation are all part of the funeral procession. God says so, but he does not command that people should act in this way. On the contrary, throughout the Bible he summons us to combat the consequences of evil. It is possible, if not to suppress them, at least to mitigate them.[20] To condemn (comparatively) painless childbirth by appeal to Genesis 3:16, to justify the enslavement of women, or to claim that the text wishes it to happen,[21] is to pervert the whole meaning of the passage.

Just as the verse for the woman, *'iššâ*, showed the change in her relationship to her husband, *'iš*, the condemnation that falls on the *man*, *'ādām*, is concerned with his relationship to the earth, *'adāmâ*. In that area too there is no mere abolition of the creation ordinances. The man was to cultivate and subdue the earth. That he will do, as already arranged. But it will not be *in*

---

[20] Young III, pp.124f. shows this cogently. Westermann *C*, pp.143f., also emphasizes that Gn. 3:16 gives an etiology, not norms.

[21] As does Gisèle Halimi in *La Cause des femmes* (Paris: Grasset, 1973), p.16. Her excuse is that she is not the first to make this contradiction.

the way that was arranged. Work will become toil. Working with the ground that is henceforth cursed will be difficult and will involve conflict. It is the weeds that will grow effortlessly. Long will be life's struggle, and its only certainty at the end of the day will be death. For 'man is the loser in his struggle with the ground, for, as it were, the ground will at last overcome him'.[22]

How are we to envisage what affects the earth here? Calvin seems ready to make the thorns and thistles in the Judge's sentence 'corruptions which originate from sin', though he adds the strange comment that God also created such things, in which we are to 'mark his anger'.[23] Arthur Lewis, on the contrary, observes: 'Nothing in the narrative suggests that the realm of nature has been altered in a fundamental way....There is no indication that the Lord God added thorns to the roses or sharp teeth to the carnivorous animals'.[24] It is a long-standing question,[25] and in case of doubt we would lean to the side of caution and keep our imagination well in hand. When Paul refers to Genesis and declares that the whole created order has been subjected to vanity because of Adam – for the fall of the head has repercussions over the whole domain that had been entrusted to him – he shows that nature did not remain intact (Rom. 8:20).[26] But he gives no indication of either the extent or, above all, the form of the change. The Psalms which sing of God's creation as we now see it and the texts in the book of Job which celebrate its awesome beauty stand as a warning against the temptation to exaggerate the difference for nature in itself. Genesis 3:17f. considers the earth in so far as it responds to man within that relationship. It is permissible to think that the disruption affects that relationship before anything else, beginning with the weakening and disorder of man himself. If

[22] Young III, p.139.

[23] Calvin, p.174. He too inclines, without pressing the point, towards the idea of a purely vegetarian diet before the fall.

[24] Arthur H. Lewis, 'The localization of the Garden of Eden', *BETS* 11 (1968), p.174.

[25] Etienne Gilson, *L'Esprit de la philosophie médiévale* (Paris: Vrin, 1932), p.263 n.21, reports that thinkers like Theophilus of Antioch in ancient times and Duns Scotus in the Middle Ages attributed the ferocity of animals, *etc.*, to the fall, whilst Thomas Aquinas on the contrary adopted the minimizing interpretation.

[26] 'Him who subjected it' in Rom. 8:20 could be God. (It certainly could not be Satan, as Karl Heim argued.) But Paul's 'because' (in the following verse) corresponds so well to the insistent 'because' of Gn. 3:17, that we may envisage applying the Romans verse to man. That would fit with what follows: it is the redemption of man that will bring with it the redemption of the cosmos, just as his fall affected the world.

man were perfectly sturdy, no microbe could do him any harm. If he had all the faculties that were his at creation, he would be able to turn the upheavals in nature to good account, without suffering at their hand. (We all know how far organisms that have become weakened suffer from conditions of life that are bracing for others.) If man obeyed God, he would be the means of blessing to the earth; but in his insatiable greed, in his scorn for the balances built into the created order and in his short-sighted selfishness he pollutes and destroys it. He turns a garden into a desert (*cf.* Rev. 11:18). That is the main thrust of the curse in Genesis 3.

By announcing that man will die at the end of a miserable time spent on earth, might the LORD be changing what he had said in Genesis 2:17: 'in the *day* that you eat of it you shall die'? This has caused difficulty to a number of commentators, but A. van Hoonacker has shown that it has a simple solution, found from the parallel in 1 Kings 2:36–46. This passage proves the meaning of the Hebrew expression: 'on that day you will fall under the power of a death sentence'.[27] The warning did not imply the threat of a death that would be carried out immediately. The Judge's sentence is in perfect agreement with his earlier warning.

The most sensitive and the most important point in Genesis 3:19 is the relationship of death to human nature. Pelagius, because he weakened the reality of original sin, claimed that death was 'natural', as, ultimately, all non-biblical systems are forced to do. The words 'you shall die' and the climax of the condemnation that falls on mankind show that death is a punishment inflicted for disobedience: 'Man would not have had to undergo death if he had observed the divine precept; that is to say, he would have enjoyed bodily immortality'.[28] 'It is death itself, and not simply premature death, that punishes sin.'[29] Paul confirms this with all the clarity you could desire. By Adam's offence, death made its entry into the world of mankind (Rom. 5:12; 1 Cor. 15:21; the primary point is the death of the body, since its antithesis is the resurrection of the body). E. J. Young reaches the firm conclusion, 'Death is not the natural end for man'.[30] But we must notice that the text establishes a connection between our return to the dust and our human consti-

---

[27] Quoted with approval by W. Goossens, 'Immortalité corporelle', in the *Supplément* to the *Dictionnaire de la Bible* 4 (1949), pp.304f.

[28] *Ibid.*, p.306.   [29] Dubarle, p.68.   [30] Young III, p.139.

tution. Man was taken from the ground, he is dust. He originates from the earth, and in the end that is what he again becomes. Death is not a possibility that in its very essence is completely alien to mankind. For man, to become mortal is not a metaphysical mutation that changes his definition. The animals who were also formed from the earth die, as man could well ascertain. He could have understood the warning in Genesis 2:17 as the prediction that he would undergo a similar fate if he ate of the forbidden fruit, and would then forfeit his privilege.[31]

☐　Many Catholic theologians posit that before the fall man was mortal by nature but that a supernatural gift of immortality was added to make him escape the consequence of his constitution.[32] Amongst them a number of modern thinkers take courage and go further. The famous Jesuit thinker, Karl Rahner, is ready to see in the dissolution of the space-time form 'the death of a metaphysical egoism' and considers that, without sin, 'Adam would have brought his personal life to its perfect consummation even in his bodily form through a "death" which would have been a pure active self-affirmation.'[33] Dubarle would like to draw a distinction between decease and the 'tragic experiences which congeal around decease'. Only the latter, he argues, are the consequence of the fall.[34] Man would have died anyway, but as a sinner he undergoes a pitiful death. What are we to make of these propositions?

Distinctions are obviously most necessary. But we must distinguish between those that have a firm basis and those that blunt the biblical texts. The distinction between 'decease' and the 'death' which enters through sin appears fabricated to meet the requirements of the case, to find a reconcilation with evolutionism.[35] There is nothing in the Bible to suggest it. Genesis does not recall any of the terrors associated with death, but simply the return to the earth, decease. But does it not show a complete lack of sensi-

---

[31] Animal death is not an evil in the Bible, it seems, despite H. M. Morris, *SC*, pp.207f., 211, 229, who takes it as the consequence of the fall of man. In order to support this, he has to interpret *nepeš* as 'consciousness' in Gn. 1 – 2; this is philologically unacceptable, for the smallest marine organisms and terrestrial animals, insects, *etc.*, are explicitly classified as *nepeš* in 1:20f., 24. In the second clause of the covenant, the man could understand the verb 'die', because it dealt with a real possibility, a fact of the animal kingdom to which man partially belonged. Evil itself was not a 'real possibility', that is to say something of which he saw a concrete example before his eyes; the word had meaning only in and by the commandment.

[32] Goossens, *op. cit.,* pp.298–313, 331f., states the classical position.

[33] Karl Rahner, *On the Theology of Death* (New York: Herder, 1961), p.35.

[34] Dubarle, p.202.

[35] Dubarle, p.203, continues: 'We may therefore admit, in conformity with the suggestions of the theory of evolution, an emergence of humanity from without the animal world'.

tivity not to sense the scandal of the death, the mere death, of a man, and not to recognize death as 'the last enemy' (1 Cor. 15:26)? As for Rahner's hostility towards the 'space-time form', is that not suspect? In spite of the subtlety of his dialectic and his cultivation of ambiguity, it looks suspiciously like a modern version of the old idealistic scorn, the old Neo-Platonist hatred, for the body and for individuality. On the contrary, space-time individuality is not a 'metaphysical egoism', but the quite untarnished image of the unity of the Creator God, fashioned by his own care. The death which brings about its disintegration is neither a liberation nor the fulfilment of the essence of humanity.

Between the constitution of man and the gifts which God is pleased to bestow on him a more legitimate distinction may be drawn.[36] But does it throw any light on the debate about death? The scholastic framework of Nature and Supernature often threatens to distort the biblical perspectives.[37] In the study of Genesis it threatens to obscure the radically relational character of a human being. Man's being as the image of God, his very nature indeed, consists of a relationship with God. The son-like communion with the Creator is not an addition to the human constitution; it is a part of its definition – and how could it be anything other than *life*? The gift of breath-spirit, the $n^e\check{s}\bar{a}m\hat{a}$ which is man's property, indicates in the second tablet (Gn. 2:7) that man is not made only of dust – and therefore that the return to the dust contradicts what man was intended to be.[38] Death cannot be called 'natural', as is attested, we believe, by a spontaneous reaction in all of us.[39] What are we to conclude, then? The created reality of mankind is dual. It is by considering that duality that we resolve the problem of whether death is natural. Man is a creature of the earth, but also the image of God; formed

[36] Calvin, *Institutes* II.ii. 12, also uses the distinction between natural gifts (corrupted by sin) and supernatural gifts (abolished).

[37] Here we are following in particular H. Dooyeweerd and C. van Til. Several Catholic theologians, including H. de Lubac and H. Bouillard, have also criticized the stock textbook concept of the two levels of nature and supernature (grace). The thesis of an added immortality seems a typical example of this concept: Adam was mortal on the first level, immortal on the second.

[38] On the $n^e\check{s}\bar{a}m\hat{a}$, cf. above, p.77, n.77 and ch. 4, p.87. Goossens, *art. cit.*, rejects the argument of the $n^e\check{s}\bar{a}m\hat{a}$ (which opposes death to the nature of mankind) by quoting Gn. 7:22. But it is not definite that this text uses $n^e\check{s}\bar{a}m\hat{a}$ for the animal; no other text does. Ec. 3:19, 21 and 12:7 (which corresponds to the earlier verses) deal with the difference in the destiny of the breath (*rûaḥ*) of man and that of the animal.

[39] Funeral rites in all cultures show that death is perceived nowhere as 'natural'. C. S. Lewis, *Miracles* (London: Bles, 1947), p.132, suggests that a large part of Christian theology can be deduced from the fact that men 'feel the dead to be uncanny'.

from dust, but endowed with the $n^e\check{s}\bar{a}m\hat{a}$. Originally death was a possibility arising from his constitution, but he was not subject to it, not destined to it by nature.[40] As the image-bearer of God and as the prince of the earth, with the power to judge and with freedom and intelligence, he seized the fruit of illusory sovereignty, he dreamed of a divine status, he proudly saw himself equal with God, and he did not escape the logic of the punishment: death came, to remind him of the other truth of his nature, his creaturely state, his earthly state. Death remains the great exposure (Ps. 82:6f.; Ezk. 28:9, 16ff.). □

In the conclusion of the narrative, the LORD takes two steps which initiate the execution of the penalty that has been announced (Gn. 3:23f.). God drives mankind out of the garden. So humanity finds itself confronting an untamed earth, a world which responds to his efforts with thistles. Secondly, God blocks the way to the tree of life. Thus mankind is deprived of the nourishment he required as the image of God, that is to say the life-giving communion with divine Wisdom. He will submit to the law of the dust. As it recounts these two acts, with a few details, what does the text seek to teach us?

The expulsion from the Paradise prepared by the LORD hurls mankind into painful toil, but at the same time also makes him an outcast. He is homeless on this earth, earthling though he is. Since man's relation to the earth is only the second relationship that constitutes his being, and since man's primary relationship is with God, he is not fully at home on the earth if God does not give him his precise place. In this way the primacy of the first relationship over the second is given a concrete imprint. Hence the endless wandering so well described by Jean Brun in *Les Vagabonds de l'Occident*; it finds expression in the myth of the Wandering Jew, the man who is homesick for his country without having a country.[41]

In order to forbid access to the tree of life, God places the $k^e r\hat{u}b\hat{\imath}m$ and adds the 'flaming sword which turned every way'. The flaming sword clearly represents the justice and the holiness of God at work in his judgments (*cf.* Je. 47:6; Ezk. 21; *etc.*). Several commentators think that the reference is to lightning

---

[40] Since man remains as the image and endowed with $n^e\,\check{s}\bar{a}m\hat{a}$, death only partly puts him in the same category as the animals. Here is the full significance of the biblical data on the state of death as a form of existence: in dying like the beast, man does not die simply like the beast. These data confirm its unnaturalness.

[41] J. Brun, *Les Vagabonds de l'Occident* (Paris: Desclée, 1976), p.21.

as a divine weapon.[42]

☐   What are the $k^e r\hat{u}b\hat{i}m$? Under the same name the ancient Near East denoted fantastic compositions of winged animals with human faces, which have been found in carvings on the doorways of royal or sacred buildings. Several times the Bible mentions $k^e r\hat{u}b\hat{i}m$. The prophet Ezekiel gives a description of them. They appear to propel or attend the chariot of God and combine the excellencies of the earthly creation: the features of mankind, the lion, the ox and the eagle (Ezk. 1:5ff.; 10:15. Rev. 4:6ff. takes up and develops this vision). Later, Ezekiel gives the $k^e r\hat{u}b$ the function of protection and then of judicial execution (Ezk. 28:14, 16). On the veil that covered the way into the holy of holies, $k^e r\hat{u}b\hat{i}m$ were woven, whilst others overshadowed the mercy seat of the ark of the covenant with their wings (Ex. 36:35; 37:7–9). Although several of the early church Fathers understood the $k^e r\hat{u}b\hat{i}m$ as symbols, as E. J. Young acknowledges,[43] by tradition they have been considered as a special class of angel, and the word has been simply transcribed as 'cherubim'. This opinion has very little to recommend it. There is no text of Scripture that identifies the $k^e r\hat{u}b\hat{i}m$ with angels, or even links them together. On the contrary, Patrick Fairbairn points out that in the book of Revelation they join with the choir of men and not with the choir of angels (Rev. 5:8, 11). Furthermore, their faces are those of *earthly* creatures.[44] Everything indicates that the biblical writers borrowed a representation that was current in their cultural environment in order to put it to symbolic use. But what use precisely? In Fairbairn's view they represent the living creation, including mankind, with the promise of its redemption. The reference to redemption, however, does not appear obvious.[45] The

[42] *E.g.,* Chaine, p.66. Lightning was the symbol of anathema amongst the Assyrians.

[43] Young III, p.162.

[44] P. Fairbairn, *The Typology of Scripture* (New York and London: Funk & Wagnalls, 1900), 1, p.234. The treatment of the subject by this evangelical theologian, pp.215–239, is famous. Calvin, p.186, keeps the idea that they are angels, but he feels the weakness of this interpretation and explains that they received the name $k^e r\hat{u}b\hat{i}m$ as an accommodation and also in the same way that the sacred bread of the Lord's Supper receives the name of the body of Christ.

[45] The emphasis on life is legitimate, since the $k^e r\hat{u}b\hat{i}m$ are also called the 'living ones', *hayyôt*, in Ezk. 1, *zōa* in Rev. 4 – 5 (Fairbairn, *op.cit.*, p.221). In order to link them with grace, Fairbairn mentions their place on the ark of the covenant (pp.225f.); but that does not require that we include redemption in all that they symbolize. For once Fairbairn has to leave the text: in order to see in the $k^e r\hat{u}b\hat{i}m$ of Gn. 3:24 the picture of living people who have been redeemed and who will regain paradise, they would have to *occupy* the garden of Eden (p.228). Now, the verse says 'at the east of the garden of Eden' (*miqqedem $l^e gan$*), *i.e.* outside, as guards to the entrance, rather than on the inside.

simplest solution is to follow Philo and Grotius and see in them the symbol of divine power, as it is manifested in the universe, or, more precisely still, a concentrated form of the universe itself, summed up in its more glorious figures, but in so far as it remains at the disposal of the LORD and acts as the instrument of his power.[46] This interpretation fits everywhere. It is indeed true that all the living forces of creation exist in order to bear the throne of God, to guard his sanctuary or celebrate his praise. At the end of the narrative concerning Eden, the $k^e r\hat{u}b\hat{i}m$ encamped on the path to the tree of life represent the total power of the world at the command of the LORD God in order to carry out his sentence. You no more brush shoulders with such guards than you dodge past the revolving barrier of the flaming sword.   □

God himself prefaces the promulgation of the two measures with a strange remark, in a sentence that is grammatically unfinished. Before finishing our review of the 'negative' and looking to see whether some glimmer of hope does not creep into our text, we must enquire into the meaning of the LORD's words in Genesis 3:22: 'Behold, the man has become like one of us, knowing good and evil; and now, lest he put forth his hand and take also of the tree of life, and eat, and live for ever'. Is the LORD resorting to irony?[47] It is objected that the God of mercy would not heap insults on the wretched couple,[48] and that irony would not provide the ground to take action.[49] Above all, in our opinion irony would ill accord with the naïve style adopted by the narrator, which he deploys so subtly. The text must be capable of being read at two levels, and the use of irony would break the naïve reading. Did the man and the woman obtain their autonomy, the power of determining good and evil, in accordance with the figurative meaning of the fruit they ate? Did they become like God, or like gods,[50] as the snake had promised? *In one sense, yes.* Here the subtlety of falsehood comes into play.

[46] Fairbairn, *op. cit.,* pp.236ff., considers these interpretations, but does not keep them. Another idea of interest is proposed by Cassuto, pp.175f., who thinks of the winds, because of their association with flame, as in Ps. 104:4, to which could be added Ps. 18:11.

[47] *Cf.* p.131, n.74 above. Those who have seen irony in Gn. 3:22 include Luther (according to Young III, p.150) and Calvin, p.182.

[48] Young III, p.150.

[49] John Murray, 'The Adamic administration', *Collected Writings of John Murray* 2 (Edinburgh: Banner of Truth, 1977), pp.51f.

[50] The 'us' is more enigmatic here than in Gn. 1:26. The inclusion of the angels in 'us' is unlikely, for why should such an association of men with angels cause such trouble? The same goes for the idea that here might be a trace of polytheism; at most one could admit that God is speaking in advance of false gods such as those of 1 Cor. 8:5. Young III, pp.151ff., after examining the other interpretations, concludes that the 'us' can only be trinitarian.

Falsehood is never anything other than a corruption of truth. The breaking of the covenant certainly gave mankind a certain independence in the choice of his conduct. Whilst in the state of innocence he was always second, receiving everything from the hand of God – the willing and the doing, the duty and the capacity – in his fallen state, under the power of evil, he comes first, for evil does not proceed from God. In so far as he is disobedient, man acts from himself and for himself, like God. In that sense, the tempter spoke the truth, and the fruit indeed had the effect promised by its name. Hence that awkward hyper-awareness and that division of the self which we described in our discussion of v.7. The 'behold' of v.22 basically certifies the fact of sin: the creature is seceding, denying his dependence and the law of the Creator. The word implies the achievement of the autonomy in a certain way. But only in a certain way, for the father of lies only ever speaks the truth by perverting it. In reality, the autonomy is illusory, a mere, pitiful aping of God. Not only is man tricked by the snake, but he is first only in evil. Now, evil is *nothing* other than the perversion of the created reality, and the whole of reality continues to depend on God. The powerlessness of evil to escape from this reality is underlined by its inclusion within the plan of God: sin itself does not occur without the sovereign permission of the Lord. Thus, mankind's pseudo-divinity, in spite of its corrupting effect, is revealed as vanity, nothing and falsehood – *'āwen* in the language of the Old Testament.

The logic of the divine remark is that of the analysis of man's pseudo-divinity. Since mankind in making himself like God does not escape from the lordship of the only true God, he cannot both be autonomous (in his negative manner) and at the same time participate in Life. To eat from one of the two trees and also to eat from the other are two absolutely incompatible options. That mankind should eat of the tree of life also is the unthinkable proposition which the divine word formulates only in order to exclude it utterly. The crazy little god with his absurd pretentions is not God and never shall be. All he can do is die.

If, however, the Lord mentions the link between the 'knowledge-of-good-and-evil' and Life, a connection that the human intelligence cannot even begin to conceive, does he do this in order to denounce it as impossible and unthinkable? Several writers have discerned that by this privation God is sparing the man and the woman that evil, no greater than which can be conceived (and which cannot in fact be conceived itself), and that thus the very punishment conceals God's mercy.[51] 'Having become like gods in respect of autonomy of choice, you are not really gods' (*cf.* Ps. 82). It is also a gentle, merciful word, for it means, 'I continue to be your God'.

Now, if God continues to be the God of mankind, there is still a future. It is not for nothing that the tree of life, planted for the sake of mankind, instead of being cut down and thrown into the fire, continues to exist and bear an abundance of fruit in the paradise of God. And with a future there is hope. The Genesis narrative itself projects the first glimmers of this reversal in the heart of the condemnation. Now we must consider how it allows us to say with E. J. Young that Adam 'having been expelled from the garden, went forth, under the power of death and yet a child of hope'.[52]

The dawn

Where in Genesis 3 do we see the first glimmer of dawn?

Before applying the punishment and driving the man and the woman out of the garden, the LORD makes an eloquent gesture: he makes them garments and covers them with them (Gn. 3:21). How could he better demonstrate that he wishes to remain the God of sinners, for their good and not for their ill? Kidner comments, not without a touch of humour: 'Social action, now delegated to human hands (Rom. 13:1–7; Jas. 2:16), could not have had an earlier or more exalted inauguration'.[53] Above all, the action taken by God is an admirable illustration of the method of grace in the face of sin and its consequences. It does not turn the clock back, it does not simply wipe out what has happened. God's intervention does not allow a return to the nudity of paradise, a point which condemns not only the nudism of 'naturist' groups but also that of the 'spirituals' and of the 'Adamite' sects which have sprung up at various times since the second century. God *covers* sin and its degradation. Here we may recall the biblical picture of justification: the gift of a new robe, rich and pure (Zc. 3:4f.; Mt. 22:11; Lk. 15:22; Gal. 3:27 and elsewhere in Paul; Rev. 19:8). History is irreversible, but God is able to do a new thing: we remain sinners, with no merit of our

---

[51] Von Rad, p.94: 'a merciful reverse side'; Young III, p.156: 'an act of kindness'; J. Murray, *art. cit.,* p.55.
[52] Young III, p.161.   [53] Kidner, p.72.

own to show, but where sin has abounded, grace has abounded all the more. And the amazing thing is that God brings to fulfilment in the garments of salvation depicted in the beginning by those of Genesis the paradoxical, revelatory function of clothing. Clothed in the grace of God, the children of God are freer and more open to the eye of God and man than were Adam and Eve. We are perfectly protected and perfectly disclosed.

The mention of Eve brings to our attention the overwhelming confession of hope which is expressed by her name (Gn. 3:20). The name comes from the Hebrew root meaning 'to live', as the Bible's own comment indicates: 'because she was the mother of all living'. In order to convey the word-play in English we should have to give her a new name like Livia.[54] So Adam called his wife 'Life', whereas in fact through her fault death has just entered the world! Where did he get such a bold idea, which almost seems blind to reality? Not from unawareness, but from a very precise awareness of the full significance of the words God has spoken. Despite death and despite the suffering that will afflict the woman, God has maintained the blessing of children. He has thus promised a stubborn perseverance of life, come what may. He has promised a future. Melanchthon was not wrong to call Eve 'the seal of grace'.[55]

The woman and her seed are still concerned in the most decisive pronouncement. We have seen that the sentence passed on the snake foretells a long warfare and the final defeat of the adversary. But now we must notice what earlier we passed over. Firstly, since by the temptation the snake showed himself to be a murderer (Jn. 8:44) and since mankind will show itself partly aware of this, the defeat of the snake will be a victory for mankind. The crushing defeat of evil is a promise! Secondly, the very hostility has an author, God himself (Gn. 3:15). Young emphasizes the point with good reason.[56] God does not simply issue a command; he makes a declaration that he himself is committed to the battle, he has his plan for victory, and in his grace he puts mankind on his side against the snake. And

[54] Daniel Lys, 'Le jeu des mots dans l'Ancien Testament', *RR* 27 (1976), p.105. The whole article is brilliant and instructive. On the etymology of Eve, *hawwâ*, and the connection that certain writers make with the Aramaic word for 'snake', *cf.* Young III, p.142. In our view, the assertion, 'Eve, the mother of all living' excludes the idea of men in the image of God who might not have descended from Adam. In this we disagree with Kidner, p.29, and his unconvincing interpretation, p.30 n.1, according to which Eve was the mother by the promise of salvation in Gn. 3:15.
[55] Quoted by W. Vischer.   [56] Young III, pp.111f.

indeed, and here is the third significant point, the crushing of the snake will be achieved by the seed of the woman. He it is who will inflict the decisive, final blow on the adversary.

☐   The prediction concerning the seed of the woman has aroused considerable discussion and demands special comment. Two questions arise: What is this seed? What will the snake do to the woman's seed, according to Genesis 3:15? The word 'seed' (posterity, descendants) has a collective meaning in current usage, and it would seem unwise to dismiss it here.[57] It is the human race that will resist the Evil One and finally triumph over him. Could the writer, however, be thinking of a particular member of that posterity, who would win the victory on behalf of, and in the name of, the human race? The old Greek translation, the Septuagint, took it that way.[58] Lagrange argues that 'the snake could only have its head crushed once and, keeping to the symbolism, by one single person'.[59] Since the adversary, who is distinguished from his own descendants, is a distinct individual, it is plausible that he had to yield in the great, final duel, according to the prediction of Genesis 3, to a single champion from the human race. The way the revelation of Scripture keeps repeating the promise of a seed in progressively individualized terms encourages us to admit that in this passage there is a latent individual meaning. From the seed of the woman, Scripture will pass to that of Abraham (Gn. 22:18 in particular), to the seed of Judah (Gn. 49:10), to the seed of David (2 Sa. 7:12ff.) and to the royal child Immanuel who will miraculously be born of the young maiden (Is. 7:14).

But what is the meaning of the very last clause in the verse? It uses the same verb that is translated 'crush' or 'bruise' for the head of the snake.[60] Certain commentators, however, believe that there is a change of meaning and that the second time it should be taken as 'strike at', 'plot against' or the like, *e.g.*: 'He will crush your head and you will aim at his heel'.[61] This translation would be admirably suited to the image of the snake trying to bite the foot raised against it. But it requires the verbal form to take on a

[57] *Ibid.*, pp.113ff.
[58] The Septuagint has the masculine pronoun (*autos*) for 'him', whereas 'seed' (*sperma*) is neuter.
[59] M. J. Lagrange, *art. cit.*, *RB* 6 (1897), p.354. He notes that ancient Jewish exegesis took this as the definitive victory of Messiah, by the keeping of the law which he would make possible. Lagrange is followed by Renckens, p.302. Young III, p.120, accepts the individual sense.
[60] *Cf.* p.179, n.13, above.
[61] Lagrange, *ibid.*, p.352. It was used in the Vulgate (despite Jerome's preference for *conterere, cf.* Renckens, p.296); *cf.* NEB, NIV. Cassuto, p.161, D. Lys, *art. cit.*, p.109.

meaning for which there is no attestation. More particularly, it obscures the idea which the text intends to express, in our view, by the repetition of the same verb, that of reciprocal action. At the climax of the struggle, the deadly blow which shall crush the snake will find its counterpart in a terrible, possibly mortal, blow for the son of the woman. It would therefore be better to use the same English verb to render the two uses of the same Hebrew verb. The traditional rendering 'bruise' (AV, RV, RSV) is perfectly satisfactory, and seems preferable to the use of the two verbs 'crush' and 'strike' found in the NIV.[62] The idea of reciprocal action no doubt belongs to the symbolic meaning of the word 'heel', which the inspired author exploits with his customary skill. For, just as *rō'š*, translated 'head', can mean the essence or the total, so *'āqēb̲*, translated 'heel' suggests its Hebrew lexical cousin *'ēqeb̲*, 'in return'. □

In the end the adversary will be bruised in an irreversible, ultimate manner, by the representative of mankind. But, mysteriously, that will not happen without the latter paying the price of suffering 'in return'.

The mysterious element in this prophecy of a reciprocal bruising remains so long as we fail to look at its fulfilment. How was victory achieved by the one who 'appeared...to destroy the works of the devil', the Son of man, born of a woman? How did he bruise the serpent's head, except by allowing its most bitter venom to be spent on him, and by undergoing 'in return' the suffering of Calvary? 'That through death he might destroy him who has the power of death, that is, the devil' (Heb. 2:14). The victory was won and its complete and utter effect will be made manifest to all in an instant at the return of the Lord Jesus Christ (Rom. 16:20). Such is the paradox of the gospel: it uncovers the hidden meaning of Genesis 3:15 and gloriously authenticates the traditional name of that verse, the Protevangelium.[63]

The one single son who had not sinned, who did not consider that equality with God was a prize to be snatched, allowed himself to be struck on behalf of his vast throng of brothers by the ever-turning sword of divine justice. Thus he thwarted for ever the snake's manoeuvres. The *k^e rûb̲îm* rushed to open the gates to him. To us who follow him, who are conquerors by his

<hr>

[62] Calvin, p.168, roundly rejects the Vulgate here, as 'without reason'. Young III, pp.116f., defends 'to bruise' for the two occasions.

[63] It is greatly to be regretted that Westermann *C*, p.100, expressly rejects this. Von Rad, sees only 'the hopelessness of this struggle', p.90.

power, he grants to eat from the tree of life which is in the paradise of God (Rev. 2:7). He gives Life – *his* Life – for the wages of *our* sin was *his* death.

9
The aftermath and the promise

The sub-title of this book, 'The opening chapters of Genesis', cautiously avoids indicating the limits of these opening chapters. Many commentators stop at the end of the Eden narrative in chapter 3. But despite the noticeable change in both tone and style, they lay themselves open to the charge of arbitrariness. Why should the opening be detached from its sequel, which is indeed its sequel since the same characters are found in it?

Several literary arguments warn us against underestimating the continuity between the first two tablets of Genesis and the sequel of the book. Claus Westermann in particular emphasizes the unity of the primordial account, Genesis 1 – 11, 'as a deliberately planned whole'.[1] Thus, chapter 5 shows how the blessing of Genesis 1 is realized in the progression of time, while chapter 10 shows its realization in spatial development.[2] The recollection of the first inventions, of the multiplication of the human race on earth and of its offensive cry in the ears of God, the recollection of the flood and of the restoration which followed for the godly hero who survived, are all found linked to the cosmogony and the account of the creation of man in the Atrahasis Epic.[3] The Babylonian story *Enuma elish* includes the construction of Babel.[4] These parallels, imperfect though they are, prove that the first three chapters of Genesis could not be separated from

[1] Westermann C, p.27.　　[2] *Ibid.*, p.25.
[3] Westermann G, pp.95ff.; A. R. Millard, 'A new Babylonian "Genesis" story', *TB* 18 (1967), pp.4–16.
[4] Speiser, p.76 (quoting VI lines 60–62).

the eight that follow. And the very plan of the biblical book forces us to say the same of the chapters that come after that, for the *tôlᵉdôt* continue uninterrupted right through to the times of Jacob and Joseph. It was clearly the author's intention in organizing his material to link the abbreviated account of the most distant times to the nearer events of the patriarchs.

As we come to the end of our study of the seven days and of the story of the garden of Eden, we can do no more than glance at the subsequent eight chapters of Genesis. But we must at least do that in order to show our concern not to isolate the initial texts. A rapid survey will not allow us to discuss, examine or prove anything; but perhaps it will bring out the main threads of the teaching and suggest a few themes for further consideration.

The leading idea will be that of development. After the expulsion from Eden, we observe the deployment of those powers with which the Creator endowed his image: the power to procreate and 'para-create', to multiply and to subdue the earth. But at the same time we see corruption prevailing, the fatal chain of events that the man and the woman set in motion by rebelling against the Father. Judgment follows; it could not be otherwise. And certain signs follow, too, which recall the Protevangelium and give hope that the LORD will show mercy. We shall emphasize the quantitative and qualitative growth of sin, then the penalties that it entails and finally the measures taken by God in his mercy which alleviate the punishments that are deserved, and which already, in a cryptic manner, announce God's salvation.[5]

Sin and its aftermath

Sin proliferates along with mankind. It takes on new aspects as human life develops in new directions. We shall distinguish four stages in this progression: Cain, his descendants, human society before the flood, and finally Babel.

With Cain there begins *violence between brothers*. From the very start, as we saw, the breaking of the covenant with God upset human relationships. Embarrassment and accusation had replaced the trustful freedom of the beginning. In chapter 4, sin against one's neighbour grows worse. We can observe in a totally different way the link between sin and death, as sin reveals its significance for inter-personal relationships in the will to

[5] The approach we are defining is close to the conclusions of David J. Clines, 'Themes in Genesis 1 – 11', *CBQ* 38 (1976), pp.483–507.

murder. And the question, 'Where is your brother?' (Gn. 4:9) corresponding to the earlier question, 'Where are you?' (Gn. 3:9),[6] shows that sin in its development can no longer be analysed solely in terms of offences against God, but also as guilt towards other men; no longer as just a 'religious' category (in the narrow sense usually given to the word), but also as an 'ethical' category.

The text is far removed, however, from an independent ethic. Rather, it shows us the religious root of crime against other persons. What bitterness fuelled the murderer's hatred? In what manner did he feel himself wronged, to cast himself in a fury of revenge on the hapless Abel? As he saw God's favour, it was solely spite which devoured all brotherly feeling in the heart of Cain.

Why did God accept Abel's sacrifice with favour and reject the offering of Cain (*cf.* Heb. 11:4; 1 Jn. 3:12)? The hypotheses usually put forward, such as the necessity of the shedding of blood, are weak, since the text is silent on the matter. Two things, however, are certain. First, the LORD was absolutely free to approve or otherwise what was brought to him; secondly, Cain's offering lacked any kind of sacrificial spirit. For the spirit of sacrifice supremely involves respect for the liberty of God. Cain's reaction shows the profound paganism of his worship. If he was disappointed, it was because by his sacrifice he hoped to build up credit with God. What made him beside himself with rage was that the LORD showed himself to be the Lord, using his freedom of choice and, by choosing the other man, showing at the same time Abel's independence of Cain.

Might that not be the deepest source of hatred against our brother, turning so swiftly to the will to murder? We tolerate other people as the objects to manipulate for our own ends, as pawns on our chess board. But we do not tolerate their showing themselves to be truly the image of God by a relationship with him which we have failed to achieve. We do not tolerate, in concrete reality, a God who is free, who does not consult us in order to act and who upsets our impersonal ideas of justice and equality. We take a dim view of his being good *and* free (Mt. 20:15). Here, no doubt, lies the hidden cause of anti-Semitism, since the only distinctive feature of Israel out of all the peoples of the earth is to have been chosen by God – like Abel. But in

[6] Westermann *C*, p.20. P. Chaunu, *La Violence de Dieu* (Paris: Laffont, 1978), p.137, observes that Abel was the first human being to die: what a proof that death comes from sin!

murder in general another element is to be found: the rejection of one's neighbour on account of our rejection of God, for our neighbour is the image of God and reminds us of the LORD's freedom to flout our own claims. His hands stained with the blood of Uriah, as were Cain's with the blood of Abel, David prayed to God this astonishing prayer: 'Against thee, thee only, have I sinned' (Ps. 51:4). That was not unawareness of his 'ethical' guilt towards Uriah; David detected within himself the cause of the abominable crime that he had committed. It was indeed basically with God that he had been offended, for God limited his freedom by forbidding him the wife of his Hittite officer, and this same God had crossed his will by *choosing* to give Bathsheba to someone else.[7]

The descendants of Cain, a race of inventors, invent *violence within civilization*. No better summary of the beginnings of civilization could be given than that found in our narrative (Gn. 4:17–24). It tells of the beginning of urbanization (v.17), of mechanical skills (v.22) and of the arts (v.21). But evil is not in abeyance. The horrendous song of Lamech glorifies his absurdly exaggerated lust for vengeance (vv.23f.). This is the second human poem in the text of Genesis, and what a contrast it makes with the first one, the lover's greeting before the fall (Gn. 2:23)! Lamech's poetry oozes hatred. The comparison with Cain's words is intructive, marking human progress on the path of violence. Just as Lamech is more 'civilized', able to forge weapons with which to deliver his 'seventy-sevenfold' blows, so also he possesses the art of words and of phrases to express brutality. Whereas Cain can only mumble his response, 'I do not know' (Gn. 4:9), Lamech celebrates his crimes as so many heroic exploits.

It is no doubt significant that progress in the arts and in engineering comes from the 'city' of the Cainites. Nevertheless, we are not to conclude from this that civilization as such is considered by the Bible to be the fruit of sin. Such a conclusion would lead us to Manicheism or to the views of Jean-Jacques Rousseau, and would overlook the fact that evil is not inherent in things, but is always the corruption and perversion of God's gifts. The Bible condemns neither the city (for it concludes with the vision of the City of God) nor art and engineering (which

---

[7] The connection we make between Cain and David does not mean that we accept the thesis of Brueggemann, criticized by Clines, *art. cit.*, pp.498f.

contributed to the sanctuary of the LORD); rather, the creation mandate in the prologue of Genesis (Gn. 1:28) is to be fulfilled. But the Bible records perversion as a fact, and evil as something actually at work. Throughout history, the Cainites dominate. The 'means' are not neutral. By *right*, they are good; but in *fact* they are predominantly found on the side of evil. Sinner that he is, mankind sins as much as he can. By increasing his power, he increases his sin.[8]

With its efficiency, the Cainite civilization provides sin with institutional consolidation. Lamech formulates a rule which his tribe will observe and which will secure it in an interminable vendetta. This violence takes its place in the social code, and at times will glorify itself by claiming the virtues of fidelity and self-denial, for the descendants of Lamech will think of vengeance in terms of duty. Sin becomes formally a part of the human tradition.

From that point onwards the growth of the earth's population is accompanied by *ever-increasing corruption*. Genesis underlines the quantitative increase: morals decline in general corruption, and degradation and filth abound everywhere (Gn. 6:5, 11). We could also speak of the 'cultural' extension of sin, by underlining that the nature of man is saturated with it from his earliest youth (Gn. 8:21). One striking formula sums up everything: *raq ra'*, 'only evil' (Gn. 6:5).

☐   The only difficulty of interpretation in this whole picture concerns the opening of chapter 6. How are we to understand this mysterious passage? Who are these 'sons of God' who took wives from among the daughters of men (*'ādām*, with the article)? Setting aside the wild inventions of science fiction, three rival theories confront us.

The majority of contemporary critics attribute to the text a meaning close to that held by Jewish apocalyptic and certain rabbis. It was probably a popular legend about oriental equivalents of the Titans. The 'sons of God' would then be heavenly beings, in line with the usual meaning of the phrase, which is used freely for the angels. They were atttracted by the beautiful creatures on earth, committed fornication with them and begot these hybrid creatures, the *nᵉp̄ilîm*, or Giants. If we set aside for the moment the doctrinal difficulties this raises, two objections in particular challenge this exegesis. Its advocates are obliged to

[8] For further development and an appreciation of the views of Jacques Ellul at this point, see our article, 'L'ordre de Dieu et la réponse de l'homme', *RR* 23 (1972), pp.120ff.

admit that the text nowhere makes the $n^e\bar{p}il\hat{\imath}m$ the fruit of the unions in question;[9] they suppose that the author of Genesis has adapted and demythologized a different version of the episode.[10] In other words, one hypothesis supports another. Furthermore, they take no account of the expression used in verse 2, which in fact would be unsuitable for the carnal offence the angels are imagined to have committed. The more usual English rendering, 'took to wife' (RSV), is accurate, for the phrase is regularly used to denote the conclusion of matrimonial unions.

Following Julius Africanus (c. 170–240) and Augustine,[11] several scholars go for an easier interpretation.[12] The 'sons of God', according to this view, represent the line of Seth, who called on the name of the LORD (Gn. 4:25f.); the 'daughters of men' are the Cainites. The text, then, stigmatizes the first mixed marriages which corrupted religious purity and whose later parallels were such a snare for Israel (*cf*. Ex. 34:16, *etc*.). This proposal lacks conviction. It is true that the LORD's elect are his sons (Dt. 14:1), and godly men address him as 'the generation of thy children' (Ps. 73:15). But the bare phrase 'sons of God' is used nowhere in the Old Testament to denote the just, the believers. It is most implausible that the phrase denotes the Sethites. Similarly, 'daughters of *'ā<u>d</u>ām*' would be a surprising term for the Cainites alone, since the sons of Seth were just as much descended from the first man, Adam.

Meredith G. Kline has revived the old interpretation of the Targum of Onkelos and of the Greek translation of Symmachus, which has been upheld until our own time by certain Jewish exegetes.[13] According to this view, the 'sons of God' are princes, 'divine beings' according to the notions about royalty current in the ancient Near East. The Bible itself can call earthly judges 'gods' or 'sons of the Most High' (Ps. 82:6, *etc*.) because they represent the LORD who has delegated his authority to them. Genesis 6 is held therefore to evoke the language of royal claims which were widespread in the pagan world by reason of corruption of the divine institution. Thus the episode describes the

---

[9] The meaning of the noun $n^e\bar{p}il\hat{\imath}m$ is by no means certain; etymologically (does it come from *nā<u>p</u>al* or *pālē*'?) no explanation has been given of the Septuagint rendering, *gigantes*. In Nu. 13:33 certain $n^e\bar{p}il\hat{\imath}m$ are giants. (*Gibbōrîm*, later, is a common word for the 'heroes' or valiant warriors.)

[10] Von Rad, pp.111f.; he recognizes that in the text the phrase merely gives an indication of time.   [11] See Chaine, p.103.

[12] Recently, Goldstain, p.224; J. Barton Payne, *The Theology of the Older Testament* (Grand Rapids: Zondervan, 1962), pp.205ff. For a fuller, older treatment, see Keil, pp.127ff.

[13] M. G. Kline, 'Divine kingship and Genesis 6.1–4', *WTJ* 24 (1961–1962), pp.187–204.

emergence, in the growing ranks of the human race, of new social structures, with power concentrated in the hands of proud potentates, claiming divine status, unbridled in their appetites. It reports the construction of vast harems, a sign of their total lack of moderation, as these 'divine' men choose at will the women of the population that they wanted. The progression, even compared with Lamech, is evident, for he was a bigamous chieftain! Kline, supported by able and learned scholars,[14] argues that this reading provides a good parallel with the Babylonian accounts of the flood. It also gives the phrase 'sons of God' a likely meaning, one indeed that is very likely, given the original setting in which the tradition recorded in Genesis 6 arose. But there is one powerful objection. In the New Testament, Jude appears to side with the angelic or demonic interpretation of the Jewish pseudepigrapha, seeing the 'sons of God' as angels who 'acted immorally and indulged in unnatural lust' (Jude 6f.).[15] Thereby Scripture appears to stand closer to the first of these interpretations, without, however, supporting the idea of a progeny of monsters. ☐

It is extremely difficult to decide finally between the first and third interpretations. Might one risk attempting to bring them together by means of the biblical notion that supernatural powers are at work behind and in league with those who wield power (Dn. 10)? In the ideas of Jewish apocalyptic which the Letter of Jude seems to authorize, the two categories tend at times to merge.[16] It is conceivable that the angels acted in association with human instruments. And if Genesis thought of divinized kings, great priests of idolatrous cults and great masters of the occult, we may be sure that these men were in

[14] K. A. Kitchen, 'The Old Testament in its context: 1. From the origins to the eve of the Exodus', *TSF Bulletin* 59 (Spring 1971), p.4; A. R. Millard, *art. cit.*, p.12. Kidner, p.84 n.5, is not convinced that 'sons of God' is a term for kings.

[15] Efforts to understand the text of Jude differently look like emergency exits (*e.g.* J. B. Payne, *op. cit.*, p.206, n.28). Jude 7 speaks of Sodom and Gomorrah and the cities around 'which likewise acted immorally and indulged in unnatural lust' (referring to Gn. 19:4ff.). In the Greek, 'likewise' is literally 'in like manner to these', where 'to these' is masculine. It cannot therefore refer to the cities (feminine in Greek); nor can it refer to the men of v.4, for that would require the pronoun 'those' and not 'these'. 'In like manner' can with difficulty be understood in a very vague way, as if the angels had sinned in an indefinite manner, the only real point in common being the fact of disobedience. 'These' must refer to the angels of v.6, and the point in common must be the quest for sexual relations between creatures of differing nature. Jude indeed does not say that he finds the fall of the angels in Gn. 6, but since the book of Enoch does, and Jude quotes that book later (v.14), there can be no reasonable doubt that that is what he has in mind. Kline and those who follow him refrain from mentioning the Jude text.

[16] Bo Reicke, *Disobedient Spirits and Christian Baptism, A Study of 1 Pet. III. 19 and Its Context* (Copenhagen: E. Munksgaard, 1946), pp.57f.

communication with the world of evil spirits. Without deciding on the precise meaning of these enigmatic verses, we may therefore read in them the testimony of an increase in sin by the proliferation of occult influences, a dangerous mixture of heavenly and earthly rebellions. The corruption is continuing to get worse.

The flood was not adequate to correct mankind's downward trend (Gn. 9:22, 25). On the contrary, the story that follows reveals a new development in the march of evil: *union in pride*, the imperial sin. At Babel (or Babylon; in Hebrew they are one and the same name) men proved that they were still capable of joining together – for the purpose of attempting to conquer heaven.

By its calculated naïvety and its play on words, the narrative of Genesis 11 bears an amazing resemblance to Genesis 3. It is basically the same project that mankind seeks to fulfil in the two chapters: to make himself equal with God and thereby gain autonomy. He wants to ascend to heaven, instead of filling the earth. He claims to make a name for himself, instead of receiving his name from his Maker. Lys observes that the deliberate assonances in verse 3 (brick/stone; bitumen/mortar, which fail to come across in English translation) express the effort to change the very nature of things as they were created,[17] and so to substitute themselves for the Creator. The 'tower' is undoubtedly an early ziggurat, a cosmic mountain figure which had the power to tame the whole mystery of reality, store the whole realm of the sacred and become the ultimate reference point for mankind. Its construction signifies mankind's seizure of the absolute, as did the eating of the forbidden fruit in Eden.

The difference between Eden and Babel is that which distinguishes the individual deed and the collective act. The name 'Babylon' evoked the most prestigious of the ancient empires. Empire brings greatness and puts within one's reach, as it were, the Absolute, Universality made concrete. A theoretical and practical system is worked out, a language and a tower, that will enclose everything. Once the system is completed, it will proclaim the autonomy of the human race, and will determine completely the lives and destinies of each individual. The ziggurat equals the System! Having become a collective enterprise, the sinful project takes on the face of totalitarianism, with technology and ideology as its means of realization. If Genesis 3

[17] D. Lys, 'Le jeu des mots dans l'Ancien Testament', *RR* 27 (1976), p.110.

reveals the religious root of human evil, Genesis 11 shows it in its most logical and perhaps most terrible political expression.

The inevitable judgment

Sin cannot fail to receive its wages. As a fugitive is pursued by his own shadow, so the procession of pain, punishment and death follows immediately in the tracks of evil as it pursues its onward march.

As far as we can tell from the facts, the harvest that Cain reaps from his crime is a *flight of terror*. He is cursed from the earth, which has swallowed his brother's blood (Gn. 4:11), whereas in chapter 3 only the soil was cursed. This worsening of the curse undoubtedly implies that no spot on earth would want to act as shelter for the murderer, and that the earth which has witnessed his act will always reject him. Adam was no more than an exile; Cain will be a fugitive, *nā'* and *nād*, a wanderer and vagabond (v.12). The land of Nod itself, to the east of Eden, where the *kᵉrûbîm* stand guard with the sword, will afford him no real shelter, since its name means 'wandering' (v.16).

His lot wrings from his hard heart the first human lament that has been recorded: 'My punishment is greater than I can bear' (v.13). The cry is excruciating. There is no question of its rehabilitating Cain, for he commiserates with himself and utters not a word of regret for the act he has committed. But it demonstrates the degree to which, by a kind of boomerang effect, the guilty sinner is the victim of the evil he has done. If the biblical Cain says nothing about the eye of conscience,[18] at least he confesses the primary consequence of the violence of fratricide, which is fear. It is fear that will make him flee. *Homo homini lupus*: one man devouring his fellow like a wolf. But as he unleashes the logic of that maxim, Cain discovers that it has a recoil, that of sheer terror.

For Cain's descendants the Bible does not specify the punishment to be undergone. No doubt it considers the answer too obvious in the very multiplication of evil to need any explanation, and close enough to the punishment of their ancestor. Lamech joins the *infernal cycle* of war between families, outbidding them in his sheer destructiveness. This increase in

---

[18] The reference is to Victor Hugo's famous poem 'La Conscience' from his epic cycle, *La Légende des Siècles* (1859), in which the eye of conscience pursues Cain relentlessly everywhere.

204

destruction is only another form of the flight that turned Cain into a wanderer – with the same driving force of anxiety and dread. Who does not know what is hidden beneath the bragging talk and flamboyant rhetoric of aggression? It is merely secret, repressed terror.

As corruption continues to grow worse, its punishment, of course, is *the flood*. An examination of the various literary, scientific and other questions that could be discussed would take us far beyond the limits of our study. But we should pause to see how the engulfment of humanity by the flood constitutes 'the wages of sin'. In short, we might suggest that the flood marks the end of God's patience and that it is a cleaning operation on the world, a kind of 'de-creation'.

The inordinate degree of human transgression in the episode of the 'sons of God' causes the LORD to announce: 'My Spirit shall not strive with man forever, because he also is flesh; nevertheless his days shall be one hundred and twenty years' (Gn. 6:3, NASB). The translation of that verse is uncertain at two points. 'Because also' could be read: 'because of (or, in) his going astray'.[19] More significantly, the verb is variously rendered by the translators: 'direct', 'strive with', 'abide in' (following the ancient versions) or even 'be humiliated'.[20] Whatever the case, it is clear that God considers that he has tolerated the ways of sinners long enough. Since men are (perhaps) yielding to the influences of other spirits, his Spirit will abandon them to their lost ways; in spite of their divine pretensions, they are mere flesh and shall submit to the sovereignty of the sole Master. The LORD grants one last reprieve of one hundred and twenty years before the disaster, but it is of the nature of patience that it should at some time come to an end.[21]

The earth is now so filled with violence (Gn. 6:11f.) that God must deploy the most gigantic ablution to wash it free of its stain. He himself uses the verb 'blot out' (Gn. 6:7; 7:4, 23). The

[19] Von Rad, p.111, strongly upholds the former interpretation, which breaks the word down into *bᵉ, še* and *gam*.

[20] *Cf.* Kidner, p.84. If one derives *yāḏôn* from *dîn/dûn*, a common Hebrew verb (to judge), you get either 'to direct' or 'to plead', 'to contest'. But the form *yāḏôn* is not used elsewhere (elsewhere you find *yāḏîn*). A root *dnn* seems to exist with the meaning to 'dwell' (the form *yāḏôn* would then be normal).

[21] A common interpretation today takes the Spirit as the breath of life which upholds the life of individuals, and takes the 120 years as the length of human life. But this seems to us less likely. In the subsequent biblical narrative, it does not appear that the human life-span settled around that length. Our interpretation fits the context better, and is in accord with 1 Pet. 3:19f.; the Spirit in which Christ went to preach to the rebellious spirits (now) in prison could be that of Gn. 6:3.

universality of the scourge corresponds to the universality of the corruption. The text also brings out this idea of a correspondence by repeating the same verb: 'Now the earth was corrupt (v.11)...and behold it was corrupt; for all flesh had corrupted their way (v.12)...behold, I will *destroy* [the same Hebrew verb] them with the earth (v.13)'. It is as if he were applying the *lex talionis,* or at least the same logic. Since men have plunged the world into moral chaos, they will be punished with physical chaos. The flood has thus the character of a just retribution.

The return to chaos is creation in reverse. The third aspect of the judgment brought out by Genesis is that of the destruction of his own work by the LORD, his 'de-creation'. He repents of having made mankind on the earth (Gn. 6:6). He undoes what he has done. He unleashes the waters that he had separated. The waters below submerge the dry land, and the waters above join them, in a return to the great turmoil of the *tōhû-bōhû* (Gn. 7:11). The earth that was formed out of water now returns into it (2 Pet. 3:5f.). The de-creation of the flood, despite its extent, was not total, merely partial. But the point is clear enough to make us think: so exceedingly evil and harmful is sin, both intensively and extensively, that there is no moderate therapy that can cure it, no satisfactory amendment of life can be expected from the old earth. The flood denounces the perversion of sin as a 'radical evil', as 'total depravity'. That is undoubtedly why in the New Testament it stands as the foremost prefiguration of the end of the world (Mt. 24:37f. and parallels; 2 Pet. 3).

The pride of Babel is doomed to *failure.* The judgment that strikes the imperial, totalitarian enterprise is the outcome that runs totally counter to the aims it had set itself. The tower remains unfinished, the target of the jibes of all who pass by it: these are the men who began to build and who were unable to finish (*cf.* Lk. 14:29f.). The union attempted by force brings about division and dispersion. The claim to reach up to heaven sinks in confusion. The derision of the LORD, who laughs at presumptuous conspirators (Ps. 2:4), emerges in the word-play on the name Babel. Whilst the Babylonians gave it the meaning 'Gate of God' (*Bab-ili*), Genesis links it with *balal,* the root of the word for 'confusion', like our 'blah-blah-blah'.[22]

The ridiculous failure of Babel signifies the failure of all totalitarian attempts. No human system manages to encompass

[22] *Cf.* Lys, *art. cit.,* p.107.

everything; there always persists the irreducible element which sows the seed of rebellion and condemns the tyranny of the masters and of the thought controllers.[23] Even the most complete of these systems, the totalitarianism of the final Babylon, the antichrist, will not be able to realize its mad imperialist design; only its sins will be 'heaped *high as heaven*' (Rev. 18:5).[24] If it seems to succeed at first, the System is able, in proportion to its success, merely to create confusion. Only the supremacy of the God of heaven permits unity and order. By usurping God's transcendence, and instituting itself as the final reference on earth, the Babel project calls forth challenges, rival projects arise, and there ensue division and dispersion. Since the story of Genesis 11 emphasizes the fate of language, which is in very truth the expression of human life, we may be permitted to point out how the same principle is confirmed in this area today. Divorced from any concern for truth, human language disintegrates into the repetition of signals and the yelling of slogans, with each universe of propaganda opposed to its rival and all words emptied of their meaning. Communication is lost and meaning is lost. The punishment for the sin of Babel is not to be underestimated.

The signs of grace

But God. But the mercy of God. If sin itself has time to develop and death has time to follow, it is because God in his mercy has something else in view. In the chapters that follow in Genesis, he gives the other signs of his grace, whether in mitigating the punishment or in preparing the future.

The LORD does not abandon guilty Cain. Having rejected his offering and observed the evil feelings that fill his heart, God does not simply turn away from Cain. He does him the honour of calling to him. God confirms that he does not leave the human race totally exposed to the power of the snake. He exhorts Cain to the manly reaction that is called for in the face of sin's zeal to cling to him. He makes an implicit offer of his help to repel temptation (Gn. 4:6f.).

When Cain has committed his heinous crime, the LORD hears the plea, repugnant though it is, of the murderer. He places on

[23] Henri Lefebvre, *La vie quotidienne dans le monde moderne* (Paris: Gallimard, 1968), pp.346f. and *passim*, insists on the inability of the system to embrace everything. Unfortunately, his utopian City is another, typical, resurgence of the spirit of Babel.

[24] The link between the two is pointed out by Kidner, p.111.

him a sign, the seal of his protection, as he had placed clothes over Adam and Eve to cover their distress (Gn. 4:15). In this manner he alleviates the terror of the poor fugitive a little. By proclaiming that he himself will punish whoever makes an attempt on the life of Cain, God seems to introduce an embryonic judicial system, since he withdraws the right of vengeance from private individuals. In any case, God proves the degree to which in his eyes the sinner remains a *man*, for whom he still wishes to be concerned.

Over against the 'civilized' consolidation of violence in the tradition of the Cainites and of Lamech, God raises up *another tradition* within the human race. In place of Abel he bestows another son, Seth (Gn. 4:25). It is interesting that the name Seth (*šēt*) should be connected by his mother with the word *šût*, 'to place', 'to designate', 'to institute'. For it is the same verb as is used in Genesis 3:15: 'I will put [or, institute] enmity'. Seth and his descendants will maintain hostility towards the snake. The text adds that with Enosh, the son of Seth, 'men began to call upon the name of the Lord' (4:26), which suggests that an organized system of worship, with its own institutions, countered the civilization of evil. Enoch who walked with God (Gn. 5:22, 24) and Noah, the instrument of relief (Gn. 5:29), show that the grace of God was not in vain in the line of Seth.

What the Lord did for Noah is, beyond all contradiction, the most glorious manifestation of divine grace in the whole history of primeval man. As the flood is *the* punishment in that era, so the salvation of Noah is the demonstration of God's favour and the great picture of redemption. One picturesque detail that stands out in contrast with the Babylonian narrative illustrates the theme of grace. Whereas the Babylonian equivalent of Noah in the Epic of Gilgamesh must himself close the door of the ark, in Genesis it is the Lord who takes this on himself and thus wonderfully shows his concern for his servant (Gn. 7:16). The New Testament does not hesitate to see in the salvation of Noah the 'type' of the deliverance obtained in Jesus Christ, of which baptism is the sign (1 Pet. 3:21). The fact that Noah and his party were eight in number takes on a symbolic significance (1 Pet. 3:20), for the eighth day, the day of the resurrection of Jesus, is that of the new creation, since the seventh day is that of the preservation of the old creation.[25]

[25] We would also point out that the numerical value of the name Jesus in Greek, *Iēsous*, is 888.

208

A new creation! If the judgment of a corrupt earth was equivalent to a de-creation, the favour bestowed on Noah and the restoration of the normal conditions of existence after the waters receded can be reckoned a re-creation. When the whole sweep of the biblical panorama is considered, it is difficult not to discern in the story of Noah the prefiguration of the new creation announced by Isaiah and inaugurated by Jesus Christ.

Furthermore, as at the original creation God made a covenant with the human race, similarly he makes a covenant with Noah. This covenant looks in both directions. The restoration of the earth after the flood was the material reconstitution of the earlier situation, but coming as it did after the judgment it was also a figure of the new creation. The covenant with Noah repeats the covenant in Eden, but also acts as a figure of the new covenant. God confirms his initial provisions which he has not abrogated. Once again he grants mankind fertility and dominion (Gn. 9:1ff.) and recalls the creation of mankind in his image (Gn. 9:6).[26] But other provisions are added because sin has entered the world with all its trail of consequences, and these provisions at times bring the new covenant to mind. Henceforth animals will be afraid of mankind (Gn. 9:2); their flesh will henceforth be his food (Gn. 9:3).[27] God makes a general principle of what he did for Cain by instituting the judicial restraint of the murderer (Gn. 9:5f.). And all these features signify the presence of tensions and hostility, of a new atmosphere, on a global scale. What is important is that God brings this new situation under his control; he does not simply wipe things out, but he takes upon himself a responsibility for what has occurred. Thereby he points already to the direction the new covenant will take. In particular, by the prohibition on blood (Gn. 9:4) he makes

[26] We consider that the clauses of Gn. 2 imply the dispositions of Gn. 1, set out in different words.

[27] Barth, pp.208ff., gives a brilliant interpretation of this addition, by supposing that animal flesh was excluded from the diet of both man and beasts in Gn. 1. But he avoids the difficulties by placing this order 'beyond the field of natural history': 'The time or "era" of this commencement is the pre-historical era in which strictly speaking ... the question can only be that of God's permission and command and not of the corresponding activity and existence of the creature' (p.211). We cannot identify with this solution, which is all of a piece with the cardinal tenets of Barthianism. We think that the addition of Gn. 9 is significant, but we must not see in it a change of law; the text does not say that we pass from prohibition (Gn. 1) to permission (Gn. 9); the omission or inclusion is merely suggestive. By anthropomorphic projection, animal death, which is not an evil in itself, *suggests* the introduction of severe violence, *etc.* In its stylized representation of the original state, Gn. 1 omits that feature in order to suggest the perfection of harmony; Gn. 9, on the contrary, adds it in order to convey the feeling that the peace has been broken.

reference to the sacrificial system. God reserves animal blood for this system in order to represent in substitutionary form the life of men and women (Lv. 17:11, 14). It is by way of sacrifice that people will be able to eat meat and benefit from the death of an animal. Now, under the new covenant it is indeed by sacrifice (which was also a judicial act) that God has brought evil under his control: he offers life to everyone who by faith 'eats' the sacrificial flesh of the Son of man (Jn. 6).

Furthermore, the LORD makes a promise, which is the heart of his covenant with Noah. He gives the human race a solemn assurance that there will never again be a flood, nor a further cursing of the ground, nor a destruction of the human race (Gn. 8:21f.; 9:9ff.). The pledge is all the more surprising because God expressly recalls the radical corruption in the heart of man (Gn. 8:21). The promise holds good in spite of sin, without sin being minimized for one moment. In other words, the promise is sheer grace – grace which abounds all the more in the very place where sin abounds. It is significant that God does this after smelling the pleasing propitiatory sacrifice (Gn. 8:21). Does God not pledge himself because he has already decided that, in order to pay the retribution for the sin that will begin to proliferate again soon, there will be a different judgment from that of the flood, a different propitiatory sacrifice from that of Noah? God promises because he has already foreordained the Lamb who will bear and carry away the sin of the world, the sacrifice of the new covenant. The associated sign of the bow in the cloud speaks of peace after battle (for the weapon has been laid aside), of a link between the reconciled heaven and earth and of the light of grace which shines over the threatening waters of the wrath of God.

The light of divine grace is so easily seen in the unfolding of events recounted by Genesis, that it is suprising at first to see no trace of it in the Babel narrative. In this final episode, might judgment perhaps be the only, the final word?

Undoubtedly an element of grace can be detected in the failure of the imperial enterprise. The LORD, as it were, takes counsel with himself in Genesis 11:6f. in a way that closely resembles Genesis 3:22, and God's two deliberations can be understood in a similar manner. The LORD appears to be afraid of the success of this human enterprise, but the intentional naïvety of the phrase demands interpretation. In 3:22 God eliminates the unthinkable notion of mankind partaking of both trees at the same time, which would be the worst possible thing that could happen. In 11:6f. he eliminates the unthinkable notion of mankind succeeding in its collective project of the domestication of the absolute, of total domination. It is unthinkable: even the antichrist will not attain it. But that too would be the worst possible thing that could happen: the nameless terror whose intolerable image is foreshadowed by the totalitarian systems that are the precursors of the final antichrist. Far better than that, the evil of dispersion and misunderstanding. By preventing the finishing of the tower, God shows mercy on those arrogant madmen.

But there is more. Why stop at chapter 11, verse 9? We must continue to read. There follow the *tōlᵉdôt* of Shem and those of Terah (from 11:27). From the family of Terah, from the heart of the dispersion of the peoples, from Ur of the Chaldeans, that is Ur in Babylonia, the LORD calls Abraham. The question of salvation remained at the conclusion of the Babel narrative; 'Our narrator *does* give an answer,' as von Rad puts it so well, 'namely, at the point where sacred history begins'.[28]

With Abram, or Abraham, the tenth from Noah, as Noah was the tenth from Adam, begins the decisive implementation of the plan of God. The sights are set on its goal: on that descendant of Abraham by whom all the nations of the earth will have their share in blessing. The sights are set on Jesus Christ and on those who in him constitute the true descendants of the father of those who believe, the humanity that is gathered together by grace.

It would require a commentary on the whole New Testament to describe the work of grace, a work which is envisaged by the call of Abraham.

That call allows the emergence of the anti-Babel, as is shown by the miracle of tongues on the day of Pentecost. By the gift of the Holy Spirit, said the Fathers, 'the humble piety of the faithful has brought the diversity of languages into the unity of the Church, so that what had been torn apart by strife is joined together by charity.'[29] The book of Revelation emphasizes the assembly of people 'from every tribe and *tongue* and people and nation' (Rev. 5:9).

It begins to set in motion the new creation (2 Cor. 5:17; Gal. 6:15; Eph. 2:10) for the redeemed humanity which passes

[28] Von Rad, p.149; *cf.* Clines, *art. cit.,* pp.503f.
[29] Quoted by Goldstain, p.261.

through the judgments of this world in the ark of salvation (1 Pet. 3:20f.).

It institutes the church, the assembly of those who, like Enosh, call on the name of the Lord in order to be saved, and walk with him as did Enoch.

It places on the forehead of those who have been pardoned a protective sign (Rev. 7:3), infinitely better than the sign on the forehead of Cain, for the blood of Jesus Christ proclaims a better message than the cry that arose from the blood of Abel (Heb. 12:24).

It allows to the descendants of the woman, through the One who allowed himself to be bruised and stricken 'in return' for his brothers, the grace to crush the adversary in the head, finally and for ever. It restores to mankind the life of the paradise of God. And it gives to them, those recreated in his image, sons in the Son, the right to call him Father for evermore.

Appendix: Scientific hypotheses and the beginning of Genesis

The interpretation of the Bible must not be overshadowed by the hypotheses current amongst scientists today. Moses knew nothing about them and we must put them out of our minds if we are going to understand his meaning properly without any interference in the meaning of the divine Word. But after that it would be irresponsible to extend this methodical neglect. The universal reign of the one true God forbids such schizophrenic compartmentalization. The believer can avoid neither cautious critical examination of the theories nor the task of linking his conclusions to the teaching of divine revelation. Everybody, obviously, must do this within the limits of his own calling.

Unfortunately in order to estimate properly the positions currently held on the origins of the universe, of life and of the human race and to judge their connection with Genesis 1 – 3, a variety of scientific disciplines must be mastered, as well as that of philology for the work of exegesis. A great number of authors with a varying array of weapons have become involved in this enterprise, in particular a group of scientists in the United States whose movement we have called 'anti-scientism' and who prefer to be called 'creationists' (they consider themselves to be the only consistent creationists) and 'catastrophists' because of the part played in their explanation of the phenomena by the catastrophe of the fall. These scientists, of whom several hundred belong to the Creation Research Society, have revived a position that was very popular amongst the Fundamentalists in the late 1920s, following the publication of George McCready Price's *The New Geology* in 1923. But the new movement has better scientific credentials. It was launched by Henry M. Morris and John C. Whitcomb with their important book, *The Genesis Flood* in 1961. Several other books have followed (see our bibliography for two of them) and Jean Flori and Henri Rasolo-fomasoandro, who are Adventists as was Price, published a moderate

213

and lucid statement in French in 1973, *Evolution ou création?* Not that they have convinced everybody! As the arguments of these people are still not particularly well known in Europe, we consider it worth while to provide a brief survey of them. At the same time we shall mention the response made by other believing scientists who are also committed to the authority of the biblical text, but who are closer to current scientific thought. We shall not attempt any kind of ruling between the two: we deny any competence in the area and can only give the opinions of a theologian and the impressions of a careful reader.

Our rapid survey must be selective. Amongst the areas of friction we shall choose questions that relate firstly to the measurement of time, secondly to the origin of living species and finally to the origin and antiquity of mankind, that is to say mankind in the strictly biblical sense. These three problems are connected but distinct and seem to cover the largest issues. True, other questions arouse controversy. In the seventeenth century Lutheran and Reformed theologians argued over the solidity of the firmament and over the existence or otherwise of an upper ocean in Genesis (*cf.* Barth, pp.135ff.; and Keil, pp.52ff. in favour of the Calvinist position). Anti-scientism has revived the dispute, supposing that before the flood the earth was covered with a very thick canopy of atmospheric waters which were rained down on the earth at the time of the flood (*The Genesis Flood*, p.77). It also rejects majority opinions on the formation of the galaxies, of the solar system and of the moon, on the basis of such difficulties as the difference in composition between the lunar rocks and the earthly rocks and the retrograde movement of a third of the satellites around their planets (*cf.* J. C. Whitcomb, *The Early Earth*, pp.41–60). However, it would scarcely carry persuasion if these propositions alone were in question. The reference to the waters 'above' (Gn. 1) is too brief for any clear theory about their meaning to be read out of the text. As for the cosmogony that is currently in favour amongst scientists, rather than stumbling over its difficulties as does anti-scientism, anyone who reads Roland Omnès' masterly *L'Univers et ses métamorphoses* admires rather the fact that so many enigmas have been resolved. Like Pierre Chaunu, he will be amazed at the agreement between the biblical affirmation about the beginning and Gamow's model, or the theory of the initial big bang, of the hadronic period (one ten-thousandth of a second), during which according to Hawking's theorem, in the finest understatement of all time, 'something odd must have happened' (Omnès, p.121). Contrary to the materialist desire to confer eternity on matter, this theory is the only one which enjoys the privilege of (embryonic) experimental verification: in 1965 Penzias and Wilson discovered an isotropic thermic radiation in the universe, as predicted by Gamow (*cf.* Omnès, pp.95ff.). Anti-scientism rejects this theory only on the basis of the conclusions they have reached on other more decisive questions and in particular those which we propose to consider.

The measurement of time

The big bang theory holds that the universe has been expanding for 13 billion years. Our planet is more recent: it is generally given 4½ billion years, its most ancient rocks being up to 3½ billion years old (*cf.* Omnès, p.173). Geochronology has been speaking in terms of that kind of time span since the eighteenth century, when geologists began to interpret numerous phenomena, such as sedimentary rocks, as the result of extremely slow processes spread over hundreds of millions of years and basically like those which can be observed today, on the principle of uniformitarianism. A table of the eras and ages was drawn up on the basis of the arrangement of the layers of rock and of indications as to how they were formed and with the corroboration of certain so-called characteristic or stratigraphic fossils which provide plentiful and specific evidence of their age. Over the last thirty years or so, radiometric methods have allowed the confirmation or correction of the old statistics. They are based on the same principle. They measure the passage of time by the constancy of the speed at which radioactive elements break down. When a radioactive body gives birth to another, to a daughter element, since the speed of the process is invariable and is known, one simply needs to know what proportion of the initial parent element has broken down in order to calculate the time. Thus it is known that a given quantity of U^{238} takes 4.5×10^9 years in order for half of it to become Pb^{206}; that is the period, or half-life, of U^{238}. If you find in a rock that there is a radiogenic quantity of Pb^{206} equivalent to three-quarters of the initial quantity of U^{238}, you will conclude that the age of the rock is $2 \times 4.5 \times 10^9$ years (two half-lives). In this way use is made of what is known about the breakdown of uranium and of thorium into lead ($U^{238} \rightarrow Pb^{206}$, and $U^{235} \rightarrow Pb^{207}$, a period of 7.13×10^8; $Th^{232} \rightarrow Pb^{208}$, a period of 1.39×10^{10}), of radioactive potassium into argon ($K^{40} \rightarrow Ar^{40}$, a period of 1.31×10^9), and of radioactive rubidium into strontium ($Rb^{87} \rightarrow Sr^{87}$, a period of 5×10^{10}). A similar method is used for dating vegetable or animal remains, based on the breakdown of radioactive carbon ($C^{14} \rightarrow N^{14}$), which is fixed by the living creature in proportion to its presence in the atmosphere and which breaks down after the creature's death with a half-life of 5,730 years; but because this is such a short period it cannot be used for measuring with any certainty above a span of 40,000 years.

The majority of Bible-believing Christians, on learning of geochronological conclusions, accept them without difficulty. If for the moment we set aside the question of the antiquity of mankind, we easily see that the days of Genesis 1 contradict the proposed datings only if interpreted literally. In fact, the majority see them as representing different eras, or see the overall passage as a literary form – Ramm, for example. For such people, including ourselves, there are no problems with Genesis.

Anti-scientism most frequently appeals to a strictly literal interpretation of Genesis. (Flori and Rasolofomasoandro appear to be an exception, as also are the group of scholars to whom we referred in chapter 1, p.21, n.9.) From there, with the assurance of their faith, its advocates proceed to question the results and methods of normal chronometry. But, without returning to a Middle Earth chronology, they cannot stretch the genealogies of the Bible over tens of thousands of years (*The Genesis Flood*, pp.474–489). Sometimes they recall the ingenious idea of Philip H. Gosse in his book *Omphalos* (1857): God must have created the world with the *appearance* of age in order to obtain instantaneously the world as he wished to have it, with its fruits *as if* they had ripened, with the sedimentary rocks *as if* they came from deposits that were thousands of years old, and with the first man perhaps having a navel (Whitcomb, *The Early Earth*, pp.30–37). But this principle, so well worked out in its own terms, can explain only a fraction of the appearances of age – unless God thought fit to scatter deliberately deceptive evidence about everywhere in order to throw the scientists off the trail! Therefore they concentrate their energies on a scientific critique of the methods of dating and complete their case by emphasizing the signs of the recent age of the earth which other scientists overlook.

The initial flaw of the generally held theory is, in the view of anti-scientism, its uniformitarianism. Why should present conditions be projected into the past while there is a refusal to imagine prodigious events that would be capable, through enormous pressures, intense heat and the like, of achieving what would otherwise take thousands of years? In elaborating a catastrophism which is quite different from that of Cuvier, anti-scientism takes Noah's flood as the sole explanation for the formation of the majority of the rocks and fossils, including the rocks of biological origin formed by 'the extraordinary density' of life in the oceans which were suddenly overwhelmed and the deposits of coal by the accumulation of wood from the forests which were swept along by marine currents. In making out their case, they argue that the solidification of the sediments into compact rocks operates much better by the rapid action of very powerful agents, and that fossilization (sometimes of an upturned tree with its roots 'in the air') suppose an almost instantaneous fixation, without which the organic form would rapidly have decayed.

As for radiometric methods, anti-scientism does not so much denounce the principal presupposition of the constant rate of disintegration, as other presuppositions which are often hidden, and the conditions for operating the methods. In all cases, to be exact, the calculation presupposes that the quantity of the genuinely radiogenic daughter element can be distinguished from the quantities of the same elements which formed part of the rock from its very beginning. But then it would be necessary to know the original distribution of the isotopes, and that is unknown. Average rates are adopted as found in non-radioactive rocks today, but those rates are variable and, anyway, it is not known what those rates were billions of years ago. The calculation presupposes further that the system has remained closed, that in the course of time there has been neither addition nor subtraction of the parent element or of the daughter element. But in fact the contrary is likely, with infiltrations, the diffusion of gases and sometimes the capture of neutrons. (For example, Pb^{206} can be changed by capture into Pb^{207}, which in that case does not result from breakdown.) Anti-scientism is not in the least surprised if the application of these methods leads to aberrant results – as in the case of the 200-year-old basalts in the Hawaiian Islands, whose dating varies from 0.22 to 42.9 million years, depending on the depth of the sample beneath the surface of the ocean. Together with the disagreements amongst methods used, that confirms that no credit should be given to official datings.

The calculations based on the breakdown of C^{14} presuppose a concentration of that element in the atmosphere of past ages which is equal to that of the concentration today, that is to say a fundamental balance between the C^{14} which is constantly being created and that which is breaking down. M. A. Cook, a Professor at the University of Utah, cites studies which show that such a balance is not in fact realized. Approximately 40% more C^{14} is created than is lost. This means that the concentration of C^{14} is constantly increasing and it must be supposed that the atmosphere in past ages contained very little of it. The ages must therefore be revised downwards; none of them in fact exceeds 10,000 years, which supports the theory of a young earth. Amongst other signs of a young earth anti-scientism points to the absence of the layer of cosmic dust which ought to be 60 metres thick across the whole earth, if the earth were 4½ billion years old; the scarcity of nickel in the ocean, whereas over that period of time the rivers ought to have carried down enough for the sea to contain several tons per square metre, and likewise for other minerals; the decrease in intensity of the magnetic field which would diminish regularly by a half every 1,400 years and would therefore imply such a high magnetic strength 10,000 years ago that it would be impossible to go back any further in time; and so forth. This ultra-short chronology is boldly asserted to be the most scientific.

The author of Genesis has shown us that he did not understand the days of his first tablet literally. It is therefore erroneous, in our view, to introduce the Bible into the geochronological debate. Divine revelation does not allow us to settle the issue. Nevertheless the scientific arguments of anti-scientism are there; what are we to make of them?

The layman reels beneath the onslaught of examples and equations! He does not even have to hand a complete point-by-point response to the case for a young earth which would allow him better to evaluate its strengths and weaknesses. Two substantial articles by scientists who are committed to the Bible have, happily, given us some light: John Byrt's article, 'The roles of the Bible and of science in understanding creation' in *Faith and Thought* 103 (1976), pp.158–188, seeks to respond to anti-scientism; and in his article 'Radiometric dating' in *Christian Graduate* 30/4 (December 1977), pp.120–127, A. Fraser, a geologist at the University of Hull, examines more specifically its criticism of the methods of dating by the breakdown of rubidium into strontium, potassium into argon and uranium and thorium into lead.

From Fraser's study it emerges that the problems raised by the application of radiometric methods are not insoluble, and that scientists are having greater and greater success in resolving them. For the rocks whose geological history is simple, excellent rates of agreements are being obtained: less than 10% difference for 75–85% of the measures compared. As for the discrepancies and anomalies, they affect samples whose history has been disturbed. They are explained by the influence of disturbances such as those mentioned by anti-scientism. Instead of being discouraged by these and completely abandoning radiometry, we can learn to take account of them and to correct their effects. Occasionally we can notice opposition between our authors on a precise fact: Cook, representing anti-scientism, asserts that 'the relation Sr^{87}/Sr^{86} goes from 0.7 to 0.9 in all specimens whether old or young' and that it was by an arbitrary 'guess' that they fixed at 0.78 the initial rate from which any excess would be interpreted as radiogenic. But Fraser shows that the relation varies from 0.70 to 0.72, or exceptionally 0.73 in rocks which contain no rubidium, and that on the contrary in those which contain it the relation Sr^{87}/Sr^{86} can rise to 3 or more (*art. cit.*, p.122). This is quite a different picture which inspires confidence as much as Cook's instilled doubt. Fraser emphasizes strongly that the catastrophist theory cannot explain the distribution of Sr^{87}: according to their theory it was the force of the flood which diffused this element in unequal degrees amongst the rocks that were then formed; how is it, then, that strong concentrations of Sr^{87} appear in rocks that are rich in rubidium? Furthermore we find similar relations and the same ages for meteorites and lunar rocks which did not undergo the flood.

It would seem imprudent to exclude a 'catastrophic' origin for a certain number of the observable data. But for many others only processes of immense length can be envisaged. Fraser cites the convincing example of the local metamorphism caused by the rising of plutonic rocks. What occurred can very easily be followed on the ground and, since it has been possible to determine the precise conditions for such a transformation (*e.g.* the temperature of crystallization, *etc.*), the time taken is known with considerable certainty, sometimes to within one million years. Byrt calculates that the earth at the time of the flood could never have borne the whole vegetable mass necessary to create the deposits of coal, as the flood theory would wish. Ramm (p.185) had already drawn attention to the 600 metres of stratification in the Yellowstone Park which reveal eighteen forests which were covered over by lava one after another, each successive forest pushing down the soil of the lava which engulfed its predecessor; how much time would have been needed for the lava to turn into soil each time and for a forest to grow on it? The signs favouring a 'young' earth belong to a class of facts which are still not properly understood or explained; they do not carry enough weight to counterbalance the much more numerous signs of a great age for the earth. As for the continued diminution of the earth's magnetic field, Flori and Rasolofomasoandro do not mention it, even when they are dealing with variations in magnetism and of the dating system based on it (*op. cit.,* pp.368ff.).

So the picture becomes clearer. The statistics of official geochronology are not absolutely certain; advances in scientific research may multiply or divide them perhaps even by two or by three, but their huge scale has the greater likelihood of being confirmed. Anti-scientism, driven on by an unduly literal exegesis of Genesis 1, has exaggerated the difficulties and forgotten the evidence supporting the consensus which predominates amongst scientists regarding the measurement of the eras.

The question of transformism

If one is permitted to count in billions of years, another debate flares up which a young earth would have closed immediately: that of transformism, or the theory of biological evolution. Convinced that it is so obliged by divine revelation, anti-scientism again opposes the majority of contemporary specialists at this point. The situation, however, is not the same as for geochronology; the dissenters are much more numerous. And their ranks are joined by scientists who make no reference to the Bible, such as Dingemans in his *Formation et transformation des espèces* (A. Colin, 1956), Jean Servier of the University of Montpellier who has taken up the torch of the great Louis Vialleton, Louis Bounoure who taught at the University of Strasbourg, while scientists who hold to the theory of evolution admit the difficulties that their theory presents, such as G. A. Kerkut of the University of Southampton in his book *Implications of Evolution* (Pergamon Press, 1960).

The essential thesis of transformism could be stated thus: there are genealogical links between living species. Or, to put it another way: the types whose diversity provides the rich variety of the biosphere appeared in succession, each one of them being produced by the transformation of an anterior type. Evolution as set forth in the theory of transformism has brought into being one single living material, which is the varied multitude of living objects which have inhabited and do inhabit the earth, in such a way that they are represented as the spreading branches of a single tree of Life.

Transformist scientists, such as G. G. Simpson in his book *The Meaning of Evolution* (Yale UP, 1951), willingly announce that evolution is not a hypothesis but a fact. By way of proof they point to the similarities and the common elements which the different species possess; they look like a family and the idea of their kinship springs up naturally in the human mind. Why, without a common genealogy, would all living beings contain exactly the same complicated types of vitamins and enzymes, why would all the higher mammals be trituberculate, and why would all walking vertebrates be quadrupeds? These arrangements do not appear to be absolutely necessary; they would not have been imposed *alone*, to the exclusion of other possible arrangements, without an original link as P. Teilhard de Chardin argues in *Le Phénomène humain* (Seuil, 1955, pp.98f.). Why in Australia, which has no placental mammals, do we find a range of marsupials which is *parallel* to the range of our placentals? 'Some fill the place of the wolves, others fill that of the ungulates, others that of the shrew mouse, of the ant-eater, of the mole, etc.' (Teilhard de Chardin, *La Vision du Passé* (Seuil, 1957), p.29, *cf.* p.121). Everything is explained if every living creature was constituted by an evolutionary differentiation from one single stock, the placentals here and the non-placentals there on the massive antipodean island. The transformists draw attention to vestigial organs, or incipient organs such as the fifty-three pairs of dentary rudiments found in the embryo of the whale which disappear before they break through, for the adult whale has no teeth. Examples of this type are suggestive even if scientists no longer assert as confidently as they did formerly that 'ontogeny repeats phylogeny', *i.e.* the embryo retraces the same path which led to the present species. (In recent years 'ontogeny' has again attracted their attention.)

It is from paleontology, however, that transformists draw their principal proof. A popular writer such as Charles Bordet provides a good summary of their conviction: 'The strongest argument that can be brought to bear in favour of transformism is the fact that none of the thousands upon thousands of fossils that have been discovered and studied has ever been discovered outside its geological stage'. The intermediate forms that were *predicted* on the basis of the evolutionary path have been subsequently discovered: 'Over the last thirty years research has been crowned with success on about ten occasions and the fossil has been found at the spot calculated', see *Teilhard de Chardin, l'actualité de son message* (Ed. Ouvrières, 1965), p.56. Anyone who arranges the fossils according to their affinities and following the main direction of the time-scale will see emerging the pattern of the evolutionary tree.

United in their assertion of the *fact* that the species have been produced by evolution, transformist scientists disagree on the *way* this has occurred.

1. Lamarck (1744–1829), the forerunner of transformism, supposed that function creates the organ: the need causes an effort in the direction of satisfying the need, the effort becomes fixed as a habit, the habit modifies the organ, and the change is transmitted to the following generation. Thus he explained that in arid regions the obligation to feed on the foliage of trees caused the elongation of the front legs and the

neck of the giraffe.

2. Charles Darwin (1809–1882), the founder, accepted the Lamarckian idea of the inheritance of acquired characteristics, but into this theory he introduced the key factor of natural selection: in the struggle for life only the most fit survive. Thus new aptitudes – whether the effects of habits on organs, of the influence of the environment, or of spontaneous variations – are soon generalized throughout the species, which thus evolves.

3. Shortly afterwards, however, August Weismann (1834–1914) showed that characteristics acquired by an individual during the course of its life are not transmitted to its descendants. Distinction must be made between the *Soma* (the phenotype) and the *Germen* (the genotype, the inherited characteristics which remain unaltered when the individual organism is modified). For Weismann, whose English translation carried a preface by Darwin, the only evolutionary factor that remains is natural selection.

4. The first discoveries in the field of genetics by Mendel (which passed unnoticed) and by Hugo de Vries confirmed Weismann's views over against Lamarckism. But they brought to light the fact that genes can undergo modifications, called mutations, apparently at random (for example when bombarded by cosmic rays).

5. From that moment today's dominant theory could be formed, which constitutes transformist orthodoxy. It is often called neo-Darwinian, although its advocates prefer to call it 'the synthetic theory' (*cf.* Simpson, *op.cit.*). According to this theory the movement from one species to another has occurred because of the combination or summation of an accumulation of small mutations, sifted by natural selection, the criterion for selection being in fact not so much the survival value as the differential rate of reproduction (*cf.* the fine exposé of M. Lamotte, 'La théorie actuelle des mécanismes de l'Evolution', in *Archives de Philosophie* 23, 1960, pp.58–78).

6. Certain others introduce into neo-Darwinism big mutations, 'systematic' mutations, producing evolutionary jumps; but these have never been observed (Schindewolf, Beurlen, Goldschmidt, quoted by Simpson, and considered by him as refuted; but S. Gould of Harvard tends to revive the idea).

7. Others, arguing from the facts of orthogenesis, appeal to a 'life force' or a 'teleology' as a way out, but they attract the scorn of those who refuse to decorate their ignorance conveniently with high-sounding, mythological names. The life force no more explains evolution than the locomotive force explains the movement of a locomotive (Simpson, *op. cit.*, pp.238f.).

8. Some look enviously towards Lamarckism, that 'superstition with its persistent foliage' as C. D. Darlington called it in 1955. Apart from Mitchourine and Lyssenko, Wintrebert can be quoted as an example of a neo-Lamarckian (according to Flori and Rasolofomasoandro, p.149).

Jean Piaget, the great Genevan scientist, has put his reputation on the block. Relying on observations of the freshwater mollusc, *Limnaea stagnalis,* which he made in 1929, he asserts the inheritance of acquired characteristics in certain cases (*Six Etudes de psychologie,* Denoël-Gonthier, 1964, pp.134f.). He builds a broad and vigorous case in favour of the same thesis 'upheld by certain free minds, but contrary to current opinion', *i.e.* neo-Darwinism, in a recent book. 'This reckless little book', as he calls it, bears a title which is completely unambiguous: *Le Comportement, moteur de l'évolution* (= *Behaviour, the driving power behind evolution*), published by Gallimard in 1976 (see pp.176, 178). In Piaget's view, neo-Darwinism has shown itself incapable of explaining macro-evolution, in particular the unbelievably precise adaptations of instinctive behaviour (such as 'the paralysing stings which the Ammophila gives to caterpillars, thus immobilizing their nervous systems without killing this prey intended for its larvae'), and the construction of new genes during the course of evolution. The fact of 'phenocopy' must be recognized, *i.e.* the inscription in the genotype of modifications which were at first exclusively phenotypical – not directly, as Lamarck maintained, but indirectly, by an internal selection (pp.100–110). Above all the genome must no longer be considered as 'a mass of independent particles', but as 'a system of interactions' integrated into the functioning of higher systems, so that the demands of behaviour (*e.g.* increased performance, auto-regulation) have repercussions on the genes, can 'sensitize' them and cause the necessary modifications of the genotype (pp. 79f., 106f., 133, 148, 172f.). The discussion is far from over.

Although Pasteur refuted the old belief in spontaneous generation, scientific evolutionists are quite willing to suppose that life arose spontaneously in the conditions of the primitive earth, by chemical 'evolution'. This opinion is not necessarily a part of transformism; it quite simply attracts the same minds because of the similarity in the ways of explaining. And they remain cautious. If scientists have been able to reproduce Oparin's 'primitive soup' in the laboratory, and obtain by synthesis the materials which constitute the cell, those are still only 'dead' molecules, without the essential elements of life, organization and metabolism. René Buvet, the leader of those who are most optimistic in France about chemical-biological continuity, observes that an aqueous environment 'selects' from organic compounds those which serve life, and he is studying the possibility of chemical reactions which are analogous to biochemical processes and yet capable of being produced without enzymes; the task is to overcome the apparently insurmountable obstacle that life requires enzymes and that enzymes are produced by life (*L'Origine des êtres vivants et des processus biologiques,* Masson, 1974, pp.94f., 104f.). But he knows that he is going against 'the principal tendency of modern molecular biology' (p.97) and that considerable research will be necessary before his suggestions can be confirmed (pp.126f.).

Transformism properly speaking does not cross the bounds of biology. But it must be noted in the past it has served as a spring-board for philosophical extrapolations. As Teilhard de Chardin said in *La Vision du Passé* (pp.36f.), 'too many evolutionists in point of fact have committed the grave mistake of taking their scientific explanation of life for a metaphysical solution of the world'. Indeed, his own synthesis of theology and evolutionism is quite discredited as science today and clearly diverges from theological orthodoxy. Darwinism has served as a weapon for atheistic propaganda and for the humanist assault on traditional Christianity. This use, or abuse, now seems out of date in Western countries (*cf.* Westermann *C*, pp.47f.). The philosophical exploitation of the theory takes various directions, often to the advantage of mechanistic materialism, as with the Nobel laureate Jacques Monod, but also of vitalist theories of pantheistic tendency.

Christians can have nothing to do with any kind of philosophical evolutionism, a vision of the world which comes down to 'reducing the development of life to a purely immanent operation within nature', as Teilhard de Chardin himself declared. Attitudes towards transformist theory vary. Many thinkers experience no difficulty in integrating it with the vision which comes from their faith, provided that the rights of the supernatural are safeguarded. The majority of Catholics, even those who are conservative, and many orthodox Protestants believe that evolution could have been the method used by the Creator; nothing prevented him from working within nature, by the manipulation of laws he himself had instituted. Ramm (pp.282ff.) cites numerous names and points out that James Orr defended theistic evolution in the fourth volume of *The Fundamentals* (pp.91–104), the series which later gave its name to 'Fundamentalism'. B. B. Warfield had a very open attitude and thought that Calvin 'teaches a doctrine of evolution' because the creatures proceed from the confused mass of Genesis 1:2; that in fact was not what Calvin meant, as John Murray has shown and as R. Stauffer confirmed (*cf.* Stauffer, *art. cit.,* ch.1, n.3, pp.260f.). Those holding a similar view in the scientific field include the late A. Rendle Short and the Frenchman Jean Humbert. Ramm prefers 'progressive creationism' which he distinguishes from theistic evolution because he posits several acts of direct, *fiat* creation and reduces evolution to the formation of new species by 'horizontal' influence (*op. cit.,* pp.116, 272). Hybrid solutions of this kind appear frequent, attributing to evolutionary method a greater or lesser role in creation. The members of the American Scientific Affiliation who collaborated in Russell L. Mixter's symposium, *Evolution and Christian Thought Today* (Paternoster, 1959) seem ready on the whole to admit evolution within the *'order'* (pp.183–206).

Daniel Vernet, who is more narrow, does not go beyond the *genus*, or at most the *'family'*. Micro- and macro-evolution, as he understands them, are acceptable, and mutations could be interpreted as creative 'miracles'. He excludes mega-evolution and insists on strictly maintaining the present framework throughout (see his article and particularly his book quoted above, p.43, n.13, pp.98f., 103ff.).

But anti-scientism will have none of this. It insists that transformism is incompatible with the Christian faith and that other opinions are nothing more than pathetic compromises. Bolton Davidheiser begins with this burning conviction in his representative volume, *Evolution and Christian Faith* (Baker Book House, 1969). They do not particularly like being called 'fixed creationists' or 'fixists' because they admit variations within different divisions of creation, but the distribution of these divisions remains fixed. The only ambiguity concerns the scale of these divisions – the 'kinds' (*mîn*) of Genesis 1. Flori and Rasolofomasoandro demonstrate amazing flexibility at this point, admitting that the kind 'is perhaps nearer to what we designate today as *genus*, even as a *family*' (p.224). F. L. Marsh, who coined the word *baramin*, an amusing barbarism for anyone who knows Hebrew, proposed as the criterion inter-fertility in a very broad sense (*SSt*, pp.148ff.; *cf.* Davidheiser, *op. cit.*, pp.255–267).

In its attack on the official theory of evolution, anti-scientism deploys every possible argument from a variety of sources. Having presented the case for, we shall now summarize its critique in order to weigh the case against.

Are the similarities observed in the diversity of living creatures proof of genealogical links? The opponents of transformism contest this postulate. They argue that these similarities can be explained just as well by the proposition of the direct creation of the various types; God made similar organs separately in order to fulfil similar functions, just as watchmakers use the same pieces throughout the world (Flori and Rasolofomasoandro, *op. cit.*, p.175; *cf.* George F. Howe, *SSt*, p.243). The critics go on to argue that evolutionists make an arbitrary choice of the features which are to count as significant; certain resemblances are considered only as parallel or as convergent, being the effects of *independent* evolutionary action, whilst others, labelled 'homological', are held to indicate a common ancestor (Howe, *SSt*, pp.243ff.; *SC*, p.74). Retractions that are sometimes made show the precarious nature of classifications (Davidheiser, *op. cit.*, pp.233f.). Anti-evolutionists reject the argument about rudimentary or vestigial organs; they seek support in the fact that organs that *appear* to be useless can be shown on investigation to be fully functional, as occurred in the case of nearly all those which in 1901 Wiedersheim listed in mankind (Flori and Rasolofomasoandro, *op. cit.*, pp.178ff.; Davidheiser, *op. cit.*, pp.235ff.). As for the embryological 'proof', they note that evolutionists distance themselves from it (Davidheiser, *op. cit.*, pp.242f.).

The data of paleontology are challenged or reinterpreted. Contrary to the allegations of evolutionists, it often happens that fossils are found outside their geological stratum: 'Human skeletons and implements have been reported deep in coal-mines, even solidly embedded in coal, pictographs of dinosaurs found on cave and canyon walls, human footprints in ancient trilobite beds, fossil pollen from modern-type trees found in the most ancient marine strata, and so on' (*SC*, p.122). Transformists are accused by their opponents of shutting themselves up in a vicious circle: fossils are dated by the rocks, but the rocks are dated only by the fossils (*SC*, p.136; Clifford Burdick, *SSt*, p.128). In numerous cases the layers that are claimed to be the most ancient are found *on top*. Science explains these and other anomalies by geological thrusting, to which such objections are raised as the absence of any trace of movement and the physical impossibility (Burdick, *SSt*, pp.124–135). How can you explain the repetition of the same strata with the same fossils as are found in five cases in Scotland and six in the Alps (*SSt*, p.126)? How can you explain fossilized trees which stand upright through *several* sedimentary layers (Davidheiser, *op. cit.*, p.286)? In order to take account of these same observations, anti-scientism brings in the currents caused by the flood, and it is also the flood which explains the habitual order of fossils – for anti-scientism does not deny the presence of a habitual order: the living creatures from the sea-bed would have been asphyxiated and imprisoned first, followed by those that live near the surface, and then those from the seashore and from the other ecological areas which were submerged in succession by the waves. In this manner would have been brought about the arrangement in strata to which appeal is made by evolutionary paleontology (*The Genesis Flood*, pp.265ff.). Other difficulties raised by the evolutionists' interpretation of fossils also receive plenty of attention: the striking absence of intermediate forms (the famous 'missing links' between the major groupings), whereas the fossils that have been recovered number millions; the already highly differentiated character, practically as rich as today, of the fauna and flora of the most ancient eras, such as the Cambrian; and the continued existence of 'living fossils' like the coelacanth (*SC*, pp.76–90).

When we move to the question of how all this took place, it is the neo-Darwinian position of evolutionist orthodoxy that the critics attack. Armed with material from the science of genetics, the critics emphasize that the mutations observed until now are on a very small scale, are nearly always lethal or deleterious, and are incapable of giving rise to complex organs. Darwin himself had written: 'When I think of the eye I become feverish', but recent discoveries show that the eye is not the only subtly composed mechanism: the tiniest cell constitutes an automated factory of unimagined functional complexity, which requires, to use Paul A. Zimmerman's fine expression, 'an exquisite symphony of co-operation' (*SSt*, p.320). The DNA code contained within a cell carries as much information as a library. As for adaptive behaviour (Jean Piaget's adaptations), the idea that such perfect arrangements could be the fruit of an accumulation of chance events is simply unthinkable.

You might as well say that Concorde assembled itself all on its own, thanks to a succession of chance events, starting from minerals dissolved in the sea (see Pearce, p.104). The calculation of the probabilities can contribute to the case: a combination of one hundred elements (which is much simpler than a cell) could be formed by chance at the odds of 10^{158} to 1 (whilst the total number of electrons in the universe is 10^{80}); even with a billion attempts per second, it would need billions and billions times more time than the billions of years it took the cosmos to form (*SC*, pp.60f.). Mathematicians who gathered for a conference have taken this line of research further and concluded that neo-Darwinism is mathematically impossible (P. S. Moorhead and M. M. Kaplan, *Mathematical Challenges to the Neo-Darwinian Interpretation of Evolution*, Philadelphia: Wistar Institute, 1967, quoted by Flori and Rasolofomasoandro, pp.206f.). In the face of such work, other objections pale into insignificance, even the objection that a complex system is not advantageous until it is complete, for natural selection would have eliminated all the superfluous, disadvantageous stages, and a gradual transformation would never have been possible.

Pushing home the argument, anti-scientism announces further that evolution is contrary to the second law of thermodynamics, that of entropy, which is the tendency to disorder and to the loss of energy (*SC*, pp.37ff.). Comparing the two rival models, 'Evolution' and 'Creation', they insist that the latter is the only one which incorporates all the data and allows verified predictions, and hence is the only one which is scientifically satisfying (*SC*, pp.8–13 and *passim*). How are we to weigh the different points in the controversy with any hope of arriving at the truth?

Because they are a minority group, academic 'underdogs', the anti-evolutionists' case deserves a sympathetic hearing. But it appears to us distinctly vulnerable in the way it handles notions and presuppositions. To talk about the alternative as 'evolution or creation', as though they were two concepts of the same order, is an unfortunate beginning. Nothing in the idea of creation excludes the use of an evolutionary procedure. Why must we tie God to one single method of action? To present creation, reduced to direct modes of intervention, as a scientific model of explanation, furthermore, is to miss the point of the function of *scientific* explanation, which interprets phenomena with the help of laws, 'regularities', and cosmic functioning; but special, transcendent creative acts elude these regularities, as does miracle in the common sense of the word. Science has no right to exclude miracle, but in the face of miracle its work stops; it admits that it has no explanation. The assertion that God has intervened does not replace it, because that assertion has its place beyond the limits of science. Science may note the emergence of living creatures as an 'irregular' event, which it cannot explain; but it will be able to do no more than admit the absence of a plausible scientific model for the genesis of life. Whether or not science can provide an explanation, God is glorified anyway; miracle draws attention to his freedom, but the ordinary course of events is no less dependent on him and does not fail to bear witness to him. Only a superficial mind cannot see that God is as necessary to provide a foundation for law as to permit exceptions to it.

If the unmodified concept of God's creative action does not exclude evolution, what are we to say about the teaching of Genesis? At this point our study again requires that we question anti-scientism. A reading which respects the forms of the language of Genesis can find no clear indication in the text for or against transformism, except in the case of the creation of mankind in his unique position. As reliable an exegete as Derek Kidner considers evolution perfectly compatible with the opening chapters of the Bible (Kidner, p.28). He adds that the language of the creative commands in Genesis 1:11, 20, 24 would suit it very well, for God appears to create in an indirect manner (*op. cit.,* p.48). Attention has sometimes been drawn for the same purpose to the contrast of the two verbs, *bārâ* (to create) and *'āśâ* (to make), in the narrative. Thus it is at least incautious to reject the idea of an evolving creation *a priori*. There is, of course, no suggestion that the Bible positively supports an evolutionary model. The question is whether it does or does not leave the method of creation and the time scale of creation much more open than anti-scientism claims.

On the other hand the objections to neo-Darwinism concerning the mechanism of evolution are on target. True, the general argument about entropy seems to us to carry little weight; recent research reconciles the principle of the decline of energy with that of evolution. According to René Buvet, 'This principle would then carry within itself its own moderating force, and the expression of that force would be constituted by what we have become accustomed to call LIFE,' which would be possible for complex open systems in a pattern of exchange (*op. cit.,* p.30). Prigogine, a Nobel laureate in 1977, is quoted in support of this, from the French magazine, *L'Express* (no. 1374, 7–13 November 1977, p.160). *But the mathematical criticism of the role given to chance in the neo-Darwinian position seems to us unanswerable.* Recent progress (*i.e.* since 1950) in molecular biology has brought out the precision and complexity of the 'simplest' organisms. If this progress had been made earlier, would neo-Darwinism ever have seen the light of day? The role of chance in causing small mutations cannot possibly be held responsible for the wonders that we observe. In these circumstances one of two things follow: either God intervened in a direct, special manner in order to make the branches of the tree of life grow, or else he used mechanisms that were open to scientific study but which are as yet unknown to the scientists. The propositions of Jean Piaget vaguely sketch the theory of such mechanisms, but, if we understand him correctly, his propositions are still rather unclear and in tension with current 'facts' of genetics. It is a pity that his recent work has nothing to say on how the DNA

227

formula could be modified (despite his cautious references to Temin, pp.67, 154, 188) and that he seems to minimize the control exercised by the genotype over adaptive variations of the phenotype.

The more obscure the possible mechanisms of evolution, the more we have the right to demand proofs of the fact that it took place, for the two problems cannot be totally separated. Therefore it seems rash to us to assert that evolution is not a hypothesis but a 'fact' (except as it is agreed by almost everybody on such a small scale that it can hardly be called evolution). In spite of the great number of favourable evidences it is still far from being verified. However, we are not saying that anti-scientism has won its case; it is not totally convincing on this question. Its weakest point is its explanation of the order of fossils in rocks in terms of stages of the flood. This hypothesis is less than plausible; Fraser emphasizes the antinomy between catastrophism and the systematic distributions that can be observed (*op. cit.,* p.126). The order that can be attested cannot possibly arise from the disorder of a cataclysm! Nor is the answer given to transformists on the question of similarities or homologies very strong; it is indeed true that God in specially creating each 'kind' *could have* used the same materials and the same general pattern, but in creating them separately he could have acted otherwise. Therefore the similarities between species argue rather in favour of a common genealogy. As for the accusation of a vicious circle, *i.e.* the dating of rocks from fossils only, it cannot be allowed to pass as a fair criticism; stratigraphy, complemented by radiometry, largely supplies independent datings. In the rest of their case the anti-evolutionists put their finger on real difficulties which weaken the case for transformism, but they overestimate their value; a theory cannot be built on anomalies nor can another be overthrown by alleging them, if the vast majority of the facts are overlooked. The observable data to which the transformist theory accords a coherent interpretation seem much greater in number than the data considered unfavourable.

To sum up: biological evolution on a large scale, distinguished of course from certain inadmissible philosophical extrapolations, remains a hypothesis, but it is a hypothesis which has a number of attractions. The Bible-believing Christian has no reason to reject it *a priori* as the procedure by which creation took place, except the scientific objection that, until now, no-one has been able to show that it is possible within the framework of known laws. Rationalist or positivist scientists, refusing the possibility of the 'miracle' of direct divine intervention, tend to minimize the objection in order to postulate an exclusive transformism. The believer can allow one way quite as well as another and can wait impartially for the result of future research. In practice he will observe that even the opponents of evolution can admit it at the level of the scientific 'family', and that it is made all the more probable by the fossil evidence when the category under consideration is more limited. Evolution seems likely up to the taxonomic level of the *order*; the probability decreases the higher we look in the scale of classification.

Adam, where are you?

The third question in our brief enquiry can borrow the wording of that asked in Eden: Adam, where are you? By that we mean, where is the man of which Genesis speaks to be situated in the schemes of pre-historical anthropology, if they must be accepted? Our discussion will be short; the arguments in this area have less material to work on than those concerning transformism. Indeed, the decision in this area appears more difficult and we do not have the data which would allow us to give clear precedence to any of the possible solutions. Furthermore the preceding discussion continues here at a number of points, including the value of chronometric methods and the possibility of an evolutionary method of creation for the emergence of man.

The great majority of mainstream scientists today admit the following reconstruction:

1. 'Our' humanity is that of neolithic man, the era of civilization involving cattle, agriculture and later metal work, which began 10,000 or 12,000 years ago.

2. This was preceded by Cro-Magnon man (of which there were various types) *Homo sapiens fossilis,* about 30,000 years earlier. Morphologically, this man is practically indistinguishable from modern man. His industry and in particular his art suggest that psychologically he resembled us. The usual interpretation of his carvings and paintings finds in them evidence of religious preoccupations.

3. From 150,000 to 40,000 – the figures become more and more approximate – lived Neanderthal man who constitutes a distinct species which is more 'primitive' in anatomy and in realizations, even if the ape-like description of this creature is today abandoned. The Neander-thals buried their dead. Certain types have a closer resemblance to *homo sapiens,* though the two could not be confused.

4. The very crude industries of the Chellean, of the Acheulean and of the Clactonian cultures are those of the various Pithecanthropic men, covering maybe roughly a million years, named after *Pithecanthropus erectus* discovered in Java at the end of the last century. Certain scientists have spoken of prehominids, for Pithecanthropus means 'monkey-man'. But today the term *homo erectus* is preferred for this category in which are classified a considerable number of fossils such as Peking man, which is associated with several specimens from Java, and a skull found in 1975 by Richard Leakey's team at Lake Turkana in East Africa, said to be 1.5 million years old. The cast of the skull gives some idea of the convolutions of the cerebrum, and the volume and shape of the skull place the Pithecanthropic men halfway between *homo sapiens* and the anthropoid apes.

5. Scientists wondered if the Australopithecan men, whose remains

were discovered in Southern Africa and East Africa, were to be linked with stones of the Pebble Culture. The discoveries of Dr Louis Leakey and his son, Richard, and of other scientists in the Olduvaï Gorges and the Omo Valley suggest that not only must we distinguish two types of Australopithecans, but also distinguish from the Australopithecans their contemporary, the real ancestor of the Pithecanthropes, who has been named *homo habilis*. The age of the first skull discovered in 1961 has been estimated at 1.8 million years, its volume being 700 cc. Since then other fossils of *homo habilis,* the first *homo faber,* have been estimated at between 2 million and 3.5 million years old.

The list that we have just reviewed passes for an evolutionary line, but with the proviso that the pattern of the evolutionary tree spreads like a bush. Scientists today categorically reject the formula, 'man is descended from the apes'; they think that man and today's apes have a common ancestor, *Dryopithecus,* who lived 20 million years ago. They concede that even their fondest theories are based on only a small number of fossil remains, and that enormous gaps exist in the chain (*cf. Time,* 7 November 1977, pp.48–54).

Anti-scientism completely rejects the kind of time scale accepted by scientists and is more critical than most about the distinct nature of these different species, especially as some are not very dissimilar from diseased states in modern mankind. It would, of course, be surprising if the anthropologists happen to have dug up diseased specimens; but it is true that the reconstruction has been too far-reaching on the basis of the actual bones and artefacts that have been found.

As we have said, the actual amount of scientific information available here is relatively very small and any conclusions based on it ought surely to be extremely tentative. There seems to be agreement that there was a remarkable development in mankind around 10,000 BC, but also that creatures that were physically similar and had some evidence of a religious culture go back much further. If anti-scientism rejects the latter, it ought probably also to reject the date of 10,000 BC on the same grounds: for there is no evidence in its favour, since anti-scientism does not accept the dating methods.

When exactly and in what way mankind became mankind-the-image-of-God seem to be questions for which at the moment we have far too little scientific evidence to make any statement. It may be better simply to note that modern man is psychologically and cultur-ally (*i.e.* scientifically) a creature of an entirely different order from the other creatures that now exist on Earth. We can conceive of the gradual emergence of some of these differences, though it is very difficult to see how some others arose gradually; but, after all, not all scientific processes are gradual. The Bible states that mankind is unique: we are the image of God, the animals are not. The scientist can discern that difference as well as anyone else, even while he detects rudimentary aspects of the same psychological and social life in other creatures. If mankind has the same kind of body, in whatever degree, it is not surprising if some animals share some features of his psychology also.

In spite of a considerable literature in this field, therefore, of which our Bibliography gives some indication, it seems best simply to say that we do not know enough to draw any very significant conclusions. It is also difficult to forecast what aspect of being the image of God would actually show up in a scientific description of mankind; so we are not quite certain what it is we are looking for when we try to discover the first man largely in terms of incomplete skeletons.

It is perhaps salutary for us thus to end on an inconclusive note, which in certain respects illustrates the attitude of faith. For faith does not have all the answers straight away. Nor does it claim that contemporary science gives it complete support. If certain factors in today's scientific picture appear contrary to the Word of God, faith is not shaken. It has such confidence in that Word that it can be quite open about its hesitations and wait patiently for the clouds to clear.

Index of biblical references

Genesis
1 39–59, 227
1:1 – 2:3 60–78
1 – 3 15–38
1:26 79–94, 189
1:27 91, 98
1:28 108, 181, 200
1:31 95, 110
2:4 30
2:5 53, 56, 114, 119
2:7 77, 82, 88, 186
2:8–17 111–134
2:17 143, 171, 184–186
2:18–25 95–110
2:19 46, 82, 91
2:20 160
2:23 149, 199
2:24 17, 104ff.
2:25 36, 109, 173
3:1–7 135–170
3:1 36, 43
3:3 126
3:5 127, 129
3:7 129, 173, 175
3:8–24 171–195
3:9 198
3:11 137
3:13 147
3:14 36
3:15 151, 208
3:16 129, 145

Genesis (*cont.*)
3:18 124
3:19 135
3:20 99, 104
3:21 37
3:22 123f., 127, 129–131, 138, 210
4 – 11 196–212
4:1 93, 128
4:6f. 207
4:7 145, 181
4:9 198f.
4:11–13 204
4:15 208
4:16 117, 204
4:17–24 199
4:25f. 160, 201, 208
5:1 30, 89f.
5:2 83, 91
5:3 85, 89
5:3ff. 160
5:22, 24, 29 208
6:3 205
6:5 200
6:6 206
6:7 205
6:9 30
6:11–13 200, 205f.
7:4 205
7:11 206
7:16 208

Genesis (*cont.*)
7:22 77, 186
7:23 205
8:21f. 200, 210
9:1ff. 209
9:6 94, 209
9:9ff. 210
9:21f. 148
9:22, 25 203
10 196
10:1 30
11 203, 207
11:6f. 210f.
11:10 30
11:27 30, 211
11:30 124
13:10 112
13:12 124
18:12 113
19:4ff. 202
19:7 129
20:7 122
22:18 193
24:50 126
25:12, 19 30
29:14 98
31:24, 29 127
34:3 104
36:1, 9 30
37:2 30
49:10 193

Exodus
3:13–15   *66*
6:3   *85*
16   *39*
20:11   *39, 43, 47f., 57*
20:26   148
22:16   *147*
23:12   *48*
31:17   *48, 57*
34:10   *61*
34:16   *201*
35:8   *78*
36:35   *188*
37:7–9   *188*

Leviticus
11:42   *179*
17:11, 14   *210*
19:19   *71f.*
19:31   *171*
20:24–26   *71*
27:33   *127*

Numbers
3:1   *30*
13:33   *201*
15:20   *62*
18:26   *85*
23:23   *153*
24:1   *153*
24:13   *133*
26:54   *180*
33:52   *84*

Deuteronomy
1:13   *85*
1:39   *127f., 132*
5:12–15   *48*
14:1   *201*
18:4   *62*
22   *106*
22:9–11   *71f.*
30:15   *127*
32:10   *65*
32:11   *68f.*
34:9   *34*

Joshua
11:4   *19*
11:14   *77*
15:5   *118*

Joshua (*cont.*)
18:19   *118*
24:20   *127*

Judges
7:16, 20   *118*
9:2   *98*
9:7ff.   *25*
9:8–15   *38, 150*
13:19   *61*
19:23   *129*

Ruth
4:18   *30*

1 Samuel
12:21   *63, 65*
13:17f.   *118*
23:3   *139*

2 Samuel
1:24   *113*
4:11   *139*
5:1   *98*
7:12ff.   *193*
11   *156*
12:1–6   *38, 156*
13:22   *127*
14:17   *127, 132*
14:20   *132*
19:12f.   *98*
19:35   *127f., 131*
24:14   *84*

1 Kings
2:36–46   *184*
3:9   *127, 132*
5:4   *90*

2 Kings
14:9   *38*
19:12   *112*
23:34   *91*
24:17   *91*

1 Chronicles
1:29   *30*

Ezra
4:18   *84*

Nehemiah
2:8   *113*
9:25   *113*

Job
9:17   *180*
15:7f.   *91, 160*
26:7   *65*
30:23   *171*
31:7   *106*
31:33   *160, 163*
33:4   *77*
36:27   *113*
37   *69*
38:10f.   *71*
38:39ff.   *42*
39:26ff.   *42*
41   *42*

Psalms
2:4   *206*
8   *90*
8:6   *83*
18:11   *189*
33:6   *65, 69*
36:9   *112*
39:6   *84*
48:2   *116*
49:8   *139*
51:4   *199*
51:10   *61*
73:5   *160*
73:15   *201*
73:20   *84*
74:16   *78*
82   *191*
82:6f.   *187, 201*
82:7   *160*
90:4   *44f.*
90:8   *78*
104   *77*
104:3f.   *69, 189*
104:9   *71*
104:19   *64*
104:29f.   *77*
104:30   *61*
110:2   *90*
111:10   *62*
126:2ff.   *61*

Index of biblical references

Proverbs
2:17 *107*
4:7 *62*
8:22–31 *68–71, 125*
9:17 *154*
15:30 *78*
20:27 *77, 87*
31:12 *127*

Ecclesiastes
2:5 *113*
3:19 *172, 186*
3:21 *186*
5:2 *83*
7:29 *164*
12:7 *172, 186*

Song of Solomon
1:11 *84*
2:16 *181*
4:13 *113*
7:10f. *181*
8:5 *126*
8:6 *109*

Isaiah
4:2 *44*
5 *38*
6:5 *178*
7:14 *97, 193*
7:15f. *127f., 132*
14 *42, 171*
14:3–23 *42*
24:10 *65*
27:1 *152*
34:11 *41, 65*
38:18f. *172*
40:14 *84*
40:17, 23 *65*
41:23 *127*
41:29 *65*
44:9 *65*
45:18f. *41, 51, 73*
46:10 *62*
48:7 *61*
54:6 *139*
62:4f. *108*
65:17 *61*
65:25 *179*

Jeremiah
2:18 *116*
4:23 *41, 65*
10:5 *127*
23:9 *69*
26:1 *62*
26:8 *122*
27:1 *62*
31:22 *61, 145*
31:32 *108*
47:6 *187*
49:34f. *62*
51:34 *113*
51:56 *172*

Lamentations
2:19 *118*
3:39 *145*

Ezekiel
1 *69*
1:5ff. *188*
10:15 *188*
16 *37, 158*
16:8 *108*
16:25 *118*
19:10–14 *38*
20 *38*
21 *187*
22 *37*
23 *38*
28 *42, 91, 112, 114, 125, 163*
28:8f. *135, 187*
28:11–19 *42, 135, 187f.*
31 *125*
31:9, 16, 18 *116*
32 *171*
32:6 *114*
47 *124f.*

Daniel
10 *202*

Hosea
1:2 *62*
6:7 *136, 160, 163*

Joel
2:20f. *61*

Amos
5:14f. *127*
9:2f. *177*
9:8 *139*

Jonah
3:3 *43*
4:11 *132*

Micah
3:2 *127*
6:8 *127*
7:17 *179*

Habakkuk
2:15 *148*
3:7 *117*

Zephaniah
1:12 *127*

Zechariah
3:4f. *191*
12:1 *82*

Malachi
2:14 *107*

Matthew
1:1 *30*
13 *37*
13:4–9 *19*
19:1–9 *105, 163*
19:4 *47*
19:5 *17*
19:6, 8, 10–12 *107*
20:15 *198*
21:33–41 *37*
22:11 *191*
24:37f. *206*

Mark
2:19 *108*
2:27 *77*

Luke
1:35 *97*
3:38 *89*
10:18f. *151*
13:31f. *18, 45*
14:29f. *206*

Luke (*cont.*)
15:22 *191*
16:23ff. *172*
23:43 *116*
24:27 *16*

John
1 *74*
1:1 *62*
3:29 *108*
5:17, 19 *57*
5:39 *16*
6 *210*
6:63 *74, 77*
7:37–39 *125*
8:41–44 *151, 163, 192*
10:35 *17*

Acts
7:22 *34*
17:28 *78, 89*

Romans
1:22–27 *103*
2:14–16 *179*
5:12ff. *136, 143, 164, 166, 169f., 184*
5:17f., 19 *136*
6:23 *171f.*
7:2 *106*
7:8–13 *122, 164*
7:14–24 *179*
8:2 *77*
8:20 *183*
11:36 *167*
13:1–7 *191*
16 *103*
16:20 *180, 194*

1 Corinthians
3:22f. *121*
6:16, 18 *105*
6:17 *108*
7 *107*
8:5 *189*
11:3 *103*
11:7 *85, 92, 94, 104*
11:8f. *98f., 104, 181*
11:11f. *98, 101, 103*

1 Corinthians (*cont.*)
13:13 *104*
14:33 *70*
15:21 *184*
15:22 *166*
15:26 *186*
15:43, 53 *172*
16:13 *145*

2 Corinthians
2:11 *151*
3:18 *85*
5:17 *211*
11:3 *147, 151, 163*
11:14 *151*
12:2f. *116*

Galatians
3:27 *191*
6:8 *172*
6:15 *211*

Ephesians
2:10 *211*
4:24 *81*
5:22–33 *108*
5:31 *105*

Philippians
2:6 *137*

Colossians
1:15 *89*
3:10 *81, 93*

1 Timothy
2:9 *175*
2:12 *103*
2:13 *104*
2:13f. *143*
2:14 *147, 163*
2:15 *143*

Hebrews
1:1 *18*
2:14 *194*
4:3–5 *56*
4:13 *177*
11:4 *198*
12:24 *212*

James
1:13 *130*
1:15 *140*
2:16 *191*
3:2ff. *142*
3:9 *86, 94*

1 Peter
1:10ff. *26*
3:7 *144*
3:19f. *205*
3:20f. *208, 212*

2 Peter
2:9 *172*
2:11 *83*
3:5f. *47, 66, 206*
3:8 *45*

1 John
1 *74*
1:5 *74, 153, 167*
2:16 *140*
3:4 *137*
3:12 *198*
4:20 *86*

Jude
4, 6f. *202*

Revelation
1:1 *38*
2:7 *113, 116, 124f., 195*
4:6ff. *188*
4:11 *60*
5:8 *188*
5:9 *211*
5:11 *188*
7:3 *212*
11:18 *120, 184*
12 *158*
12:9 *151, 163*
12:12, 17 *42*
18:5 *207*
19 *74*
19:8 *191*
20:2 *151, 163*
21 – 22 *96*
22:1–5 *77, 124f.*

Books of the Apocrypha

2 Esdras
7:48   *165*
8:44   *80*

*The Wisdom of
Solomon*
1:13f.   *30, 166*
2:23f.   *80, 166*
2:24   *151*

Ecclesiasticus
17:3–5   *80*
18:1   *49*
25:24   *166*

General index

Aalders, G. C. 133
Aharoni, Y. 116
Albright, W. F. 32
Allmen, J. J. von 88, 109
Alonso-Schökel, L. 36, 159
Aquinas, T. 50, 64, 89, 99f.,
  116, 179, 183
Aristotle 15, 93
Atrahasis epic 34, 82, 196
Augustine 15, 36, 44, 49, 56,
  58, 64, 89, 100, 112, 123,
  151f., 158, 201
Avi-Yonah, M. 116

Bacon, F. 43, 120
Barr, J. 85
Barth, K. 17, 21, 31, 52, 58, 61,
  63f., 68f., 70, 76, 81f., 85f., 88,
  91f., 97f., 102, 108f., 115f.,
  120, 123, 126f., 129, 133, 150,
  153, 209, 214
Bavinck, H. 83
Beauchamp, P. 32f., 39, 51–53,
  57–59, 61, 63–66, 68–71, 73,
  75, 90, 92
Beauvoir, S. de 101, 103
Berdyaev, N. 92
Berkhof, L. 112
Berkouwer, G. C. 81–83, 86,
  94, 133
Bianchi, U. 160
Blocher, H. 105

Bonhoeffer, D. 17, 21, 58, 64,
  70, 75f., 91f., 102, 104, 115,
  122, 128, 152, 174
Bonnet, J. 69
Bordet, C. 220
Bouillard, H. 186
Bounoure, L. 219
Bruce, F. F. 70
Brueggemann, W. 199
Brun, J. 72, 187
Brunner, E. 81, 92, 168f.
Bullinger, E. W. 19
Bullinger, H. 112
Bultmann, R. 88
Burdick, C. 225
Buvet, R. 222, 227
Buytendijk, F. J. J. 76, 100f.
Byrt, J. 217f.

Cajetan 36
Calvin, J. 63, 69, 81–83, 89f.,
  108, 114f., 118, 123f., 133,
  144f., 151, 172, 179, 183, 186,
  188f., 194, 223
Cambier, J. 125
Camelot, T. 80, 89, 92f.
Cameron, N. M. de S. 21
Caquot, A. 62, 65, 69
Cassuto, U. 30–33, 36, 40, 62f.,
  74, 84, 87, 96, 100, 112–114,
  126, 128f., 139, 189, 193f.
Ceuppens, J. 49f., 144

General index

Chaine, J. 30, 34, 188, 201
Chalmers, T. 41
Chaunu, P. 20, 198, 214
Clement of Alexandria 80
Clines, D. J. A. 77, 80, 83–86, 90, 94, 197, 199, 211
Cocceius 112
Condillac, E. B. de 91
Cook, M. A. 217f.
Copernicus, N. 168
Coppens, J. 127–130, 133, 139, 147–149
Corte, N. 23, 35
Cross, F. M. 66
Cunstance, A. C. 41

Dana, J. 43
Darlington, C. D. 221
Darwin, C. 221
Davidheiser, B. 224f.
Dawson, J. W. 43
Delitzsch, F. 44, 118, 127
Devaux, H. 43
Dibelius, M. 147
Dillmann, A. 128
Dingemans 219
Dooyeweerd, H. 186
Driver, S. R. 30, 46
Dubarle, A.-M. 37f., 153, 155–159, 162f. 165, 168, 184f.
Duns Scotus 183

Eichrodt, W. 65, 153
Eliade, M. 15, 123, 159, 161
Ellul, J. 200
Engnell, I. 31, 120
Enuma elish 63, 65, 67, 196

Fairbairn, P. 188f.
Feuerbach, L. 100
Flaubert, G. 16
Flori, J. 213–215, 219, 221, 224, 226
Foh, S. T. 181f.
Fraine, J. de 21, 35, 99f., 104, 131, 139, 161
Francis of Assisi 82
Frankfort, H. 60, 96
Frankfort, H. A. 60, 96
Fraser, A. 218, 228
Fueter, P. D. 146

Gersonides 49f.
Gilgamesh epic 113, 128f.
Gilson, E. 183
Goldstain, J. 71f., 77f., 81, 99, 130, 147–149, 151, 160f., 201, 211
Goossens, W. 184–186
Gordis, R. 35, 91, 127–129, 160
Gosse, P. H. 216
Gould, S. 221
Graf, K. H. 30
Gregory of Nyssa 25, 77, 92, 148
Grelot, P. 147, 149
Gretillat, A. 41
Gross, H. 80, 85
Grotius, H. 189
Guardini, R. 148
Gundry, R. H. 88, 171
Gunkel, H. 128, 148

Halimi, G. 103, 182
Harris, R. L. 113, 117
Harrison, R. K. 30
Hasel, G. F. 61–63
Heidegger, M. 120
Heidel, A. 33f., 61–63, 65, 67, 82, 152, 160
Heim, K. 183
Henry, M. 99f.
Herder, J. G. von 51, 96
Hobbes, T. 128
Honeyman, A. M. 127
Hoonacker, A. van 149, 184
Hornung, E. 86
Howe, G. F. 224
Hugo, V. 204
Humbert, J. 223
Hummelauer 40

Ibn Ezra 62f., 128
Irenaeus 80

Jacob, E. 80, 85, 88
Jéquier, G. 65, 68
Jeremias, A. 65
Jerome 180, 193
Jervell, J. 85
Jewett, P. K. 57
Josephus 115
Julius Africanus 201

Junker, H.   65

Kant, I.   24, 168f.
Kaplan, M. M.   226
Keil, C. F.   30, 34, 46, 56, 112f.,
   118f., 124, 127f., 133, 139,
   151, 180, 214
Kerkut, G. A.   219
Kidner, D.   25, 30, 40, 43–45,
   64, 84, 106, 112–114, 118,
   124, 139, 156, 191f., 202, 205,
   207, 227
Kierkegaard, S.   109f., 137f.,
   144, 168f.
Kipling, R.   21
Kitchen, K. A.   202
Kline, M. G.   46, 50, 53, 56, 69,
   85, 114, 201f.
Köhler, L.   82
Kuyper, A.   83

Lagrange, M. J.   34, 36, 40,
   50f., 98, 112, 130, 152, 158,
   193
Lamarck, J. B.   220, 222
Lamotte, M.   221
Laplantine, F.   153
Lapparent, A. de   20
Leach, E.   162
Leakey, L.   230
Leakey, R.   229f.
Leenhardt, F.–J.   164f.
Lefebvre, H.   207
Leibniz, G. W.   138
Lévi-Strauss, C.   161, 176
Lewis, A. H.   112, 116f., 123,
   183
Lewis, C. S.   186
Lilar, S.   101
Linnaeus, C.   71
Lorenz, K.   23
Loretz, O.   53, 57, 79, 85–87,
   89f., 93
Lubac, H. de   186
Luther, M.   16, 58, 81, 139, 189
Lys, D.   192f., 203, 206
Lyssenko   22, 221

Maag, V.   86
Mackenzie, J. L.   42
MacRae, A. A.   32, 46

Maillot, A.   102
Marsh, F. L.   224
Melanchthon, P.   192
Mendel, G. J.   221
Merleau-Ponty, M.   89, 101
Michaëli, F.   31, 52, 126
Millard, A. R.   34, 82, 196, 202
Miller, H.   43
Milton, J.   130
Mitchell, T. C.   77, 118
Mixter, R. L.   223
Monod, J.   223
Moorhead, P. S.   226
Morris, H. M.   45, 47, 185, 213
Murray, J.   56, 88, 94, 112,
   123f., 133, 143, 145, 164, 189,
   191, 223

Nautin, P.   70
Noordtzij, A.   50
Noth, M.   37

Olievanus   112
Omnès, R.   214f.
Origen   70, 107, 128
Orr, J.   157, 223
Ovid   89

Pascal, B.   16, 79, 159
Pasinya, M.   33, 67
Pasteur, L.   222
Payne, D. F.   31, 34, 39, 44,
   50f., 77, 93, 120, 161
Payne, J. B.   136, 201f.
Pearce, E. K. V.   46, 118f., 226
Pedersen, J.   88
Pelagius   184
Pfeiffer, C. F.   19, 152
Philo   80, 148, 189
Piaget, J.   222, 225, 227
Pindar   61
Plato   17, 88, 92
Price, G. M.   213

Rad, G. von   31f., 34–36, 39, 43,
   56, 63, 66, 68, 75, 85, 90, 113,
   131, 139, 150, 152, 159, 191,
   194, 201, 205, 211
Rahner, K.   159, 185f.
Ramm, B.   40–43, 46, 50, 215,
   218, 223

General index

Rasolofomasoandro, H.
213–215, 219, 221, 224, 226
Reicke, B. 202
Reisner, E. 154
Rémi de Saint-Germain 100
Renan, E. 23
Renckens, H. 21, 31, 39, 48,
51, 61, 65f., 69, 90, 100, 115f.,
149, 155, 159, 162, 180, 193
Resplandis, C. 131,137, 140,
148
Reymond, R. L. 139
Ricoeur, P. 19, 37, 133, 135,
142, 144, 152f., 157f., 160f.,
165–169
Ridderbos, N. H. 50, 64
Rousseau, J.–J. 199
Rousselot, J. 25, 66
Rowley, H. H. 80

Sartre, J.–P. 101
Sayce, A. H. 118
Schiller, F. von 76
Schmidt, K. L. 82, 85
Scofield, C. I. 41
Servier, J. 219
Shakespeare, W. 144
Shedd, W. G. T. 143
Short, A. R. 223
Simpson, G. G. 219, 221
Solignac, A. 16, 49
Speiser, E. A. 68, 112f., 117f.,
139, 179f., 196
Spicq, C. 80, 85
Stalin, J. 22
Stauffer, R. 16, 58, 63f., 223

Teilhard de Chardin, P. 220,
223
Theophilus of Antioch 183
Thompson, J. A. 37f., 46, 50

Til, C. van 186
Tillion, G. 119
Touati, C. 50
Tresmontant, C. 34, 60f., 157

Vadja, G. 65
Vaux, R. de 130, 133, 149
Vernet, D. 20, 43, 223
Vialleton, L. 219
Vischer, W. 17, 86, 91f., 192
Vries, H. de 221
Vriezen, T. C. 153

Walsh, J. T. 30, 35
Waltke, B. K. 34, 41–43, 51,
62–64
Warfield, B. B. 17, 223
Weeks, N. 23f., 46f., 51, 53, 56
Weismann, A. 221
Wellhausen, J. 30, 126
Westermann, C. 24, 31f., 34,
49, 56, 62f., 65, 74, 80, 85f.,
90f., 96, 118, 120, 122, 152,
157, 178, 182, 194, 196, 198,
223
Whitcomb, J. C. 41, 43, 46, 64,
213f., 216
Whitehead, A. N. 22
Wiedersheim 224
Wiseman, P. J. 27, 40
Woudstra, M. H. 30

Young, E. J. 30, 32, 34, 36f.,
46–48, 50f., 53, 56, 61–65, 68,
113, 124, 126, 130, 133, 137,
141, 144, 150–152, 156, 164,
175, 178–180, 182–184, 188f.,
191–194

Zimmermann, P. A. 75, 225